THE MYTH OF INEVITABLE
US DEFEAT IN VIETNAM

C. DALE WALTON
Southwest Missouri State University

With a Foreword by
W.W. ROSTOW

FRANK CASS
LONDON • PORTLAND, OR

First published in 2002 in Great Britain by
FRANK CASS PUBLISHERS
2 Park Square, Milton Park,
Abingdon, Oxon, OX14 4RN

and in the United States of America by
FRANK CASS PUBLISHERS
270 Madison Ave,
New York NY 10016

Transferred to Digital Printing 2005

Website: www.frankcass.com

British Library Cataloguing in Publication Data

Walton, C. Dale
   The myth of inevitable US defeat in Vietnam. – (Cass
series. Strategy and history; v. 3)
   1. Vietnamese Conflict, 1961–1975
   I. Title
   959.7'043373

ISBN 0-7146-5187-7 (cloth)
ISBN 0-7146-8191-1 (paper)
ISSN 1473-6403

Library of Congress Cataloging-in-Publication Data

Walton, C. Dale, 1971–
   The myth of inevitable US defeat in Vietnam / C. Dale Walton.
      p. cm. – (Cass series – strategy and history, ISSN 1473-6403;
3)
   Includes bibliographical references and index.
   ISBN 0-7146-5187-7 (cloth) – ISBN 0-7146-8191-1 (paper)
   1. Vietnamese Conflict, 1961–1975 – United States. 2. United
States – Politics and government – 1945–1989. I. Title: Myth of
inevitable United States defeat in Vietnam. II. Title. III. Series.
   DS558 .W34 2001
   959.704'3–dc21

2001047765

Typeset in 10½/12 Minion by Vitaset, Paddock Wood, Kent

For Antonia

Contents

Foreword

In the vast literature on the war in Vietnam, this book – to use an apt cliché – is like a breath of fresh air. It is a solid piece of scholarship with abundant references in the notes and extensive comments on them; it is well written; it has a clear thesis, which its title suggests; it is deeply felt but closely argued. In short, this is just the kind of book that should be read and debated some 30 years after the denouement in Saigon.

Dr Walton marches through the initial decision to defend Vietnam and the confusion in public opinion about Southeast Asia; criticisms of the management and organization of the forces in the field; the failure to cut the Communist supply lines through Laos and Cambodia; the misunderstanding of China's view of Vietnam; the use and misuse of airpower in Indochina; and Nixon's attempt at peace, frustrated by Watergate.

The author argues persuasively that the United States could have achieved its limited objectives in Vietnam in a number of ways: by a better use of the ground, naval, and air forces at its disposal, but above all by cutting on the ground the trails through which the Communist forces were supplied via Laos and Cambodia.

Put another way, Kennedy and Johnson chose to fight a war of attrition within Vietnam, giving supply lines and sanctuary to the Communist forces, rather than blocking the trails on the ground with US forces. General Matthew Ridgeway defeated the Chinese Communist and North Korean forces at the 38th Parallel in Korea by making them fight our kind of war using massed artillery and air supremacy. That is the kind of battle we could have forced on the North Vietnamese if we had chosen to cut the Ho Chi Minh trails.

Why, then, did Johnson stick to his initial rules of engagement and deny a showdown within his grasp? He remembered – as did Secretary Rusk – the traumatic entrance into the Korean War of the Chinese forces. Johnson feared a larger war and quite possibly a nuclear war. He explained his dilemma, as he saw it, in his speech at San Antonio on 29 September 1967:

> I cannot tell you tonight as your President – with certainty – that a communist conquest of South Vietnam would be followed by a communist

conquest of Southeast Asia. But I do know there are North Vietnamese troops in Laos. I do know that there are North Vietnamese trained guerrillas tonight in Northeast Thailand. I do know that there are communist-supported guerrilla forces operating in Burma. And a communist coup was barely averted in Indonesia, the fifth largest nation in the world.

So your American President cannot tell you with certainty that a Southeast Asia dominated by communist power would bring a third world war much closer to terrible reality. One could hope that this would not be so.

But all that we have learned in this tragic century strongly suggests to me that it would be so. As President of the United States, I am not prepared to gamble on the chance that it is not so. I am not prepared to risk the security – indeed, the survival – of this American Nation on mere hope and wishful thinking. I am convinced that by seeing this struggle through now, we are greatly reducing the chances of a much larger war – perhaps a nuclear war. I would rather stand in Vietnam, in our time, and by meeting this danger now, and facing up to it, thereby reduce the danger for our children and for our grandchildren.

I sided at the time and in retrospect with the view taken by Dr Walton. The risks of Chinese intervention because of US operations on the supply trails far from Hanoi were minimal. And the Geneva Accords on Laos, which the USSR signed, explicitly ruled out supply through third parties against South Vietnam. But the American people elected Johnson to make that judgement, not a national security advisor.

One of the best sections of this book is the analysis of the Chinese view of the war in Vietnam. The men in Beijing were inhibited by the aftermath of the Great Leap Forward crisis; by the Cultural Revolution; by Mao's decline and the impending succession crisis; and by the continuing awkward, if not hostile, relations with Moscow. The author captures well the hard-pressed defensive mood of Beijing in the 1960s and early 1970s.

One can regret that the author largely rules out of his book the motives which led to the US commitment to South Vietnam and the Asian framework of the struggle there: Churchill's talk with Eisenhower before his Inaugural at the Waldorf-Astoria of 1955; the run-up to the bipartisan SEATO Treaty and the failure in Laos of Plan 5; the great economic boom in Asia in the 1960s and 1970s; the emergence of the Asian Development Bank and ASEAN. Johnson gave serious and sustained attention to these matters, which had a great deal to do with Southeast Asia's survival and the view that Communism was not the wave of the future in that part of the world.

Dr Walton stays narrowly within his thesis, and by doing so puts the endless debate over Vietnam on a good track. He is to be congratulated. He has made a distinguished contribution to the Cass series.

W.W. ROSTOW
Rex Baker Jr Professor of Political Economy at the University of Texas at Austin

Series Editor's Preface

The Myth of Inevitable US Defeat in Vietnam is a full-frontal assault upon mainstream scholarly and popular views. There are two reasons why Dale Walton's book is in this Series on 'Strategy and History'. First, his argument constitutes a superior protracted exercise in strategic reasoning. Second, considered as a whole, his text offers a quite distinctively new approach to understanding the American war in Vietnam. Treating the existing literature on Vietnam very much as a free-fire zone, Dale Walton does not take prisoners and leaves his scholar-targets with very few sanctuaries in which to hide. Whatever our personal conclusions about the great American adventure in Southeast Asia in the 1960s and 1970s, we – the Series Editors – are thrilled to endorse publication of a book which subjects so many underexamined assumptions to rigorous strategic scrutiny.

Walton takes the US decisions to fight for and in South Vietnam very much as a given. His book is a reconsideration of US strategy writ large in the war; it is not about the basic wisdom, or otherwise, of the policy determination to support an independent non-communist government in South Vietnam. However, since the author argues that '[i]t required massive miscalculation on the part of US policy-makers to make North Vietnamese victory possible' (p. 3), we can surmise that he does not find fundamental fault with US policy. In short, US high policy did not ask the impossible of US strategic performance.

Many readers probably will be startled to learn from Walton that 'once Washington decided to enter the conflict, it required numerous major errors on the part of the United States to make Hanoi's conquest of South Vietnam feasible' (p. 4), and that 'even a minimally competent [US] strategy would have prevented the conquest of South Vietnam' (p. 5). Unlike many counterfactual speculations, Walton's radical reinterpretation of Vietnam does not hinge upon some single, purportedly critical matter. On the contrary, we are told that '[t]here was no single, key error that fundamentally undermined the American effort in Vietnam' (p. 154). Moreover, 'it is demonstrated herein that there were *numerous* roads to victory, but that Washington chose none of them' (p. 2). Bold words, indeed!

To summarize, Walton argues: (1) that the preservation of a non-communist government in South Vietnam should not have proved an exceptionally challenging mission for the US superpower in the 1960s, *ergo* the decision to intervene, though debatable, was strategically not unreasonable; (2) there were no true showstoppers for US success, aside from a pervasive poverty in US strategic thought and planning;

(3) there were several ways to win the war, but the United States decided against all of them; and (4) despite repeated, even systematic, strategic error, by the early 1970s the United States had still come very close indeed to succeeding.

This book gores a whole herd of orthodox oxen. For but one example, Walton's argument is not tolerant of the following kind of claim that is more assertion than anything else: 'The asymmetry of social mobilization and political control capacity within Vietnam as a whole was the crucial factor ... the main problem was not that US strategy was too conventional or not conventional enough [referring to the debate between Colonel Harry Summers and Andrew Krepinevich], but that no US effort could make up for the asymmetry in political motivation, mobilization, and organization between the Vietnamese communists and noncommunists. That difference meant that the war could not be won by any primarily *American* strategy at an acceptable price' (Richard K. Betts, 'Is Strategy an Illusion?', *International Security*, Vol. 25, No. 2 (Fall 2000), pp. 36–7). Betts is plausible, but, on the evidence of the state of play in South Vietnam in the early 1970s, he is wrong. The citadel of opinion on Vietnam, even as garrisoned by thoughtful strategic commentators, comprises many beliefs that do not appear to have been exposed to fresh ideas for a very long time. Much as the on–off–on debate about ballistic missile defense shows a persisting terrain of unchanging views, so Vietnam appears to be firmly settled country as far as American scholars are concerned. Most are agreed that it was a fundamental error for the United States to have committed itself to the defence of Saigon. It should be needless to add that that apparently absolute judgement is, of course, dependent upon supportive judgements about the course and outcome of the war. If, following Walton, we discover that the United States ought to have found the preservation of South Vietnam to be an eminently feasible strategic project, then, presumably, we should be open to the thought that the decisions of 1964–65 to intervene were not so foolish after all.

The mainstream view that the US task in Vietnam was mission impossible will have extraordinary difficulty coping with Walton's total approach to the subject. Such revisionist literature as there has been on Vietnam has tended to push a particular counterfactual (for example, *if only* the US had closed the Laotian corridor; *if only* the US Army had practised counterinsurgency more extensively and effectively; *if only* the United States had conducted a militarily sound bombing campaign, and so on and so forth). Walton does not do that. He has noticed that whenever a revisionist comes along with a highly persuasive 'what if', the orthodox mission-impossible view can locate other showstoppers to US strategic success.

The Myth of Inevitable US Defeat in Vietnam is a milestone in the literature interpreting the American war in Vietnam, as well as a *tour de force* of strategic reasoning. We cannot know whether or not Dale Walton is correct in his argument, as there is no 'proof' available beyond strategic logic, but the strong possibility that he is on the right lines is disturbing and, we believe, instructive. This is an important book that should shake up many scholars who have allowed themselves to become complacent in their approach to understanding what happened, and why, in Vietnam 30 years ago.

COLIN S. GRAY
Series Co-Editor

Acknowledgments

A wide variety of friends and colleagues assisted this project directly or obliquely. First, I am deeply grateful to my parents, Clevelan Dale and Gleora J. Walton; they have helped me more than they know. Throughout the publication process, my editor, Andrew Humphrys, has been accommodating and professional, and Penny Rogers deserves much credit for her sharp-eyed copy-editing. James Kiras assisted in many ways with the manuscript and certainly improved the final product. The staff of the National Archives, College Park, MD, and the Vietnam Archive, Texas Tech University, Lubbock, TX, provided research assistance. Col. Harry G. Summers, Jr (USA, ret.) and Adm. Elmo R. Zumwalt, Jr (USN, ret.) kindly consented to lengthy, and very enlightening, interviews. Sadly, both of these officers have since passed away, but their contributions to the US military will be remembered by history.

Many people have read and commented on the material herein, but Professor Martin S. Alexander and Dr Eric J. Grove are due particular thanks. Their comments on an earlier version of this work were most valuable. The ideas herein were discussed long into the night with colleagues at the University of Hull, particularly Thomas M. Kane and Lawrence W. Serewicz. The H.B. Earhart Foundation and the National Institute for Public Policy provided financial support. Professors J.D. Crouch II and William R. Van Cleave merit recognition for supplying me with the intellectual tools required for this project. Finally, I wish to give special thanks to Professor Colin S. Gray, a mentor whose contributions both to this work and to my strategic education have been great indeed.

Abbreviations

AID	Agency for International Development
ARVN	Army of the Republic of Vietnam
CAP	combined action platoon
CCP	Chinese Communist Party
CHICOM	Chinese communist
CIA	Central Intelligence Agency
CINCPAC	Commander-in-Chief, Pacific
COMUSMACV	Commander, US Military Assistance Command, Vietnam
DMZ	demilitarized zone
DPRK	Democratic People's Republic of Korea (North Korea)
DRV	Democratic Republic of Vietnam (North Vietnam)
GVN	Government of Vietnam (South Vietnamese government)
JCS	Joint Chiefs of Staff
MAAG-V	Military Assistance Advisory Group, Vietnam
MACV	Military Assistance Command, Vietnam
NCO	non-commissioned officer
NLF	National Liberation Front
NSCWG	National Security Council Working Group
NVA	North Vietnamese Army
PF	Popular Forces
PLA	People's Liberation Army
POL	petroleum, oil, and lubricants
PRC	People's Republic of China
PROVN	'A Program for the Pacification and Long-term Development of Vietnam'
ROC	Republic of China (Taiwan)
ROK	Republic of Korea (South Korea)
RVN	Republic of Vietnam (South Vietnam)
SAM	surface-to-air missile
SOG	Studies and Operations Group
USAAF	United States Army Air Forces
USAF	United States Air Force
USIA	United States Information Agency
USMC	United States Marine Corps
USN	United States Navy

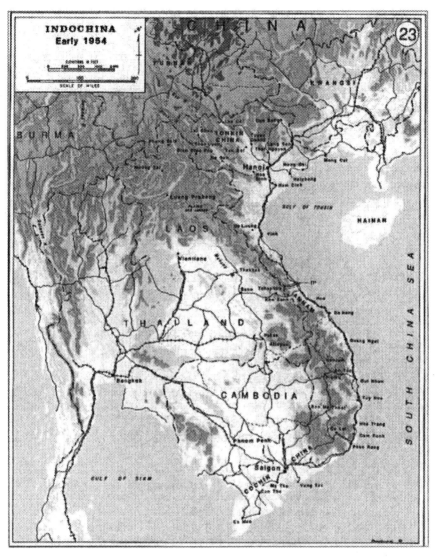

MAP 1

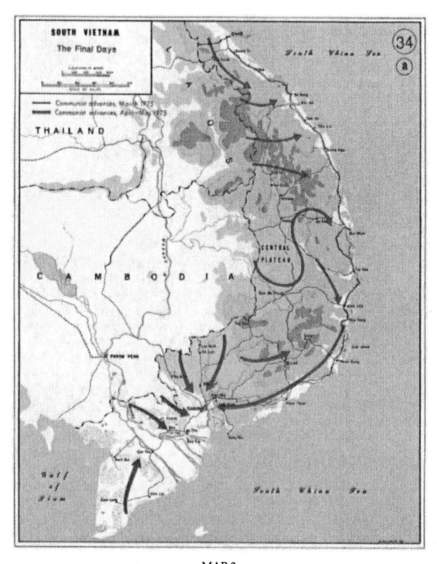

MAP 2

Introduction:
A Tangle of Myths

There has been an immense amount of debate on the role of the United States in Indochina. Almost every aspect of the US intervention in that region has been tirelessly studied, explored, and argued in thousands of books and articles. Nevertheless, the debate on Washington's strategy in the war is surprisingly stagnant: there is a paper ocean of material addressing civilian and military decisionmaking during the war, and many of these works are admirable, but a multitude of intriguing questions are rarely posed and even more rarely discussed in an enlightening manner.

Over time a stifling conventional academic wisdom about the Vietnam War has taken root. The 'lessons of Vietnam' are constantly referred to in academia and in the popular media, but the exact nature of those supposed lessons is usually vague; even when specific lessons are cited, they are generally no more than clichés that reflect the preconceptions of the person imparting them.[1]

There have been some attempts to draw general strategic lessons from the Vietnam War[2] but, relative to the vast amount of material that has been produced on the conflict, little effort has been made to challenge and test numerous areas of conventional wisdom on the US strategy in Indochina. Vietnam is an American popular fixation but, although academics, journalists, filmmakers, novelists, and others have tirelessly attacked the subject, the strategic lessons of the conflict remain elusive.

Almost all observers are in agreement that the United States made dire errors in the Vietnam War, and many also agree that the main error was the decision to defend South Vietnam in the first place – that the Vietnam intervention was a doomed adventure from the beginning.[3] It can certainly be argued logically that defending South Vietnam was a mistake; indeed, it is an obvious truism that if the United States had never embarked on the Vietnam enterprise it would never have suffered the consequences of its decision to do so (this observation, however, reveals nothing about why the United States lost).

1

The contention that the US effort in Vietnam was therefore preordained to failure does not necessarily follow. While it may be maintained that, to paraphrase (and adapt) Bismarck, 'the whole of Indochina is not worth the healthy bones of a Nebraskan paratrooper',[4] that is irrelevant to the question of whether or not the United States could have effectively defended Saigon's independence. Some enterprises are unwise *because* they almost certainly cannot be completed successfully, but the US effort in Vietnam was not in this category: the United States was an immensely wealthy superpower, while its major opponent was a small, impoverished country with little industry and less-than-reliable great power allies. There was no fundamental reason why – compared to most weighty military–political tasks undertaken by great powers throughout history – the odds for US success in Vietnam should not have been very high.

Nevertheless, it is commonly presumed that communist victory was inevitable – that the United States, for one or more reasons, could not realistically have guaranteed the survival of a non-communist South Vietnamese regime.[5] Academic tidiness aside, events are fluid and are shaped by men and women.[6] Analysis that relies on *post hoc ergo propter hoc* arguments is common to historical post-mortems, and is usually misleading.[7] This is certainly not to say that power in all its forms does not matter in a contest between polities. Indeed, the opposite is true: relative power matters greatly, and grants advantages to one polity over another that are sometimes enormous. Nonetheless, the outcome of a conflict is determined by how that power is used; there is no advantage so great that it cannot be frittered away or even turned against its owner.

Even when authors allow that the United States could have prevailed in Vietnam, they tend to argue the advantages of one particular form of warfighting – for example, some authors contend that the consistent application of innovative counterinsurgency techniques would have made a significant difference in the outcome of the war.[8] There is merit in many of these claims, but this book does not argue that there was a unique path that the United States had to choose in order to secure victory. Rather, it is demonstrated herein that there were *numerous* roads to victory, but that Washington chose none of them. For the purposes at hand, 'winning' for the United States is defined as securing the long-term political autonomy of South Vietnam because, as in the Korean War, the preservation of a friendly non-communist regime was *the* central goal of the United States. Thus, for example, if the Paris Peace Agreement had held and the Republic of Vietnam (RVN) in South Vietnam had not been subsequently conquered by Hanoi, the outcome of the Vietnam enterprise would have been victory for the United States. The United States would have achieved its main objective, while the Democratic Republic of Vietnam (DRV) in North Vietnam would have been unsuccessful in securing its key goal (national unification under Hanoi's rule).

This should not, however, be construed to mean that 'all victories are created

2

equal'. Obviously, simply forcing North Vietnam to concede in 1964–65 would have been preferred by Washington over an arguably pyrrhic victory in 1973. In the former case, the human, financial, and diplomatic costs of victory would have been much lower, while friends and foes would presumably have been more impressed by the puissance of the United States. The preservation of South Vietnamese autonomy is, however, a sound 'victory baseline', as Washington would have found even the latter far preferable to what actually occurred (the 1975 conquest of South Vietnam).[9]

The United States was a superpower possessing enormous diplomatic and financial resources, as well as a well-trained and copiously equipped army, immense strategic and tactical airpower, the largest navy in the world, and a multitude of other military resources. In all material terms the United States possessed staggering advantages over North Vietnam. Richard Nixon implicitly acknowledged this relative power relationship in November 1969 with his famous statement that 'North Vietnam cannot defeat or humiliate the United States. Only Americans can do that.'[10] It required massive miscalculation on the part of US policymakers to make North Vietnamese victory possible.[11]

This book asks both why the United States acted in the way that it did and, more importantly, how the outcome of the war might have been altered if the US government had chosen to act differently. While it is not possible to 'predict the past' any more than it is to predict the future, it is perhaps useful to put forward interesting facts and intriguing but infrequently mentioned possibilities; the current Vietnam debate is unimpressive, but this certainly does not mean that there is nothing strategically interesting about the American experience in Vietnam.

It is unusual for a country to enjoy such a material advantage over an opponent as the United States did in Vietnam, and Washington was able to shape its involvement in Indochina to a great degree. Not only was the United States militarily superior to its communist opponents but, as an intervening power, it could control the manner and tempo of its involvement. The United States was free to enter combat at the time and in the manner of its choosing: it could opt to operate (or not to operate) in Laos, Cambodia, and/or North Vietnam, construct its strategic air campaign according to its preferences, and fight the ground war in South Vietnam in any number of ways. Yet Washington elected for a route that neutralized most of its advantages and surrendered the momentum of the war's conduct to its opponents – with calamitous results for the United States and its South Vietnamese ally.

This book explores a wide variety of subject matter, and draws on diverse sources; both contemporary[12] and postwar[13] histories have been extensively consulted, as well as memoirs and other writings of major US decisionmakers[14] and other resources. Unfortunately, as is often the case in academic endeavors, the quantities of material available to researchers can obscure important issues: given the vast number of primary and secondary sources, an author can find evidence for almost any contention. This work does not, however, claim to explore heretofore obscure documents and consequently to offer a new explanation for the US failure in Vietnam.[15]

Indeed, the information vital for a judicious strategic analysis of the war has long been known *and was known or potentially knowable to US policymakers while the war was ongoing.* Policymakers had reason to believe that graduated pressure would likely fail against Hanoi; they knew that North Vietnam was making use of Laos and Cambodia to support its war in the South; they knew they did not have enough troops in South Vietnam to promise rapid success in the counterinsurgency effort; and so forth. US leaders were not simply ignorant and their lack of success was the result of a series of errors in strategic judgment, not a failure of intelligence.[16] Indeed, not only policymakers could see the flaws in US policy. While any claims that a particular observer was 'right about everything from the beginning' are dubious (it is rare for any individual to be so prescient) many figures outside of government commented incisively on specific aspects of the US effort in Vietnam.[17]

STRATEGIC ANALYSIS AND HISTORY

This book is written from the perspective that human actors have a decisive outcome on historical events and rejects any methodology that argues otherwise. It is of course acknowledged that geography is a critical factor in human events, and that cultural, economic, demographic, technological, and other trends have an impact on societies and therefore on history. Nevertheless, human actors are primary, because they ultimately make the decisions that shape the course of events. Even the broadest, most seemingly impersonal trends are the ultimate result of human actions.

This book makes use of counterfactual analysis in support of its strategic argument.[18] This methodology is a necessary and proper tool for strategists, whose field is both practical and based on historical study: strategic scholarship is blind if it is unable to judge 'better' from 'worse' in the conduct of statecraft, and the latter requires that a degree of counterfactual analysis be utilized. It is appropriate to ask what would have been the result of varied courses of action; if the relative merits of decisions cannot be judged, meaningful strategic analysis is impossible.[19]

The analysis herein demonstrates that a successful outcome was possible for the United States in Vietnam and, moreover, it would not have required political–military genius to bring the Vietnam enterprise to a satisfactory conclusion.[20] A major difference in perspective between this work and most conventional interpretations of Vietnam is the argument herein that, once Washington decided to enter the conflict, it required numerous major errors on the part of the United States to make Hanoi's conquest of South Vietnam feasible.

4

There are three reasonably plausible candidate 'theories of victory' for a successful US intervention in Indochina. First, the North Vietnamese could have been convinced that their theory of victory was implausible and seriously detrimental to the health of their polity (by, for instance, persuading the communist leadership that continuing the war in the south could lead to an American occupation of the DRV) thereby dissuading them from further action against South Vietnam. It is, however, highly unlikely that such a strategy, pursued exclusively and without actual displays of force by the United States, would have been successful. Second, the United States could have denied North Vietnam the societal ability to conduct the war in South Vietnam. This would have required measures such as massive bombing of the North Vietnamese infrastructure, destruction of the railroad link to China, the mining of Haiphong harbor, or even the invasion of North Vietnam. There were militarily plausible ways that the United States could have carried out such a strategy. Third, the United States could have prevented North Vietnam from having the opportunity to apply its military force against South Vietnam (but not necessarily brought grave pressure against North Vietnam itself, as in option two). This would have required, most importantly, American activity in Laos and Cambodia.

Overall, the US government's prosecution of the Vietnam conflict was exceedingly clumsy. The best US strategy would have combined aspects of all three of the alternative strategies outlined above, but even a minimally competent strategy would have prevented the conquest of South Vietnam. US policymakers did not make a single, excusable imprudent decision that eventually resulted in the fall of South Vietnam; rather, they made many errors and, long after realizing that the effort in Vietnam was being seriously impeded as a result, continued to pursue their chosen course. The United States would likely have won if it had made any one of *several* key decisions differently. Indeed, as is demonstrated below, the United States almost did succeed in securing Saigon's independence, and if not for a related historical event (the Watergate scandal), the Paris Peace Agreement might well have proven a satisfactory conclusion to the US military effort in Indochina.

A WEB OF DELUSIONS

A great number of myths and partial myths are perpetuated in scholarship about the Vietnam War. Some of these myths contradict others; some have little or no truth, while others are partially valid. Taken together, these myths do not form a truly coherent whole, but that has not been a barrier to their dominance of the literature – authors usually choose to reinforce their favored myths and to ignore or attack those they do not endorse. What ties the myths together is that they can all be used to buttress the belief that the United States was incapable of creating circumstances under which the RVN would survive as an independent state. These myths, in their totality, constitute the 'legend of Vietnam'.

The fundamental barrier to an accurate understanding of the broad strategic lessons of the Vietnam conflict is *not* that essential details are hidden from view; it is that a set of assumptions has captured the Vietnam literature. All the information necessary to enable scholars to derive reasonable conclusions about the strategic errors of the US policymaking establishment has long been known – indeed, most of the relevant information was available and in the public domain while the conflict was ongoing.

An accurate understanding of the war requires that *all* the major myths of Vietnam be attacked – it is not sufficient that one or more Vietnam myths be overturned; the entire 'myth superstructure' must be razed. It is only then that the fundamental errors in US decisionmaking become clear, and the previously obscured truth is revealed. As of the time of the 1962 Laos Crisis, it was highly improbable that North Vietnam would eventually emerge victorious. The actual outcome of the conflict was the result of numerous (and often gross) strategic errors on the part of the United States. Washington lost in Vietnam because of a series of military–political errors unmatched in the history of the American republic: for well over a decade the US government regularly made important strategic errors in Indochina, and eventually succeeded in 'snatching defeat from the jaws of victory'.

A convenient way to categorize the myths of Vietnam is to separate those that pertain to South Vietnam's general viability as a state and the competence of its political–military institutions from those that primarily concern the ability of the United States to undertake successful military operations in Indochina. Regarding the former, the conventional wisdom that South Vietnam was simply an unviable state is rejected outright. Although Saigon did suffer from a high degree of corruption and, compared with its North Vietnamese foe, strategic ineptitude, it was viable. The apparatus of the South Vietnamese state functioned, albeit imperfectly, and generally proved capable of maintaining a reasonable degree of internal order despite the military conflict extant within its borders; South Vietnam collapsed because of external, not internal, pressures.[21] The RVN was vulnerable to Hanoi, but only if its protecting power failed to guard it successfully; the independent variable in the 'RVN survival equation' was the United States.

Because it was the political–military success or failure of the United States that would determine the survival of the RVN, the question of how the United States could have triumphed militarily in Indochina is studied in depth. It is established herein that the United States was clearly capable physically of prevailing in Indochina, but that US policymakers lacked a credible theory of victory in Vietnam.[22] Washington did not treat Indochina as a unified theater, wrongly assumed that the DRV could be pressured into abandoning its war

Table 1: The Myths of Vietnam

The Viability of South Vietnam	The US War in Indochina
The ARVN was an extremely poor force that improved little over the course of the war	Almost all the communist troops that the US military encountered were South Vietnamese, and most were local guerrillas
The ARVN officer corps was irredeemably corrupt and incompetent	Despite a huge expenditure of effort, the United States did little permanent damage to the NLF
The failure of American advisors radically to improve the ARVN demonstrates that the South Vietnamese military was beyond redemption	There was no way that the bombing of North Vietnam could achieve very much because it was not an industrialized country
The events of 1975 vindicate the view that the ARVN was inept	The United States lost because it relied too much on technology – heavy artillery, armor, and high-performance aircraft were of little use in Vietnam
The overwhelming majority of South Vietnamese favored the overthrow of the GVN or, at best, were apathetic	There was no way to control infiltration into South Vietnam and attempts to do so were certain to be futile
The NLF was essentially independent of Hanoi	A conflict with the PRC would certainly be extremely costly for the United States; defeat in Vietnam was undoubtedly preferable to a Sino–American conflict
South Vietnam was always unstable and constantly plagued by military coups	The US involvement in Vietnam was just as threatening to the PRC as was US intervention in Korea in 1950
The RVN was extremely authoritarian and most South Vietnamese enjoyed no more freedom than did the North Vietnamese	Mining North Vietnam's ports in the 1960s would likely have led to conflict with the Soviet Union and/or the PRC
The fall of South Vietnam was mainly the result of internal instability and/or the unpopularity of the GVN	The great majority of the American people turned against the war during or shortly after the Tet Offensive
	The US war in Indochina was, by the standards of modern war, unusually brutal; very large numbers of North and South Vietnamese, Cambodian, and Laotian civilians were killed by indiscriminate use of firepower
	The United States illegally bombed neutral Laos and Cambodia and trampled the sovereignty of those countries; essentially there was peace in eastern Laos and Cambodia before the United States 'expanded the war' into those areas
	The 1973 Paris Peace Agreement was little more than a surrender by the United States and essentially ensured the eventual fall of South Vietnam; the United States had no ability or intention to enforce the Agreement.

goals by incremental pressure, and misassessed the military capability and intentions of China.

This book examines the reasons why the strategy it did implement was faulty and explores the various ways in which the United States could have created an effective strategy for achieving its key goals in Indochina – and shows that there were several ways in which the United States could have constructed and implemented such a strategy. At the same time, it demonstrates the mythical character of many long-cherished beliefs about Vietnam, and shows that, despite its myriad errors, the United States almost secured the permanent independence of South Vietnam.

NOTES

1. One of the alleged lessons of Vietnam that Robert S. McNamara cites in his memoirs is the observation that 'we must recognize that the consequences of large-scale military operations – particularly in this age of highly sophisticated and destructive weapons – are inherently difficult to predict and to control. Therefore, they must be avoided, excepting only when our nation's security is clearly and directly threatened.' (*In Retrospect: The Tragedy and Lessons of Vietnam* (New York: Vintage, 1996), p. 332.) Aside from the questionable claim that war is currently less predictable than it was in the past, there is nothing unique to the Vietnam conflict, the United States, or even to the last thousand years of warfare, about this observation. The former defense secretary also discusses 'lessons of Vietnam' in Robert S. McNamara *et al.*, *Argument Without End: In Search of Answers to the Vietnam Tragedy* (New York: Public Affairs, 1999), pp. 373–98.
2. Most famously in Harry G. Summers, Jr, *On Strategy: A Critical Analysis of the Vietnam War* (Novato, CA: Presidio, 1982).
3. Allan E. Goodman describes this phenomenon well: 'For some the dénouement in Vietnam in April of 1975 is now and was then seen as something akin to original sin; the collapse of the ARVN and the Saigon government, according to this view, was inevitable. Because of the flawed nature of the US commitment, including especially the lies we told ourselves about why we were there and what could be accomplished, the truth about what would really happen was always shrouded. To believers in this school of thought, therefore, even policies and programs premised on a realistic appreciation of the Vietnamese and their situation and outlook would at best postpone the collapse of the GVN.' ('The Dynamics of the United States–South Vietnamese Alliance: What Went Wrong', in Peter Braestrup (ed.), *Vietnam as History: Ten Years After the Paris Peace Accords* (Washington, DC: University Press of America, 1984), p. 91.)
4. On the question of 'selective intervention', see Hans J. Morgenthau, 'To Intervene or Not To Intervene', *Foreign Affairs*, 45, 3 (April 1967), pp. 425–36.
5. This is a common theme of historians who are critical of US policy in Vietnam. One such author writes that '[t]he United States utterly failed to develop a credible limited-war doctrine and technical capability to intervene in the Third World, a crucial symbolic objective of the entire campaign for three administrations. Yet ultimately this was even less decisive than its intrinsic inability to create a viable political, economic, and ideological system [in South Vietnam] capable of attaining the prerequisites of military success … America, locked into its mission to control the broad contours of the world's political and socioeconomic development, had set for itself inherently unobtainable political objectives.' (Gabriel Kolko, *Anatomy of a War: Vietnam, the United States, and*

the *Modern Historical Experience* (rev. edn, New York: New Press, 1995; originally published 1985), p. 545.)

6. See C. Dale Walton, 'Vietnam: Avoidable Tragedy or Prudent Endeavor?', Review essay, *Comparative Strategy*, 19, 4 (October–December 2000), pp. 355–60.

7. One historian sagely observes that '[w]ar as a narrative of risk and hazard is not universally admired by historians (the "drum and trumpet" school has long been out of fashion), no more than is emphasis on personalities (the "great man" school). But strategy divorced from its consequences is singularly desiccated and – to use a necessary if unpleasant word – bloodless. The effectiveness of a strategy is a function of its execution. Bad strategies produce bad battles; men die to no good effect and causes just and unjust are consigned to the dustheap.' (Eric Larrabee, *Commander in Chief: Franklin Delano Roosevelt, His Lieutenants, and Their War* (New York: Simon & Schuster, 1987), p. 7.) Also noteworthy are the comments of A.J.P. Taylor in *From Napoleon to the Second International: Essays on Nineteenth-century Europe* (London: Penguin Books, 1995; essay originally published 1977), pp. 12–13.

8. See Victor H. Krulak, *First to Fight: An Inside View of the US Marine Corps* (Annapolis, MD: Naval Institute Press, 1984), *passim*.

9. In this regard, it should be noted that in the 1950s and 1960s a substantial number of observers believed that the United States had lost the Korean War – or at best fought to a 'losing draw' – but it seems unlikely that many historical commentators would agree with that assessment today.

10. Quoted in Stanley Karnow, *Vietnam: A History* (New York: Penguin, 1984), p. 600.

11. This is not to imply that North Vietnam played no part in its own victory. On the contrary, Hanoi played its hand tenaciously and well, refusing to surrender its ultimate goals and working diligently to bring about the circumstances in which military victory would be possible. For a highly positive assessment of the capability of Gen. Giap in particular, see Cecil B. Currey, *Victory At Any Cost: The Military Genius of Viet Nam's Gen. Vo Nguyen Giap* (Washington, DC: Brassey's, 1997). Also see Peter Macdonald, *Giap: The Victor in Vietnam* (London: Fourth Estate, 1993).

12. Such works include Harry Brandon, *Anatomy of Error: The Secret History of the Vietnam War* (London: Andre Deutsch, 1970); Russell H. Fifield, *Southeast Asia in United States Policy* (New York: Praeger, 1967); Marvin E. Gettleman (ed.), *Viet Nam: History, Documents, and Opinions on a Major World Crisis* (New York: Fawcett, 1965); Eric F. Goldman, *The Tragedy of Lyndon Johnson* (New York: Alfred A. Knopf, 1969); Senator Mike Gravel (ed.), *The Pentagon Papers: The Defense Department History of United States Decisionmaking on Vietnam*, four vols (Boston, MA: Beacon, 1971–72); David Halberstam, *The Making of a Quagmire* (London: Bodley Head, 1965); *idem*, *The Best and the Brightest* (New York: Penguin, 1986; originally published 1972); Marguerite Higgins, *Our Vietnam Nightmare* (New York: Harper & Row, 1965); George McT. Kahin and John W. Lewis, *The United States in Vietnam* (rev. edn, New York: Delta, 1969); Alexander Kendrick, *The Wound Within: America in the Vietnam Years, 1945–1974* (Boston, MA: Little, Brown, 1974); Marcus G. Raskin and Bernard B. Fall (eds), *The Viet-Nam Reader: Articles and Documents on American Foreign Policy and the Vietnam Crisis* (rev. edn, New York: Vintage, 1967); and Robert Shaplen, *The Road From War: Vietnam 1965–1970* (New York: Harper & Row, 1970).

13. Examples include Larry Berman, *Planning a Tragedy: The Americanization of the War in Vietnam* (New York: W.W. Norton, 1983); Michael R. Beschloss (ed.), *Taking Charge: The Johnson White House Tapes, 1963–64* (New York: Simon & Schuster, 1997); Robert Buzzanco, *Masters of War: Military Dissent and Politics in the Vietnam Era* (New York: Cambridge University Press, 1996); James William Gibson, *The Perfect War: The War We Couldn't Lose and How We Did* (New York: Vintage Books, 1988); George C. Herring,

LBJ and Vietnam: A Different Kind of War, An Administrative History of the Johnson Presidency Series (Austin, TX: University of Texas Press, 1994); Lloyd C. Gardner, *Pay Any Price: Lyndon Johnson and the Wars for Vietnam* (Chicago, IL: Ivan R. Dee, 1995); William Conrad Gibbons, *The US Government and the Vietnam War: Executive and Legislative Roles and Relationships*, 4 vols (Princeton, NJ: Princeton University Press, 1986–95); Marvin E. Gettleman *et al.*, *Vietnam and America: A Documented History* (rev. 2nd edn, New York: Grove, 1995); Karnow, *Vietnam: A History*; Guenter Lewy, *America in Vietnam* (New York: Oxford University Press, 1980); H.R. McMaster, *Dereliction of Duty: Lyndon Johnson, Robert McNamara, the Joint Chiefs of Staff, and the Lies that Led to Vietnam* (New York: HarperCollins, 1997); Bernard C. Nalty (ed.), *The Vietnam War: The History of America's Conflict in Southeast Asia* (New York: Smithmark, 1996); John M. Newman, *JFK and Vietnam: Deception, Intrigue, and the Struggle for Power* (New York: Warner, 1992); James S. Olson and Randy Roberts, *Where the Domino Fell: America and Vietnam, 1945–1995* (2nd edn, New York: St Martin's, 1996); Dave Richard Palmer, *Summons of the Trumpet: A History of the Vietnam War from a Military Man's Viewpoint* (New York: Ballantine, 1984; originally published 1978); Mark Perry, *Four Stars* (Boston, MA: Houghton Mifflin, 1989); John Prados, *Keepers of the Keys: A History of the National Security Council from Truman to Bush* (New York: William Morrow, 1991); Robert D. Schulzinger, *A Time for War: The United States and Vietnam, 1941–1975* (New York: Oxford University Press, 1997); Neil Sheehan, *A Bright Shining Lie: John Paul Vann and America in Vietnam* (London: Jonathan Cape, 1989); Barbara W. Tuchman, *The March of Folly: From Troy to Vietnam* (New York: Ballantine, 1985); and Brian VanDeMark, *Into the Quagmire: Lyndon Johnson and the Escalation of the Vietnam War* (New York: Oxford University Press, 1991).

14. Including George W. Ball, *Diplomacy for a Crowded World: An American Foreign Policy* (Boston, MA: Little, Brown, 1976); *idem*, *The Past Has Another Pattern: Memoirs* (New York: W.W. Norton, 1982); Joseph A. Califano, Jr, *The Triumph and Tragedy of Lyndon Johnson: The White House Years* (New York: Simon & Schuster, 1991); Clark Clifford, 'A Viet Nam Reappraisal: The Personal History of One Man's View and How it Evolved', *Foreign Affairs*, 47, 4 (July 1969), pp. 601–22; *idem*, with Richard Holbrooke, *Counsel to the President: A Memoir* (New York: Random House, 1991); Chester L. Cooper, 'The Complexities of Negotiation', *Foreign Affairs*, 46, 3 (April 1968), pp. 456–7; *idem*, *The Lost Crusade: The Full Story of US in Vietnam from Roosevelt to Nixon* (London: McGibbon & Kee, 1970); Philip B. Davidson, *Vietnam at War: The History, 1946–1975* (Novato, CA: Presidio, 1988); Gerald R. Ford, *A Time to Heal: The Autobiography of Gerald R. Ford* (New York: Berkley, 1980); J. William Fulbright with Seth P. Tillman, *The Price of Empire* (New York: Pantheon, 1989); Roger Hilsman, *To Move a Nation: The Politics of Foreign Policy in the Administration of John F. Kennedy* (New York: Delta, 1967 [1964]); *idem*, 'Must We Invade the North?' *Foreign Affairs*, 46, 3 (April 1968), pp. 425–41; Townsend Hoopes, *The Limits of Intervention: An Inside Account of How the Johnson Policy of Escalation in Vietnam was Reversed* (rev. edn, New York: David McKay, 1973); Lyndon Baines Johnson, *The Choices We Face* (New York: Bantam, 1969); *idem*, *The Vantage Point: Perspectives on the Presidency, 1963–1969* (New York: Popular Library, 1971); Henry A. Kissinger, 'The Viet Nam Negotiations', *Foreign Affairs*, 47, 2 (January 1969), pp. 211–34; *idem*, *American Foreign Policy* (expanded edn, New York: W.W. Norton, 1974); *idem*, *White House Years* (Boston, MA: Little, Brown, 1979); *idem*, *Years of Upheaval* (Boston, MA: Little, Brown, 1982); *idem*, *Diplomacy* (New York: Simon & Schuster, 1994); *idem*, *Years of Renewal* (New York: Simon & Schuster, 1999); Krulak, *First to Fight*; McNamara, *In Retrospect*; Paul H. Nitze with Anne M. Smith and Stephen L. Rearden, *From Hiroshima to Glasnost: At the Center of Decision – A Memoir* (New York: Grove Weidenfeld, 1989); Richard M. Nixon, 'Asia After Viet Nam', *Foreign Affairs*,

46, 1 (October 1967), pp. 111–25; *idem, RN: The Memoirs of Richard Nixon* (New York: Grosset & Dunlap, 1978); *idem, The Real War* (New York: Warner, 1981); *idem, No More Vietnams* (New York: Avon, 1985); Fredrick Nolting, *From Trust to Tragedy: The Political Memoirs of Fredrick Nolting, Kennedy's Ambassador to Diem's Vietnam* (New York: Praeger, 1988); Bruce Palmer, Jr, *The 25-Year War: America's Military Role in Vietnam* (Lexington, KY: University Press of Kentucky, 1984); W.W. Rostow, *The Diffusion of Power: An Essay in Recent History* (New York: Macmillan, 1972); *idem, The United States and the Regional Organization of Asia and the Pacific, 1965–1985,* Ideas and Action Series, No. 6 (Austin, TX: University of Texas Press, 1986); U.S. Grant Sharp, *Strategy for Defeat: Vietnam in Retrospect* (Novato, CA: Presidio, 1978); William C. Westmoreland, *A Soldier Reports* (New York: De Capo, 1989; originally published 1976); Elmo R. Zumwalt, Jr, *On Watch: A Memoir* (New York: Quadrangle, 1976); and *idem,* and Elmo Zumwalt III, with John Pekkanen, *My Father, My Son* (New York: Dell, 1987).

15. Indeed, the author has a skeptical general attitude toward scholarship that relies on archival 'magic bullets' to buttress a radical reinterpretation of one or more aspects of the Vietnam conflict. A prominent example of a work incorporating excellent archival research to support dubious arguments is Buzzanco, *Masters of War*. For comparative negative, mixed and favorable reviews of *Masters of War* see Harry G. Summers, Jr, 'Vietnam: A Truncated History', *Diplomatic History*, 21, 4 (Fall 1997), pp. 652–6; Douglas Kinnard, Untitled Review, *Naval War College Review*, 50, 3 (Summer 1997), pp. 143–5; and Andrew J. Rotter, 'Operation Exculpation', *Diplomatic History*, 21, 4 (Fall 1997), pp. 657–62.

16. Many US policymakers have attempted to portray their mistakes as the result of a sort of grand intelligence failure: the United States did not understand Vietnam and therefore US leaders could not possibly have made correct decisions. McNamara argues that one of the key reasons for the US defeat was '[American] misjudgments of friend and foe alike [that] reflected our profound ignorance of the history, culture, and politics of the people in the area, and the personalities and habits of their leaders.' (*In Retrospect,* p. 322; also see pp. 32–3.) This contention is inconsistent with the historical record. In fact, US leaders possessed a vast amount of information on Indochina from government and non-government sources. For example, in mid-1963 McNamara enjoyed a 'long interview' with a certain Professor Smith, an individual who, according to McNamara's report on the conversation, 'speaks Vietnamese fluently, is an oriental [*sic*] scholar, possesses wide contacts among the leaders of both North and South Vietnam, and in the course of his daily work has access to transcripts of [North Vietnamese] radio broadcasts and to personal letters and other documents smuggled out of [North Vietnam].' ('Report of McNamara 26 September 63 Interview with Professor Smith', McNamara files, United States National Archives, RG 200, Box 63, NN3-2000-092-001 HM 92-93.)

17. For a small sample of the enormous number of interesting contemporary articles analyzing the situation in Indochina see Chester L. Cooper, 'The Complexities of Negotiation', *Foreign Affairs,* 46, 3 (April 1968), pp. 454–66; Bernard B. Fall, 'Viet Nam in the Balance', *Foreign Affairs,* 45, 1 (October 1966), pp. 1–18; Lionel Gelber, 'History and the American Role', *Orbis,* 11, 1 (Spring 1967), pp. 199–209; Samuel P. Huntington, 'The Bases of Accommodation', *Foreign Affairs,* 46, 4 (July 1968), pp. 642–56; Herman Kahn, 'If Negotiations Fail', *Foreign Affairs,* 46, 4 (July 1968), pp. 627–41; Stanley G. Langland, 'The Laos Factor in a Vietnam Equation', *International Affairs,* 45, 4 (October 1969), pp. 631–47; Franz Michael, 'The Stakes in Vietnam', *Orbis,* 12, 1 (Spring 1968), pp. 121–31; Jeffery Race, 'How They Won', *Asian Survey,* 10, 8 (August 1970), pp. 628–50; Robert Shaplen, 'Viet Nam: Crisis of Indecision', *Foreign Affairs,* 46, 1 (October 1967), pp. 95–110; and Sir Robert Thompson, 'Squaring the Error', *Foreign Affairs,* 46, 3 (April 1968), pp. 442–53;

18. It should be noted that this work differs from many counterfactual analyses in that it does not 'shift the pieces on the chessboard' – there are no detailed discussions of questions such as whether, for example, the United States would have won in Vietnam if Richard Nixon had been elected president in 1960. The effect of key actual events such as Watergate on the US effort in Vietnam, however, is discussed. It should also be noted that that the options most palatable in terms of US political–strategic culture are given the most comprehensive treatment. None of the options that receive the most attention herein – including ongoing operations in Laos and Cambodia, alterations in US bombing, the mining of North Vietnamese ports, and changes in how the United States bureaucratically organized its Vietnam effort and conducted the war on the ground – cut deeply against the grain of American culture. Although US leaders did not pursue these options, a notional rational actor (a 'Policymaker X') plausibly could have done so.

19. A compelling defense of the use of counterfactual analysis for historical investigation is offered by Niall Ferguson in 'Introduction: Virtual History: Towards a "Chaotic" Theory of the Past', in *idem* (ed.), *Virtual History: Alternatives and Counterfactuals* (London: Papermac, 1997), pp. 1–90.

20. This is in contrast to many authors. Robert A. Divine notes in a review of Vietnam War literature that '[a theme] which runs though the postrevisionist books is the fatal American ignorance of the force and vitality of Vietnamese nationalism. In contrast to the revisionists, who keep wondering if the war could have been won, these scholars answer with a resounding, "No!"' (Robert A. Divine, 'Historiography: Vietnam Reconsidered', *Diplomatic History*, 12, 1 (Winter 1988), p. 92.)

21. The clash between Buddhist factions and the Diem government is commonly believed to demonstrate the non-viability of South Vietnam. However, at most the events of 1963 demonstrated that Diem himself could no longer lead his country effectively and, of course, he was actually overthrown by military officers – servants of the state – not Buddhist rioters. Indeed, it is worth noting that South Vietnam's one-time colonial hegemon suffered repeated bouts of internal turmoil in the 1960s, yet no one would claim that France is not a viable state.

22. Colin S. Gray argues persuasively that 'Washington … fundamentally misread the nature of the war upon which it was choosing to embark, and hence – inevitably – it designed a theory of victory for that war which could not succeed'. (*War, Peace, and Victory: Strategy and Statecraft for the Next Century* (New York: Simon & Schuster, 1990), p. 115.)

1

The Temptation to Intervene: US Policymakers and Vietnam

> Returning home after years of service in Viet Nam, I am nagged by the insistent thought that we have not yet adequately answered a plain question: What is it, exactly, that we seek in Viet Nam?
>
> Gen. Edward G. Lansdale[1]

One of the many questions related to the war in Vietnam is the matter of what reasoning motivated key US policymakers, who represented a superpower with overseas security interests and obligations that were centered in Europe, to take a military stand against communism in Southeast Asia, an area of dubious strategic value in which it was difficult to use US military advantages to maximum effect. The question is an important one: the United States made a series of commitments that eventually culminated in US forces taking an active combat role in an ongoing war of considerable size despite a traditional lack of US interest in the area.

Leaving aside the obvious point that the United States failed to prevent the communist victory in Indochina, many observers doubt the wisdom of choosing to defend South Vietnam under any circumstances and, given the known risks and difficulties inherent in such a project, question the strategic acumen of US policymakers who supported the progressive deepening of the US commitment to Vietnam. This issue is still controversial: most authors claim that the Vietnam enterprise was grossly ill-conceived from the beginning, but some still defend it as being strategically and morally justifiable.[2] While the question of whether the United States should have actually been in Vietnam is beyond the scope of this work, the manner in which Washington 'constructed the war' is not. Acting in response to the situation in Indochina, and in what they believed to be a reasonable manner, US policymakers set the parameters of the conflict in Vietnam (and unknowingly contributed to the US defeat). By exploring briefly some of the quandaries facing policymakers, particularly in the Johnson administration, it is possible to see why the United States was in Vietnam.[3]

The motives of US policymakers for defending South Vietnam were mixed and the strategic thinking behind the Vietnam commitment was sometimes muddy. Policymakers approached the Vietnam problem from a variety of personal perspectives and with widely varying notions as to how the war should be fought. Disagreement between civilian and military policymakers on this question tended to be strong even though their general goals were virtually identical[4] – almost all US policymakers wanted a non-communist, stable South Vietnam and were in return willing to tolerate a communist regime in Hanoi. Moreover, it is important to note that the desire of US policymakers to guard the prestige of the United States and its role as protecting power played a vital role in Vietnam decisionmaking. Even policymakers who were dubious of South Vietnam's strategic value did not tend to question the importance of maintaining the reputation of the United States.[5]

Indeed, after the introduction of US combat troops, the prestige and credibility of the United States as a protecting power was at stake to such an extent that, regardless of the question of South Vietnam's strategic value, an ongoing commitment was arguably merited to avert the loss of face that would, and eventually did, result from a US withdrawal. Though such reasoning might have risked the creation of an 'ape on a treadmill' mentality – the fact of the initial commitment to South Vietnam justifying an ongoing, and steadily increasing, commitment to that country – Washington's credibility as a protecting power was a serious matter. Many US policymakers believed that the reputation of the United States was a major, if not decisive, factor in determining whether or not a Third World War would be fought over Western Europe. If the United States saw the Vietnam commitment through to a successful conclusion, so it was reasoned, the Soviet Union would be impressed by American fortitude. This in turn would impact Soviet behavior in Europe, increase the credibility of the NATO threat to make first use of nuclear weapons to repulse a Soviet invasion of the West, and so forth.

Unsurprisingly, at no point was the Vietnam conflict entirely separate from the Cold War in the minds of US leaders. The situation in Vietnam was part of a world struggle against communism. Reference to this fact is important to understanding the reluctance of policymakers to annul the commitment to South Vietnam.[6]

THE PERCEIVED NEED TO INTERVENE

For the purposes at hand, it is useful to distinguish between the US financial commitment to South Vietnam and the commitment of US troops to battle against communist forces in Vietnam. The US provision of military and financial aid to South Vietnam was not particularly unusual during the 1950s and 1960s. As part of its effort to contain the spread of communism and Soviet influence, the United States provided aid to a variety of regimes throughout the world, and the degree to which the recipient states were democratic, free of corruption, and internally popular varied considerably.

During the Eisenhower and Kennedy years, the Vietnam situation was mainly exceptional because of its unusual combination of problems: the simmering guerrilla war, the unsteadiness of the South Vietnamese government, the National Liberation Front's (NLF) inclination to undertake high-profile terrorist actions, and the perceived threat to other Southeast Asian countries. These circumstances resulted in a comparatively high-profile situation which kept the attention of US decisionmakers and the American media.

US support to the government of South Vietnam (GVN) before the introduction of combat troops was not difficult to justify in the minds of most policymakers. The financial commitment to South Vietnam in the early 1960s was not burdensome and even the provision of American advisors to the Army of the Republic of Vietnam (ARVN) was not very difficult; the number of advisors was small and did not place a noticeable strain on military personnel resources. Americans were killed in Vietnam even before US forces undertook major combat operations and this did present a potentially significant domestic political problem to policymakers. Nevertheless, there was little reason to believe that the American public would not have been willing to tolerate the ongoing assignment of several thousand military advisors to South Vietnam.

The deployment of large numbers of US combat troops to the defense of South Vietnam represented a very different type of commitment from the American perspective. It was difficult for the US military to meet its personnel needs elsewhere in the world while also fighting in Vietnam, and after the experience in Korea the American public was suspicious of wars of containment at the fringes of the communist bloc in Asia. To a citizenry that took a proprietary interest in its army, sending large numbers of US troops to battle represented a very serious commitment. The Korean War had already illustrated the American public's impatience with limited conflicts waged for vague goals. Of particular relevance to the Vietnam situation, Korea had confirmed that a communist great power might come to the direct military aid of a neighbouring minor communist power, even when such intervention meant combat with US troops.

In light of such factors, US policymakers had good reasons to choose their ground for a war of containment carefully. They had to contend with limitations on available resources – the United States was certainly not going to place its society on a war footing as it had in the Second World War – and had grounds for the belief that the public tolerance of such a war would be restricted. Furthermore, policymakers were aware that the military–political situation in Vietnam was volatile and presented the United States with many and varied challenges.

Nonetheless, despite the obvious difficulties inherent in fighting in Vietnam – an unstable Saigon government and a troubled South Vietnamese army, a North Vietnamese government with fairly solid nationalist credentials, a peasantry largely disaffected from the central government and a strong and potentially self-sustaining guerrilla insurgency, an inability to isolate the battle-field without either invading North Vietnam or occupying the territory of nominally neutral countries, and so forth – US policymakers chose to fight there rather than to pull back and wait for a later, and perhaps more manageable, communist challenge (probably in Thailand). Claims by some US policy-makers to complete ignorance of the potential problems of defending South Vietnam appear questionable, if not disingenuous, on close examination.[7] Many observers realized that the problem in South Vietnam was not strictly military and that the weakness of the South Vietnamese government presented a major difficulty for the United States.[8]

The domino theory, or perhaps more importantly the strategic–political paradigm subscribed to by those policymakers who were intellectually responsive to the domino theory, weighed heavily in this decisionmaking process. US leaders saw the expansion of communism, and with that the expansion of Soviet Union and/or Chinese power, as a threat that had to be addressed and were willing to fight under conditions that were far from ideal if circumstances so demanded. Yet at the same time, the feelings of policymakers and the public about the war were always somewhat ambivalent and the intellectual commitment to containment was tempered by a worry that the Vietnam enterprise was ultimately not worthwhile. This ambivalence was a vital dimension to the Vietnam policymaking process: concern about the expansion of Soviet power led the United States into Vietnam, but decisionmakers usually lacked the intellectual and emotional conviction that the survival of the RVN was important enough to justify the assumption of high risks.

CONTAINMENT IN CONTEXT

A popular 'myth of containment' postulates that during the entire period from 1947 until the collapse of the Soviet Union in 1991, the United States chose to challenge communist power everywhere that it threatened to expand, regardless of the nature of the regime that communists threatened to replace. This image is one of a hegemonic United States rushing to plug any holes in its complex system of alliances and to exploit weaknesses within the enemy camp. But this is clearly overstated; the reality was much less neat – at times the United States displayed considerable vigor in its containment effort, and at other times its reactions to important events were belated, tepid, and uncertain.

Other than military aid and unenthusiastic political support, the United States offered little resistance to Mao Zedong's 1949 victory over the Nationalist Kuomintang, despite the feeling of many Americans that a 'special relationship' existed between the United States and China. The rhetoric of John Foster Dulles aside, the United States also declined to attempt communist 'rollback' in Eastern Europe by taking self-liberated Hungary under its protection in 1956. Washington even allowed a communist regime to take root in Cuba. Any of these events could, in theory, have occasioned direct United States military intervention, but for various reasons US policymakers chose not to risk acts of war against communist forces (except, of course, for American organization and backing of the farcical 'Bay of Pigs' invasion by Cuban exile forces in 1961).[9] Yet despite taking a cautious course toward a communist government less than 100 miles from Florida, the Kennedy administration greatly deepened the US presence in South Vietnam. Essentially the same policymakers who chose to reject the possibility of changing the government of Cuba by force of American arms, a project for which many contemporary observers argued,[10] and that probably could have been brought rapidly to a successful conclusion, took on – with considerable alacrity – the very difficult long-term project of providing major assistance to South Vietnam to protect that country from a communist take-over.

Whatever the real merits of the decision to defend South Vietnam vigorously, the Indochinese situation was perceived as demanding such strong action. A broad policy consensus formed around intervention in Vietnam because of accidents of circumstance, not because Vietnam was necessarily the most important or best area in which to oppose communist expansion.[11] In a different political context, the United States might have done little for South Vietnam and allowed that government to disintegrate, but the intellectual atmosphere that surrounded US policymakers encouraged the belief that a commitment to Indochina should be part of the worldwide effort to contain communism.[12] Despite the problems inherent in involvement in a Southeast Asian war, US policymakers were willing to intervene in Indochina and to increase their involvement with a series of steps that led eventually to large-scale US commitment to combat.

Part of the explanation for policy choices in Southeast Asia almost certainly lies in the dynamics of the US involvement. The United States first became involved in Vietnam in a limited and seemingly low-risk fashion – the provision of assistance to the French in their war against the Viet Minh.[13] As the US involvement grew the sense of obligation to South Vietnam and the importance of Vietnam to US international prestige increased. Yet, since the Vietnam problem was a chronic condition that never commanded the undivided attention of policymakers there was a tendency to drift into an ever-greater commitment without a careful assessment of the risks, problems, or possible benefits for the United States.

This observation about the slow entanglement of the United States in South Vietnam is perhaps best described as the 'quagmire thesis'.[14] It is key to conventional explanations of how the United States became trapped in Vietnam. To a degree it is a credible explanation, especially when accompanied by discussion of how the 'domino theory' impacted the thinking of decision-makers and helped create an intellectual environment in which the United States was susceptible to entanglement in the war. Many policymakers believed that the loss of Vietnam to communism could be an important propellant for the spread of communism throughout Southeast Asia. Considering the perhaps simplistic framework within which some US policymakers viewed the Cold War struggle – viewing the spread of communist rule to any previously non-communist country as a significant setback rather than carefully assessing the relative strategic values of threatened areas and accepting that the loss of marginal lands might be less costly than defending them – these reasons provided a compelling rationale for US involvement in South Vietnam.

Nonetheless, merely invoking the tendency of military quagmires to consume unsuspecting great powers and noting the containment-minded intellectual environment in Washington is ultimately not sufficient to explain why the situation in Vietnam seemed, from the perspective of US decisionmakers, to demand strong action. The United States, a power that was not innocent of the subtleties of foreign entanglements, embarked on a 'policy journey' in which an ever-deepening commitment was made to the independence of South Vietnam, and it did so despite the fact that there was little about South Vietnam, or even all of Indochina, to indicate that the area was particularly vital to US interests.[15]

Presidents Roosevelt and Truman gave relatively little attention to Indochina.[16] Eisenhower attached considerable importance to South Vietnam,[17] but only dispatched a small number of advisors to that country; his significant assistance to Saigon was in the form of aid.[18] Moreover, it would seem likely that communism in South Vietnam would have virtually no direct effect on the defensibility of Western Europe, the region about which the United States was most concerned. In addition, American historical links to Indochina were minimal, the South Vietnamese contribution to the American economy was negligible, and a notoriously corrupt government with suspect democratic credentials ruled Saigon.

In addition, many observers understood that the United States military was not intellectually and psychologically well prepared to fight in Vietnam. The military was intellectually focused on possible war with the Red Army in Western Europe and, except for speciality units like the Green Berets, was not particularly interested in, or proficient at, counterinsurgency operations. Though some observers believed that the US involvement in Vietnam would be a relatively quick and painless exercise, many knew that it would be neither, and some even understood the importance of political patience to ultimate success in Vietnam.[19] Such leading figures as Senator Richard Russell and Senate majority leader Mike Mansfield, a former professor of Asian history, warned against the United States making a serious military commitment to Vietnam.[20]

Less than 20 years before the commitment of large numbers of US troops to the defense of South Vietnam, the US government put forth only a feeble effort to 'save' China, but the generation of policymakers that occupied high office during the Kennedy and Johnson years operated in a considerably different political environment. The necessity of the Cold War struggle against the spread of communism was accepted by most policymakers (and by most Americans), and the containment of communism in general and of Soviet and Chinese power in particular was the linchpin of US foreign policy. Furthermore, the political and bureaucratic environment in which leaders operated shaped decisions. Public opinion, current military capability, and the willingness of foreign governments to cooperate with initiatives all influenced policy; actions which would be almost unthinkable to the Truman administration later become politically feasible. Many of the policymakers who shaped the effort in Vietnam had been in government during the Korean War and they were determined to 'get it right this time' by conducting an effective, highly controlled limited war in Vietnam.

The Truman administration had been unsure how to proceed with containment from 1945 to 1950; Washington did not want to alienate the Soviet Union unnecessarily – or, after 1949, the People's Republic of China (PRC) – and certainly did not want to provoke a war. Indeed, in the early years of that period Truman himself believed the American public was unwilling to countenance military action to prevent the spread of communism.[21] After the announcement of the Truman Doctrine on 12 March 1947, an inconsistent but conspicuous program of worldwide communist containment started to take shape, but US troops were only committed to combat against communist forces after the June 1950 invasion of South Korea.

The Kennedy and Johnson administrations, however, were confident that the Soviet Union and the People's Republic of China were highly, and perhaps irredeemably, antagonistic to the United States.[22] Kennedy and Johnson, and their top officials, expressed an interest in negotiations that might lead to improvements in Soviet–American relations, but saw the Soviet and communist Chinese regimes as being intensely committed to undermining vulnerable non-communist governments and damaging the position of the United States in the world. It was clear to all parties involved that the relationship between the United States and the communist powers was highly adversarial. Policymakers in both administrations believed that a forceful response to attempted communist expansion was necessary to prevent communist success (an unsurprising attitude for a group of policymakers steeped in the then not-so-distant 'lessons of Munich').[23]

At a time when the Soviet Union was probing the Third World and various forms of Marxist ideology appealed to sizeable elements of the elite and general populace in some newly-independent countries, any surrender of territory to communist control was viewed by most US policymakers as a practical setback and an indication of weakness that would be noticed by both friends and foes.[24] Though often dismissed by critics as excessive, or even irrational, the reaction of US policymakers to the perceived communist threat was understandable. Although US leaders were confident in the superior virtue of their system of government, the Soviet Union's military establishment was growing progressively more powerful and the deepness of the inherent flaws in the Soviet economy was not apparent to most observers.[25] Victory over communism was not in sight to US policymakers, and they had reason to believe that the containment of communism might require numerous small wars in various parts of the Third World.[26] Particularly after the embarrassment in Cuba, there was a determination to draw a line against further communist expansion as quickly as possible and thereby to shore up the confidence of US allies in their protector while simultaneously warning the Soviet Union and the PRC that future imperial expansion on their part would be difficult, if not impossible. As Robert McNamara wrote in a 7 January 1964 memorandum to President Johnson:

> In the eyes of the rest of Asia and of key areas threatened by Communism in other areas as well, South Vietnam is both a test of US firmness and specifically a test of US capacity to deal with 'wars of national liberation'. Within Asia, there is evidence – for example, from Japan – that US disengagement and the acceptance of Communist domination would have a serious effect on confidence. More broadly, there can be little doubt that any country threatened in the future by Communist subversion would have reason to doubt whether we would really see the thing through. This would apply even in such theoretically remote areas as Latin America ... My assessment of our important security interests is that they unquestionably call for holding the line against further Communist gains. And, I am confident that the American people are by and large in favor of a policy of firmness and strength in such situations.[27]

In the policymaking environment then prevailing, numerous factors came together to reassure decisionmakers in their belief that the situation in South Vietnam demanded US intervention while not clarifying the potential negative outcomes of a failed effort to save that country. Among other considerations, they were reluctant to cede ground anywhere,[28] confident that they had learned from the mistakes of the Korean War, eager to confirm that the United States was still an authoritative protecting power, largely convinced that if communist expansionism were not met with countervailing force then communism would continue to flow into vulnerable areas and overtake them, and fearful of the consequences of a national debate over 'who lost Vietnam'.[29] Also, the US presence in Vietnam increased slowly, which increased the sense of obligation to Vietnam on the part of policymakers without simultaneously throwing up prominent 'red flags' that would warn policymakers that there was a very good chance that the United States would fail to achieve its goals in Vietnam and would thereby greatly damage its international prestige and damage its foreign policy credibility throughout the world.[30]

American civilian leaders understood intellectually that a severe negative result was, theoretically, a possible outcome of the Vietnam enterprise, but the high likelihood of a negative outcome to a very constrained war was not apparent to most of them. They were understandably confident in the quality of both their military instrument and strategic analysis, and failure in Vietnam seemed unlikely regardless of whether or not the United States fought in an unusually constrained fashion.

CONCLUSION: THE CLASH OF 'INEVITABLE' OUTCOMES

US policymakers had a complicated notion about what they stood to gain by preventing a communist take-over of South Vietnam, but their assessment of the risks involved in defending Vietnam was incomplete. It appears that most US policymakers did not appreciate at crucial decision points in 1964 and 1965 how serious the consequences of a failed intervention in Vietnam might be, *or how likely it was that the US intervention would in practice prove not to be politically viable.*[31] This was a major oversight in the US decisionmaking process – most policymakers seem not to have considered seriously the long-term political viability of the Vietnam project. They worried about matters related to the popularity of US involvement in Vietnam, but they never developed a real plan to cope with public-relations problems, made no concerted propaganda effort on the home front, and eventually alienated most of the national press corps.

Ultimately, policymaking requires leaps of faith. Some problems are acknowledged as not being immediately fixable; it is simply hoped that they will at some future point be solved, neutralized, or at least will be no more than minor handicaps. The course of action taken by the United States in response to the problems experienced by South Vietnam in the mid-1960s indicates that most US policymakers implicitly assumed that the Vietnam project was politically sustainable as a 'small war' until such time as the South Vietnamese insurgency could be defeated outright or an acceptable accommodation could be reached with North Vietnam. That assumption had a major impact on decisions about the US role in Vietnam.

For example, this assumption of success is well illustrated in a November

1964 National Security Council Working Group (NSCWG) paper that played a major role in shaping the Washington debate on Vietnam at a crucial decision point.[32] Stating that 'the loss of South Vietnam to Communist control, in any form, would be a major blow to our basic policies',[33] while also noting potential flaws in the 'domino' theory and stating that '[w]ithin NATO (except for Greece and Turkey to some degree), the loss of South Vietnam probably would not shake the faith and resolve to face the threat of Communist aggression or confidence in us for major help',[34] the paper then describes three broad policy options for the United States, which vary from continuing the status quo (Option A), to a program of military pressure against North Vietnam that is to involve 'increasing pressure actions to be continued at a fairly rapid pace and without interruption until we achieve our present stated objectives' (Option B),[35] to a policy of escalated response (Option C).

All of the options mention the possibility that South Vietnam might collapse before the United States had an opportunity to take substantial action to assist that country, but none discusses the possibility that the US position in Indochina might prove to be politically untenable at home. There are references in related documents to the United States' will to stay in Vietnam,[36] but – like so much of the early Vietnam debate in the United States – the discussion is essentially policy-oriented in a narrow sense. The debate between policymakers was about 'options' rather than questions of national will; in hindsight, this appears to be a flawed perspective that left a vital element out of the Vietnam debate.

Ironically, Lyndon Johnson felt that he must intervene in Vietnam to prevent a North Vietnamese victory that would bring about a 'divisive debate' that would 'shatter my presidency, kill my administration and damage our democracy'.[37] Johnson's fear of a debate similar to that conducted over 'who lost China' following Mao's victory in 1949 was reasonable. If the United States did not oppose the communists in Vietnam militarily some American political leaders would, for understandable reasons, accuse the Johnson administration of deserting an ally and showing weakness in the fight against communist expansion. While the South Vietnamese government was unsavory in some respects, it was non-communist, friendly to the United States, and so weak that it obviously required US support in order to survive.[38]

It is commonplace to assume that the United States stumbled into war in Vietnam, but that image is misleading. As US policymakers 'climbed the escalation ladder', they were well aware of the fact that they were taking their country into an ongoing war.[39] For example, in an 18 June 1965 memo to President Johnson, Under Secretary of State Ball argues that, 'In raising our commitment from 50,000 to 100,000 or more men and deploying most of the increment *in combat roles* we are beginning a new war – the United States *directly* against the Viet Cong.'[40] Nevertheless, most US policymakers – including President Johnson and Secretary of Defense McNamara – seemed to have only nebulous ideas about war termination. US leaders wanted North Vietnam to cease its attempts to overthrow the Saigon government, but they had rather vague ideas on how to convince Hanoi to abandon its drive for unification.

Furthermore, the unhealthy condition of the Saigon government presented policymakers with a variety of difficulties that drove the United States toward direct military intervention. Corruption and ineptitude within the ARVN made it difficult for the South Vietnamese to defend themselves. If the ARVN had been in a reasonably healthy condition in the mid-1960s and if the GVN were stable, it might have been sufficient for the United States to send only military aid and advisors to South Vietnam. This would have been far preferable from the perspective of US policymakers – the Kennedy administration had avoided a major combat commitment in Vietnam, and the Johnson administration also tried to do so for as long as possible.[41] Yet, in the (almost undoubtedly correct) estimation of US leaders the South Vietnamese Army was not adequate to the task of defending its country from the communist forces. In the period between the November 1963 overthrow of Diem and the March 1965 introduction of ground combat units South Vietnam appeared to many observers to be on the verge of internal collapse.[42] To most policymakers the introduction of US troops seemed the best way to stabilize a very wobbly government. They therefore felt it necessary to overcome their aversion to the introduction of ground troops and to commit US forces, even though the very instability of the GVN was, in turn, thought likely to hinder the effectiveness of any US military effort.

Any search for a single, overriding factor that led to US combat involvement in Vietnam is probably misguided. There is no compelling evidence that a single policy consideration led to the US commitment to South Vietnam; certainly, there is no single memorandum that would explain comprehensively the reasoning behind the Vietnam involvement. Rather, the pressures on policymakers repeatedly made it appear that an ever-increasing commitment to South Vietnam was the best available alternative out of a set of unattractive options. With hindsight, this was a serious error of analysis that occurred chiefly because US leaders did not accurately judge the long-term political sustainability of the Vietnam project at an early point in the process of entanglement. Furthermore, they were unwilling to take the escalatory measures necessary for rapid war termination because they believed that the risk of war with the PRC would be too high. By the time a 'critical mass' of policymakers concluded that the Vietnam project was not politically sustainable for the time necessary to secure victory through an attritional style of war, US troops had already participated in substantial combat and US prestige and credibility were at stake to a very great degree. Thus, US policymakers had trapped themselves in a war that they no longer considered worthwhile, but from which they were unable to withdraw with dignity.

US policymakers chose some of the worst plausible options for securing their Vietnam goals, but they did so for some of the best conceivable reasons, including a desire to prevent Vietnam from providing the spark that might ignite a great power war, or even a Third World War. Whatever the motives of US decisionmakers, however, they *chose* to undertake a long-term anti-guerrilla struggle that did not play to the strengths of the US military – a course that made their task in Vietnam immensely difficult.

Other courses that the United States could have chosen would almost certainly have proven militarily more fruitful. The United States had the means, for example, to undertake a consistent strategic air campaign and naval blockade against the DRV, crippling its infrastructure and cutting its logistical links to China and USSR, and to occupy large swathes of Laos and Cambodia and undertake a serious campaign to cut the Ho Chi Minh Trail. These options were militarily realistic,[43] but policymakers believed, not unreasonably, that all involved a risk of touching off a war against China;[44] as we shall see, their behavior was constrained enormously by perceptions of grave risks. Johnson administration policymakers never resolved satisfactorily the tension between their desires to preserve the RVN, limit the military role of the United States in Indochina, and maintain public support for their efforts. Thus, Washington took the 'middle of the road' course and the reward for the modesty of its commitment was a war more costly in every sense than any but the most pessimistic US policymakers imagined – and eventual defeat.

NOTES

1. Edward G. Lansdale, 'Still the Search for Goals', *Foreign Affairs*, 46, 1 (October 1968), p. 92.
2. For a defense of the US effort in Vietnam by a major Johnson administration policymaker, see W.W. Rostow, 'The Case for the Vietnam War', *Parameters*, 26, 4 (Winter 1996/97), pp. 39–50.
3. Some of the many works concerning the question of how the United States came to be entangled militarily in Vietnam include David M. Barrett, *Uncertain Warriors: Lyndon Johnson and His Vietnam Advisors* (Lawrence, KS: University Press of Kansas, 1993); Larry Berman, *Planning a Tragedy: The Americanization of the War in Vietnam* (New York: W.W. Norton, 1983); George McT. Kahin, *Intervention: How America Became Involved in Vietnam* (New York: Alfred A. Knopf, 1986); Herbert Y. Schandler, *The Unmaking of a President: Lyndon Johnson and Vietnam* (Princeton, NJ: Princeton University Press, 1977); Robert D. Schulzinger, '"It's Easy to Win a War on Paper": The United States and Vietnam, 1961–1968' in Diane B. Kunz (ed.), *The Diplomacy of the Crucial Decade: American Foreign Relations During the 1960s* (New York: Columbia University Press, 1994), pp. 183–218; and Brian VanDeMark, *Into the Quagmire: Lyndon Johnson and the Escalation of the Vietnam War* (New York: Oxford University Press, 1991).
4. For instance, National Security Advisor McGeorge Bundy complained 'that the military thought of the war in Vietnam too much in terms of regular conventional warfare with an identifiable enemy and specific military objectives'. (US Department of State, 'Memorandum for the Record of the White House Daily Staff Meeting, Washington,

March 30, 1964. 8 a.m.', 30 March 1964, *Papers Relating to the Foreign Relations of the United States, 1964–1968* (Washington: GPO, 1992), p. 1:197. Hereafter cited as *FRUS*.)

5. In a paper written by Assistant Secretary of Defense McNaughton and distributed to McNamara and other top policymakers, he estimated that the US goals in South Vietnam were '70% – avoid a humiliating US defeat (to our reputation as guarantor)'. ('Paper Prepared by the Assistant Secretary of Defense for International Security Affairs (McNaughton)', 10 March 1965, *FRUS, 1964–1968*, p. 2:427.) On McNaughton's role in Indochina decisionmaking, see Lawrence Freedman, 'Vietnam and the Disillusioned Strategist', *International Affairs*, 72, 1 (January 1996), pp. 133–51.

6. Henry Kissinger observes that '[a]s the leader of democratic alliances we had to remember that scores of countries and millions of people relied for their security on our willingness to stand by allies, indeed on our confidence in ourselves. No serious policymaker could allow himself to succumb to the fashionable debunking of "prestige" or "honor" or "credibility" … We could not revitalize the Atlantic Alliance if its governments were assailed by doubt about American staying power. We would not be able to move the Soviet Union toward the imperative of mutual restraint against the background of capitulation in a major war.' (*White House Years* (Boston, MA: Little, Brown, 1979), p. 228.)

7. At important escalation decision points, high-level US policymakers realized that they were pursuing a difficult course and apparently there was little illusion that the war in South Vietnam would be brought to a quick, successful conclusion. See Leslie H. Gelb, with Richard K. Betts, *The Irony of Vietnam: The System Worked* (Washington, DC: Brookings Institution, 1979), p. 24, and R. Buzzanco, *Masters of War: Military Dissent and Politics in the Vietnam Era* (New York: Cambridge University Press, 1996), *passim*. On the vital period from January to July 1965 see Robert S. McNamara, with Brian VanDeMark, *In Retrospect: The Tragedy and Lessons of Vietnam* (New York: Vintage, 1996), pp. 169–206.

8. See Bryce F. Denno, 'Military Prospects in Vietnam', *Orbis*, 9, 2 (Summer 1965), pp. 411–17.

9. On the flawed planning for the Bay of Pigs invasion see Trumbull Higgins, *The Perfect Failure: Kennedy, Eisenhower, and the CIA at the Bay of Pigs* (New York: W.W. Norton, 1987).

10. As one author notes, in early 1961 many American newspapers 'were calling for following up the failure of Bay of Pigs with a full-scale invasion of Cuba'. (Richard Reeves, *President Kennedy: Profile of Power* (London: Papermac, 1994), p. 108.)

11. It should however be noted that many policymakers took very seriously the possibility that the fall of South Vietnam would have significant 'ripple' effects. For example, a memorandum from McNamara to Johnson warned that '[w]ithout [American] support … Vietnam will collapse, and the ripple effect will be felt throughout Southeast Asia, endangering the independent governments of Thailand and Malaysia, and extending as far as India on the west, Indonesia on the south, and the Philippines on the east.' ('Memorandum Prepared in the Department of Defense', 2 March 1964, *FRUS, 1964–1968*, p. 1:119.)

12. Bernard Fall describes well the US government's preoccupation with demonstrating steadfastness in Asia. 'With each successive blow [to US foreign policy in Asia], the American determination to make a stand somewhere became stronger. A success in the Far East, far from remaining essentially a political, military, or diplomatic objective, became an internal American issue. "Firmness" became a policy *per se* rather than a style of policy, since all flexibility was immediately associated with previous periods of "weakness".' (Roger M. Smith (ed.), *Anatomy of a Crisis: The Laotian Crisis of 1960–1961* (Garden City, NY: Doubleday, 1969), p. 158.)

13. On the origins of the US military advisory role in Vietnam see Ronald H. Spector, *Advice and Support: The Early Years of the US Army in Vietnam, 1941–1960* (New York: Free Press, 1985).

14. For a work that challenges many of the assumptions of the quagmire thesis see Gelb, *The Irony of Vietnam*.

15. The Joint Chiefs of Staff (JCS) effectively said this in a May 1954 memo to Secretary of Defense Charles Wilson. Indochina was described as 'devoid of decisive military objectives' and it was noted that 'the allocation of more than token US armed forces to that area would be a serious diversion of limited US capabilities'. (Quoted in William Conrad Gibbons, *The US Government and the Vietnam War: Executive and Legislative Roles and Relationships*, Part I: 1945–1960 (Princeton, NJ: Princeton University Press, 1986), p. 236.)

16. See Schulzinger, *A Time for War*, p. 17.

17. For example, 'in speaking of Southeast Asia, President Eisenhower had said that South Viet Nam's capture by the communists would bring their power several hundred miles into a hitherto free region. The freedom of 12 million people would be lost immediately, and that of 150 million in adjacent lands would be seriously endangered. The loss of South Viet Nam would set in motion a crumbling process that could, as it progressed, have grave consequences for us and for freedom'. (Clark Clifford, 'A Viet Nam Reappraisal', *Foreign Affairs*, 47, 4 (July 1969), p. 605.)

18. A detailed study of the Eisenhower administration's Vietnam policy is offered in David L. Anderson, *Trapped by Success: The Eisenhower Administration and Vietnam, 1953–1961*, Contemporary American History Series (New York: Columbia University Press, 1991).

19. '[T]he real test of South Vietnam's (and the United States') ability to withstand the pressures of the Second Indochina War is going to come in the political field. Yet it is precisely in that field the whole first year after Diem's overthrow can be written off, at best as a total loss or at worst as a fatal step backwards.' (Bernard Fall, 'The Second Indochina War', *International Affairs*, 41, 1 (January 1965), p. 70.)

20. Stanley Karnow, *Vietnam: A History* (New York: Penguin Books, 1984), pp. 326–7.

21. Truman writes that 'I knew that peace in the world would not be achieved by fighting more wars. Most of all, I was always aware that there were two enormous land masses that no western army of modern times had ever been able to conquer: Russia and China ... In 1945 and 1946, of all years, such thoughts would have been rejected by the American people before they were even expressed.' (*Years of Trial and Hope: 1946–1953* (London: Hodder & Stoughton, 1956), p. 96.) It is notable, however, that even in 1948–49 Mao was gravely worried about the possibility of US intervention in the Chinese Civil War. See Hao Yufan and Zhai Zhihai, 'China's Decision to Enter the Korean War: History Revisited', *China Quarterly*, 121 (March 1990), pp. 95–9.

22. For example, in a speech on 7 April 1965, President Johnson claimed that '[t]he rulers in Hanoi are urged on by Peking. This is a regime which had destroyed freedom in Tibet, which has attacked India and has been condemned by the United Nations for aggression in Korea. It is a nation which is helping the forces of violence in almost every continent. The contest in Viet-Nam is part of a wider pattern of aggressive behavior.' (Quoted in Marcus G. Raskin and Bernard B. Fall (eds), *The Viet-Nam Reader: Articles and Documents on American Foreign Policy and the Vietnam Crisis* (rev. edn, New York: Vintage, 1967), p. 345.)

23. On the anticommunism of John F. Kennedy, one author writes that '[Kennedy] had always known about the Communists. They were tough and we had to be tougher; they responded only to force so we had to have more force than they. Reminiscent of Theodore Roosevelt, President Kennedy called for Americans to get into geopolitical

shape to adopt a sort of athletic patriotism to meet the future's challenges.' (Loren Baritz, *Backfire: A History of How American Culture Led Us into Vietnam and Made Us Fight the Way We Did* (New York: Ballantine, 1985), p. 90.) The macho culture of the Kennedy White House and its relation to the effort in Vietnam is explored in Robert D. Dean, 'Masculinity as Ideology: John F. Kennedy and the Domestic Politics of Foreign Policy', *Diplomatic History*, 22, 1 (Winter 1998), pp. 29–62.

24. See Gelb, *The Irony of Vietnam*, p. 366.

25. Indeed, even two decades later, many Western commentators grossly overestimated the productivity of the Soviet Union's economy. One author points out that as late as 1984 the celebrated economist J. Kenneth Galbraith 'assured the West that labour productivity per person was higher in the USSR than in America'. (Quoted in Mark Almond, '1989 Without Gorbachev: What If Communism Had Not Collapsed?', in Niall Ferguson (ed.), *Virtual History: Alternatives and Counterfactuals* (London: Papermac, 1997), p. 395.)

26. General Maxwell Taylor stated in a report to President Kennedy concerning Vietnam that '[i]t is my judgment and that of my colleagues that the United States must decide how it will cope with Khrushchev's 'wars of liberation' which are really para-wars of guerrilla aggression. This is a new and dangerous communist technique which bypasses our traditional political and military responses.' (Quoted in Lyndon Baines Johnson, *The Vantage Point* (New York: Popular Library, 1971), p. 58.)

27. 'Memorandum From the Secretary of Defense (McNamara) to the President', 8 January 1964, *FRUS, 1964–1968*, p. 1:8.

28. For instance, McNamara stated in a speech on 26 March 1964 that South Vietnam was 'a member of the free-world family, [and] is striving to preserve its independence from Communist attack ... Our own security is strengthened by the determination of others to remain free, and by our commitment to assist them. We will not let this member of our family down, regardless of its distance from our shores.' (Quoted in Raskin and Fall (eds), *The Viet-Nam Reader*, p. 194.)

29. On the latter, see VanDeMark, *Into the Quagmire*, p. 216.

30. McNamara argues that '[w]e [Rusk and McNamara] failed to ask the five most basic questions: Was it true that the fall of South Vietnam would trigger the fall of all Southeast Asia? Would that constitute a grave threat to the West's security? What kind of war – conventional or guerrilla – might develop? Could we win it with US troops fighting alongside the South Vietnamese? Should we not know the answers to all these questions before deciding whether to commit troops? It seems beyond understanding, incredible, that we did not force ourselves to confront such issues head-on. But then, it is very hard, today, to recapture the innocence and confidence with which we approached Vietnam in the early days of the Kennedy Administration.' (*In Retrospect*, p. 39.)

31. One influential author makes the case that 'the highest-ranking officers of the Vietnam era simultaneously made war and played politics', being aware of 'the uncertain, if not bleak, chances for success, these officers consistently requested the very measures – massive reinforcement, activation of Reserves, mobilization, total air war – that the White House would never authorize' in the hope of shifting blame for failure in Vietnam to civilian policymakers. (Buzzanco, *Masters of War*, pp. 10–11.) This argument is, however, fundamentally flawed, because it confuses the best military judgment of senior military officers with their political goals: it is highly probable that the Joint Chiefs of Staff (JCS) suggested most of the above measures (as we shall see, 'total' air war of the sort practiced against Japan in the Second World War was not recommended by the JCS) because they were militarily sound. Unless available evidence is viewed in a highly selective manner, it is difficult to conclude that many high-ranking officers believed in the mid-1960s that the United States would not prevail in Vietnam. Most JCS members

disapproved of the 'Johnson–McNamara way of war' because they correctly saw it as a poor strategy that would prolong the conflict, *not* because they believed that the American effort was inevitably doomed and that it was necessary to 'pin the rap' for defeat on civilian policymakers. Indeed, during the mid-1960s the JCS, far from practicing deft manipulation of civilian policymakers, was unusually weak, with McNamara ensuring that the president heard little of the intense military disapproval for Johnson administration policy in Vietnam. A convincing alternative to the Buzzanco view on the relationship between civilian and military policymakers in the Johnson administration is offered in H.R. McMaster, *Dereliction of Duty: Lyndon Johnson, Robert McNamara, the Joint Chiefs of Staff, and the Lies that Led to Vietnam* (New York: HarperCollins, 1997).

32. 'Paper Prepared by the National Security Council Working Group', 21 November 1964, *FRUS, 1966–1968*, pp. 1:916-29. As the *FRUS* editors explain in a footnote, this paper was circulated repeatedly in draft form and no copy of the actual 21 November draft has been found; the copy printed in *FRUS* is identical to that draft except for small changes made on 26 November.

33. Ibid., p. 917.

34. Ibid., p. 919.

35. Ibid., p. 920. It should be noted that the Joint Chiefs of Staff released a memorandum countering the NSCWG paper and rejecting NSCWG Option B as 'not a valid formulation of any authoritative views known to the Joint Chiefs of Staff'. The Joint Chiefs proposed an alternative 'Course B' which included a program of 'intense military pressures against the DRV' that 'would be carried through, if necessary to the full limits of what military actions can contribute toward US national objectives'. This Course B – a more vigorous military option than any proposed in the NSCWG paper – is endorsed by the JCS in the memo. See 'Memorandum From the Joint Chiefs of Staff to the Secretary of Defense (McNamara)', 23 November 1964, *FRUS, 1964–1968*, pp. 1:932-5.

36. For example, an NSCWG intelligence assessment puts forth the view that communist actions against South Vietnam 'implies a fundamental estimate on their part that the difficulties facing the US are so great that US will and ability to maintain resistance in that area can be gradually eroded – without running high risks that the US would wreak heavy destruction on the DRV or Communist China'. (Quoted in William Conrad Gibbons, *The US Government and the Vietnam War: Executive and Legislative Roles and Relationships*, Part II: 1961–1964 (Princeton, NJ: Princeton University Press, 1986), p. 369.)

37. Karnow, *Vietnam*, p. 320.

38. Some authors critical of US foreign policy would go so far as to describe South Vietnam as essentially an American client regime. 'The assassination of Ngo Dinh Diem … marked the end of the myth of an independent South Vietnam. From now on, the US government, which had conspired with Vietnamese generals in its pay to overthrow Diem, it own chosen ruler of South Vietnam, had to operate through a succession of military dictators, all linked directly to the Pentagon's military command structure.' (Marvin E. Gettleman *et al.* (eds), *Vietnam and America* (rev. 2nd edn, New York: Grove, 1995), p. 239.)

39. Writing of his July 1965 decision to increase US troop levels in Vietnam, Johnson makes clear that he was choosing to embark on a conventional ground war of some size and that the hostilities in Vietnam could potentially escalate into a superpower conflict. 'Now we were committed to major combat in Vietnam. We had determined not to let the country fall under Communist rule as long as we could prevent it and as long as the Vietnamese continued to fight for themselves. At the same time, I was resolved to do everything possible to keep this a limited war, to prevent it from expanding into a nuclear conflict.' (*Vantage Point*, p. 153.)

40. 'Memorandum From the Under Secretary of State (Ball) to President Johnson', 18 June 1965, *FRUS, 1964–1968*, p. 3:18. Emphasis in original.

41. During the 1964 campaign, Johnson repeatedly made statements to the effect that 'American boys should not do the fighting that Asian boys should do for themselves.' (*Vantage Point*, pp. 240–1.) Although he carefully avoided any explicit promise not to send US combat units to Vietnam, many observers later accused Johnson of lying to the electorate. In his memoirs Johnson indirectly answers the charges of bad faith often leveled against him, stating that 'I was answering those who proposed, or implied, that we should take charge of the war or carry out actions that would risk a war with Communist China. I did not mean that we were not going to do any fighting, for we had already lost many good men in Vietnam. I made it clear that those who were ready to fight for their own freedom would find us at their side if they wanted and needed us ... A good many people compared my position in 1964 with that of [Goldwater], and decided I was the "peace" candidate and he was the "war" candidate. They were not willing to hear anything they did not want to hear.' (Ibid.) However, Johnson's explanation is disingenuous: it is clear that he was attempting to portray the election to the public as a choice between peace and war and misleading voters on the likelihood of sustained US involvement in ground combat. See Robert D. Schulzinger, *A Time for War* (New York: Oxford University Press, 1997), pp. 155–6.

42. The sentiments expressed in the minutes of a 30 May 1964 meeting involving many of the major US foreign policymakers are typical of the period. 'Mr [George] Ball asked for comment on his assessment that the general situation in Viet-Nam was deteriorating. Secretary McNamara agreed with this assessment. He said he agreed with UK representative [Robert] Thompson who was in Washington this week, who said that his assessment was that nothing much was happening and that there was lots of talk but little action. He said that Thompson had stated that he did not know whether we were beyond the point of no return, and that if the present deterioration continues the situation would disintegrate in anywhere from three to four months to nine months from now. If the situation is to be retrieved Thompson favored getting rid of the Dai Viet. Secretary McNamara said these conclusions were approximately the same as his own.' ('Summary Record of a Meeting, Department of State, Washington, May 30, 1964, 10:30 a.m.', 30 May 1964, *FRUS, 1964–1968*, pp. 1:397-8.)

43. For a discussion by the Joint Chiefs of Staff of some of the military options available to the United States see 'Memorandum for the Secretary of Defense, 2 March 1964', Papers of Robert S. McNamara, RG 200, Box 82, United States National Archives, NN3-2000-092-001 HM 92-93. The role of the JCS in Vietnam decisionmaking is explored in detail in Buzzanco, *Masters of War*; McMaster, *Dereliction of Duty*; and Mark Perry, *Four Stars* (Boston, MA: Houghton Mifflin, 1989).

44. The possibility of a war with the Soviet Union was taken much less seriously by policymakers. For example, see the JCS 'Memorandum for the Secretary of Defense, 2 March 1964'; 'Special National Intelligence Estimate', 25 May 1964, *FRUS, 1964–1968*, pp. 1:378-80 and 'Intelligence Memorandum', 21 April 1965, *FRUS, 1964–1968*, p. 2:596. A more alarmist view is offered by George Ball in a memorandum to the president, but even Ball does not speak directly of a US–Soviet conflict, although it does warn that the Soviet Union might place 'ground-air missiles – probably with Soviet missile crews in North Vietnam' and states that in the case of a direct Sino–American clash the Soviet Union 'would probably seek to limit their contribution to advanced military equipment. But, again, the contribution to [sic] Soviet and other personnel or volunteers could not be excluded'. ('Memorandum From Acting Secretary of State Ball to President Johnson', 13 February 1965, *FRUS, 1964–1968*, p. 2:254.)

29

2

A People Bewildered:
American Public Opinion and
the Vietnam War

The American public did not pressure its government to fight in Vietnam. In some wars, such as the Spanish–American War and the world wars, public passion to a considerable degree drove the US government's decision to enter the conflict.[1] Nonetheless, although there was a broad anticommunist and pro-containment consensus within the American voting public, this did not automatically result in a high level of public concern for the fate of South Vietnam. Most Americans knew little about the situation in Southeast Asia until after the US government made a considerable political commitment to Saigon. Certainly, few Americans would have shown much daily concern about the RVN if the United States had not been involved deeply in that country. Vietnam's importance in the public imagination was directly related to the actions of the US government: the policymaking elite placed Vietnam prominently on the public agenda, and, as the commitment to the defense of South Vietnam increased, the fate of Saigon became an increasingly important issue. The American people did not demand a war in Vietnam but their leaders gave them one.

FROM KOREA TO VIETNAM

The first US war to contain communism was fought on the Korean peninsula, and it was a mixed success. US policymakers – concerned about geostrategic issues, unwilling to fight on the Chinese mainland, and worried that a declaration of war against North Korea and China might lead to war with the Soviet Union – had attempted to secure US objectives in Korea without declaring war against either North Korea or China. The experience in Korea, however, had not been one that would tend to reinforce the belief by US policymakers that undeclared war was an effective instrument for the government of the United States. Policymakers were disappointed by the level of public support for the war and found the ultimate outcome of the conflict to be tolerable but unsatisfying. The United States succeeded in its principal war aim of ensuring that South Korea remain an independent non-communist state, but to do so it had to fight an unanticipated war with the People's Republic of China (PRC); Washington failed to accomplish its secondary war aim, the unification of the peninsula on US terms.[2]

The Korean War offered US decisionmakers numerous lessons about public opinion and displayed the effect of an unpopular war of containment on presidential popularity. It is possible that the conflict was a significant element in President Truman's 1952 decision not to run for re-election,[3] because the negative impact of the war on Truman's popularity was considerable.[4] Policymakers of the Vietnam era were well aware of the unpopularity of the Korean War and understood why the war was rejected by a sizeable percentage of the voting public; indeed, many figures in the Johnson administration had served in government during the Truman years. Nonetheless, policymakers in the mid-1960s pursued a military–political course in Vietnam similar to the one that resulted in the unpopularity of the Korean War.[5]

Despite their considerable, and ever-increasing, concern about public opinion, US leaders nevertheless pursued a course of action that was likely to lead to considerable public and Congressional opposition to the war. Maintaining long-term support for the conflict required that the public be convinced that the war was both important and winnable; also, it was necessary to be able to demonstrate verifiable medium- and long-term military progress. Korea had shown that large segments of the American public would cease to support a war that was not clearly waged in the defense of vital national interests and that appeared to be unwinnable (or at least unwinnable at an acceptable price and within a reasonable time frame). The combination of the government's tepid prosecution of the war and the dubious importance of Vietnam to the vital interests of the United States would inevitably result in public relations problems for the US government.

Although policymakers needed military success in Vietnam to maintain public support, they also feared that an imminent victory could provoke Chinese intervention. The experience of the Korean conflict had resulted in an understandable belief on the part of many US policymakers that China would intervene to prevent an American triumph in Vietnam. Both North Korea and North Vietnam were communist regimes that bordered China and, when the United States was on the verge of conquering the former, the Chinese had intervened militarily. The potential parallels between the Korea and Vietnam situations were all too obvious. The possibility of Soviet intervention in Vietnam, and of such actions resulting ultimately in a major war between the superpowers, also loomed in the background (albeit as a much less likely possibility). These constraining factors forcefully shaped US policy in Vietnam and deterred decisionmakers from potentially decisive actions such as a large-scale invasion of North Vietnam (the concern of US policymakers about possible Chinese intervention in Vietnam is studied in greater detail below).

US leaders pursued their course in Vietnam in 1964–65 with an understanding of the significance of the constraints they were placing on the military effort. They were not ignorant of the military situation in Vietnam and their warfighting decisions did not result from a fundamental misunderstanding of the tactical aspects of the war. For example, it was commonly understood that General William Westmoreland's strategy of attrition would not result in a quick victory (and this knowledge was reinforced with every passing month) and policymakers conducted the bombing campaign against North Vietnam primarily as a diplomatic exercise – the campaign was intended to pressure Hanoi into committing to a peace agreement advantageous to the United States, not to terminate North Vietnam's ability to conduct the war in the South. US leaders were aware that their decisions would not result in rapid military victory. Indeed, they specifically rejected the very options that could have resulted in a short and favorably decisive war because it was feared that definitive victory might bring about a great-power confrontation.

Policymakers had good reasons to believe that, if it were a necessary prerequisite for victory, the communist government of North Vietnam could and would accept high casualty levels for long periods of time. If the North Vietnamese government were willing to pay the price, it could continue the conflict for an unknown, but presumably long, period;[6] the American citizenry, however, certainly would not accept an open-ended military commitment to South Vietnam. In addition, the US decision actively to seek out the enemy, rather than to remain ensconced in defensive enclaves, allowed the communists a high level of control over American casualty levels. This, combined with other factors, placed decisions about the momentum of the war in North Vietnamese hands (although on occasion the United States would increase the tempo of its operations and seize the initiative; the Linebacker II air campaign is an example of this).

US policymakers understood that their choice to fight a highly constrained war in Vietnam entailed significant public relations problems. Nevertheless, they accepted these handicaps because they believed that victory was achievable within an acceptable time frame, either through negotiation (the preferred method) or, if necessary, through the military defeat of the communist forces in South Vietnam. This belief was incorrect, though the error is understandable in the intellectual context of 1964–65: the concept of utilizing a strategy of graduated pressure to win a limited war against communist aggressors was untested but seemed plausible to many strategists. Even from 1967 onward, however, after policymakers had recognized the gravity of their error, they did not undertake a rapid, massive escalation of the war because they remained unwilling to accept the perceived risks that would accompany a truly radical shift in US strategy. US policymakers were not willing to take the risks necessary to solve their strategic and public relations problems, so they took a different gamble, accepting the existence of these problems and attempting to work around them.

By doing so, US leaders committed a fatal error: the United States enjoyed a robust military advantage in Vietnam, but the American home front was vulnerable. The strategic military errors of the United States were not, in themselves, fatal for the war effort, but, in misjudging the patience of the American people and the tenacity of their enemy, US leaders provided a key strategic opportunity to Hanoi.

THE ONE-HALF WAR

In several senses, policymakers chose to fight a limited war in Vietnam: their objectives fell far short of requiring the surrender of North Vietnam, the means employed were strictly rationed, and the area of operations was highly limited for US forces. Moreover, the knowledge that the conflict was being fought for limited ends with limited means became intertwined in the minds of many policymakers with the notion that the emotional stake of the American public toward the conduct and outcome of the war should be minimized.[7]

The actions of President Johnson played an important role in the shaping of American public attitudes toward the Vietnam effort. As previously mentioned, Johnson was wary of declaring war against North Vietnam or of undertaking ambitious military operations against that country and greatly feared the possibility of an expanded conflict that would involve China; also, he was fearful that a large war in Vietnam would destroy the momentum of his domestic 'Great Society' program even if China was not drawn into the conflict.[8] Thus, he decided not to mobilize the American public for the war and even adopted the politically difficult position of aligning himself with neither the hawks nor the doves: even though he headed the executive branch directing the war in Vietnam, Johnson attempted to navigate a 'middle path' between his pro- and antiwar critics.[9]

The government's inability to set out before the public a clear and convincing case for US involvement in Vietnam did much by default to strengthen the case against the war;[10] the government offered no satisfying 'one paragraph' (let alone a one-line bumper sticker) explanation of why the effort in Vietnam was important to US national interests.[11] The domino theory and related geostrategic formulations could be used to relate the importance of Vietnam to the public, but the theory was open to attack and its ability to convey a sense of immediate danger was questionable.[12] Another public relations obstacle recognized by Johnson administration policymakers was the scarcity of effective spokespersons for the government position.[13]

There was also a degree of incoherence in the statements of US officials about the war. Policymakers, including the president, tended to describe the actions of North Vietnam publicly in very harsh terms and to use frequent references to North Vietnamese aggression to justify military action against that country.[14] But at the same time policymakers wished to secure a negotiated settlement to the Vietnam problem and were wary of creating a public outcry against the restrictions placed on military actions by civilian leaders.[15] This placed policymakers in the uncomfortable position of having to attack the activities of North Vietnam with sufficient ferocity to maintain public approval of the Vietnam commitment, while at the same time not inciting a 'war fever' that would create public demand for drastic action against North Vietnam.[16]

Thus, the US government indirectly gave the public the puzzling message that South Vietnam was important enough to justify the expenditure of American lives, and the aggression of North Vietnam was sufficiently abominable to warrant retaliatory bombing and other measures, but the former country was not vital enough and the latter country not hostile enough to justify a 'real' war. The government made it reasonably clear that the fear of a wider war was driving its policy, but never adequately explained to its own people in a coherent and believable manner why a highly constrained war was strategically and morally appropriate and why the American people should be willing to fight for years in Indochina.

Despite these constraining factors, the government was able to muster an impressive amount of support for the war during the early period of US involvement. However, much of this support was 'soft', and many citizens rapidly tired of the war as fought; opposition to the Johnson administration's conduct of the war came from both the hawk and dove camps (each of which was well represented in Congress).[17] This was reminiscent of the Korean War, when Truman's unwillingness to strike targets within China, to use nuclear weapons, and so forth provoked opposition to the warfighting policy of the administration. In Vietnam, as in Korea, hawks were unwilling to accept an indifferently prosecuted war of containment that lacked a clear theory of victory.

Over time, a substantial number of hawks, frustrated over the conduct of the war, drifted away from their initial support for a spirited effort in Vietnam. Johnson administration policymakers had of course wanted to restrain the hawks, but found they were more effective than they wished: many hawks did not move toward support for the government's conduct of war and, disillusioned, they turned against the Vietnam enterprise altogether. The move away from hawkishness is demonstrated in a series of surveys conducted between December 1967 and November 1969 which asked: 'People are called "hawks" if they want to step up our military effort in Vietnam. They are called "doves" if they want to reduce our military effort in Vietnam. How would you describe yourself – as a "hawk" or a "dove"?' [18] During the early part of this 'middle period' of the war, the initial confidence of Americans was decreasing, but the belief that the military effort in Vietnam was best diminished or abandoned had not fully taken hold. Indeed, after the launch of the Tet Offensive on 30 January 1968, hawkishness *increased*. [19] From March 1968 onward, however, the trend was very clear: Americans were tiring of a conflict that seemed to defy positive resolution.

Table 2: The Decline of 'Hawkishness' [20] (in %)

	Dec. 1967	Late Jan. 1968	Early Feb. 1968	Late Feb. 1968	March 1968	April 1968	Early Oct. 1968	Nov. 1969
Hawk	52	56	61	58	41	41	44	31
Dove	35	28	23	26	42	41	42	55
No opinion	13	16	16	16	17	18	14	14

A SKEPTICAL PRESS AND A DIVIDED CONGRESS

It would be excessive to claim that the press was primarily responsible for the unpopularity of the US effort in Vietnam and was *the* agent accountable for the final US withdrawal from Vietnam. Nonetheless, the great majority of Americans had most of their information about Vietnam filtered through the independent news media, a fact which automatically gave journalists some influence over public opinion. Further, the American news media – particularly, in the context of the Vietnam War, the television networks and prestige newspapers – played a major role in the forging of government policy in Vietnam from the Kennedy period to the fall of Saigon. [21]

In the Vietnam context the media was exceptionally influential because it was situated to fill an 'opinion vacuum'. With the US government unable to articulate clearly why the preservation of South Vietnam was important to the national security of the United States, media figures – in their roles as strategic commentators and guardians of the public conscience – were unusually prominent, and had a greater impact on public opinion than would normally be expected. [22] By failing to defend their own case convincingly, US policymakers indirectly enhanced the influence of outside commentators, including those with an antiwar disposition. Thus, when journalists – particularly those who were respected by the public, such as Walter Cronkite [23] – turned against the war their opinions carried considerable weight. [24]

The hostility of the press to US policy toward Vietnam was a phenomenon that began well before the entry of US troops into the war and gained momentum over time. In the early and mid-1960s this hostility was evident mainly within the Saigon-based American press corps in Vietnam. By contrast, the editors and owners, as well as many columnists, in the United States tended to be sympathetic to the arguments of the government, though the reluctance of policymakers to make clear the depth of the US commitment to South Vietnam resulted in criticism.[25]

Much of the American press corps in Vietnam was (to a degree, understandably) cynical about the truthfulness of US government spokesmen long before the Tet Offensive or the other events that are generally credited with creating the 'credibility gap' – the broad public mistrust of government statements about Vietnam.[26] Most of the Saigon reporters of the early 1960s despised the Diem government, believing it to be shamelessly corrupt and authoritarian, and their relations with US officials in Saigon tended to be poor. Indeed, several of the early reporters hoped that their dispatches would help topple Diem.[27] While there is little that the US government could have done to mollify these critics, the Saigon-based reporters were merely the first group of journalists hostile to US policy in Vietnam. Over time an increasing segment of the press corps grew dissatisfied with Washington's effort, and hundreds of influential journalists and editors were eventually opposed to US participation in the Vietnam conflict.

Given the way in which US policymakers chose to conduct the war, this was unavoidable; the government's decisions on how to conduct the diplomatic side of the conflict and to finesse public opinion poisoned relations with the press. The energetic use of deception was an inherent part of the government approach to the war: because US political strategy required that Hanoi be convinced that its war effort was not worthwhile and controlled escalation was the chosen technique for pressuring that country into abandoning its war aims, North Vietnamese uncertainty about the speed and severity of US escalation was an important aspect of the diplomatic approach. This method would have been undermined if the United States truthfully informed the media of its intentions in Vietnam.

To make matters worse, government statements that were sincerely expressed might appear a few months later to have been deliberate lies, because the government approach to the war was fluid and did not involve a coherent long-term plan. Moreover, the US strategy for victory gave few clear guideposts that would indicate that the war was being won: at any given time, the progress against communist guerrilla forces and the success of the effort to win the hearts and minds of villagers was debatable and the exceedingly optimistic reports emanating from official sources tended to undermine the credibility of the government. The same justifiable impatience that marked the public attitude toward the war in Vietnam was evident in the press.

As time passed and the war dragged on, there was a substantial 'boomerang effect': many reporters became convinced that official statements were totally untrustworthy, and tended to seek out and believe information that would discredit the official version of events, even when that information came from communist sources.[28] As disillusionment with the war increased, the antiwar and anti-government bias in Vietnam reporting intensified.[29]

THE ANTIWAR MOVEMENT AND CONGRESS

The organized antiwar movement did not end US involvement in Vietnam. The movement was unpopular with most of the electorate, lacked internal cohesion and authoritative leadership, and alienated many potential supporters who were sympathetic to the idea of withdrawing from Vietnam but did not want to be affiliated with radicalism or hatred of the United States. Antiwar forces did succeed in securing the 1972 Democratic presidential nomination for 'peace candidate' Senator George McGovern, but McGovern lost the general election by a margin of 60.7 to 37.5 per cent,[30] a resounding defeat.

The publicity surrounding the antiwar movement was a vexing domestic political problem for both the Johnson and Nixon administrations, but the goals of the peace movement were irreconcilably opposed to those of the US government. Ultimately, if policymakers were to continue to conduct the war, they had to reject the criticism as unwarranted or overblown, and most felt morally justified in doing so.[31] Indeed, the Nixon administration even counter-attacked the antiwar movement, most notably in the president's famous 'silent majority' speech of 3 November 1969,[32] and enjoyed a fairly high degree of success.[33]

However, the antiwar movement did constrain the actions of decision-makers indirectly. The existence of the movement gave policymakers a constant cause for concern.[34] Government officials were aware that any US escalation would result in an organized outcry – and, as the antiwar movement gained momentum, the opposition to the war took on dramatic proportions. Tens of thousands of protesters attended the large antiwar protests in Washington and elsewhere and the antiwar gatherings garnered extensive national media coverage; celebrities also became involved in the antiwar movement, which further increased the publicity of the movement and provided an additional attraction for the media.[35] This vocal opposition, combined with media coverage sympathetic to the antiwar cause,[36] presented US policymakers with a problem of 'protest management'.[37] These domestic political difficulties created numerous embarrassing incidents, placed the war effort in disrepute, and served as encouragement to the North Vietnamese in their belief that the United States would eventually withdraw from Indochina.

While the radicalized 'authentic' antiwar movement was itself unable to rally the support necessary to force a withdrawal from Vietnam, there was a parallel antiwar effort operating in more respectable circles, and this endeavor was more directly influential and better able to rally large segments of the public against the war.[38] Although Congress at first stood strongly behind the Johnson administration on Vietnam, the legislative branch quickly became a center of debate about the war, and many senators and representatives stood in public opposition to the Vietnam commitment. Intense Congressional opposition to an ongoing war was unusual for the twentieth century (although there was solid precedent for such opposition in the nineteenth century); even the Korean War had created few vehement opponents like Senator J. William Fulbright, the 'archcritic of [Johnson] Administration Vietnam policy',[39] or Senator Edward Kennedy, who called the Vietnam War 'senseless and immoral'.[40] In addition, of course, some candidates for the presidency in 1968 and 1972 ran in opposition to the war; Democratic Senators Eugene McCarthy, George McGovern, and Robert Kennedy are particularly notable antiwar candidates.[41]

Opposition to the Vietnam commitment from large numbers of sitting members of Congress legitimized opposition to the war; the legislative effort to end the involvement in South Vietnam was the comparatively reputable side of the peace movement that most Americans could relate to and see as a legitimate form of opposition to executive branch policy. Of course, this did not make a stridently antiwar stance popular with all Americans (McGovern's weak showing against Nixon is evidence of that fact) but it helped to remove some of the shame associated with opposition to an ongoing war. The combination of the authoritative Congressional and media figures was a powerful counter to those who spoke in favor of the war.

As the prospects for victory dimmed in Vietnam and the desire for a quick end to the fighting increased, establishment opposition to the war placed great pressures on the executive branch and ultimately damaged the US negotiating position with North Vietnam.[42] Even more importantly, it effectively eliminated the ability of the United States militarily to compel the DRV to abide by the Paris Peace Agreement.[43] Congressional activity limiting executive freedom of action in Indochina and the breakdown of executive branch prestige and authority that resulted from the Watergate scandal were essential conditions for North Vietnam's ultimate military conquest of South Vietnam: as the disastrous 1972 invasion of South Vietnam demonstrated, a vigorous response by the United States could halt a conventional DRV invasion.

A WAR NOT DECLARED

There were two primary reasons why US policymakers chose not to declare war over Vietnam: they wished to maximize escalatory control and to minimize the possibility of Chinese military intervention. A declaration of war against the DRV would place an expectation of conclusive victory in the public mind, but US policymakers did not want such a victory against North Vietnam: they only wished to coerce North Vietnam into ceasing its campaign for compulsory Vietnamese unification under communist rule. A decisive military victory against the DRV, and especially one that involved the occupation of part or all of North Vietnam, was considered extremely dangerous because the possibility of such a victory was perceived as being likely to draw Beijing into the war.[44] In short, China's status as a great-power protector to Hanoi and other factors made a declaration of war against North Vietnam unacceptable to US policymakers.

A Congressional declaration of war against North Vietnam would have been the surest method by which to rally the support of the American public for the Vietnam intervention. Johnson administration policymakers were aware that a declaration of war was likely obtainable, at least for a limited time in 1964 and 1965, but the administration was unwilling to pursue that course, largely because it would have required that the American citizenry be rallied.[45] Declaring war would have clearly placed the Vietnam situation at the top of the domestic political agenda and would have put enormous pressure on the president to take decisive measures against North Vietnam, including unrestricted bombing and the invasion of that country.

Washington considered the disadvantages of declaring war so weighty that, despite the obvious importance of the matter, the question received little serious consideration. The desire within the executive branch for a highly limited conflict precluded the option of declaring war against North Vietnam,[46] and, although Congress solely possessed the power to declare war, it relied on the executive to provide leadership on the Vietnam issue. Only after US entry into the ground war did Congress exert meaningful authority over Vietnam decisionmaking, and Congressional influence was then used to constrain the war effort.

Along with the refusal to declare war the United States chose repeatedly to offer to enter into negotiations with North Vietnam. Though the initial terms offered amounted to the denial of North Vietnamese war aims, a clear and harsh penalty for long-term defiance of the United States was never clearly stated to the government of the DRV or to the American people. At no point did the US government pledge to take specific actions that would grievously damage North Vietnam, topple its government, or even prevent it from conducting an expeditionary war by, for example, striving to curtail imports to and disrupt road traffic within that country. This vague and irresolute position put steel in the negotiating posture of the North Vietnamese, and confused the American public about the nature of the war.

The constant public calls by the president and others for negotiations and the enticements offered to the North Vietnamese (including bombing halts) did assure the American citizenry that its government was attempting to find a peaceful solution to the war. However, this public 'peace offensive' also strongly suggested that policymakers were uncertain of victory, were desirous of a quick solution to the Vietnam problem, and psychologically were undercommitted to the war – and by 1966 the desperation of US policymakers for a peace settlement was apparent to many observers. The government demonstrated in public a lack of commitment that undermined both its position vis-à-vis the North Vietnamese and its efforts to maintain public support for the war.[47]

CONCLUSION: A FAILURE TO DEMONSTRATE RESOLVE

The common public complaint that the United States 'was fighting the war with one hand tied behind its back' was a crude description of US policy but was essentially accurate. Because of their cautious attitude, US policymakers concluded that they had to conduct the conflict in a manner that made isolation of the battlefield a practical impossibility. This in turn made decisive military victory in South Vietnam difficult, if not unrealizable. US policymakers did not explain these uncomfortable facts to the American public in a candid manner, even though the imperative responsibility not to widen the war was frequently cited as reason for restraint.

Policymakers were unwilling to explain candidly *why* they believed it was necessary to fight a long counterinsurgency war rather than a short one that applied great force against North Vietnam. This bred public impatience and led to peculiar trends in opinion polls; for instance, there were 'sharp temporary increases in Johnson's popularity when there were dramatic moments in the bombing of North Vietnam and also when there was apparent hope for a negotiated movement toward peace, like the Glassboro meeting of June 1967'.[48] Both intensive bombing and intensive negotiations – determined use of the sword or the olive branch – were more popular than an everyday government procedure that attempted to conflate war and diplomacy in a form that pleased few Americans.

Policymakers held irreconcilably contradictory desires: to maintain public support and to fight a highly limited war over which they could maintain effective control of escalation. Although the American public was committed to the containment of communism in a general way, the rationale offered by policymakers for involvement in Vietnam in particular was vague, and did not resonate strongly with the American public. Nonetheless, this problem was not necessarily disastrous in itself – victory is an excellent tonic for uncertainty, and demonstrable success in the field would have rallied public support. Indeed, almost despite itself, the US government was able to muster broad support for US involvement in Vietnam; that support was, however, not solid enough to withstand a long, frustrating war.

There was little that policymakers could do to improve the prospects for long-term public support of a counterinsurgency war in South Vietnam, but decisions about the geography and tempo of the war were largely within their control. The United States could have placed enormous military pressure on North Vietnam and obliged that country to fight a style of war that did not play to its natural advantages.

The conflict in Vietnam presented policymakers with a public relations trap and, with the benefit of hindsight, it is apparent that in order to solve their public relations problem it would have been necessary for Washington to pursue a more aggressive military campaign against North Vietnam.[49] Certainly, by declaring war and undertaking intensive operations, at least for a few years, the half-hearted public backing for the US effort in Vietnam could have been channeled into loyal support for an ongoing conflict. The public image of the antiwar movement would have been extremely poor – indeed antiwar activity would have been disloyal and illegal – and Congressional opposition to the war would have been marginal, at least for a time.

This does not mean, however, that a declaration of war would have been necessary or even particularly desirable. Although a declaration of war did offer advantages in regard to public opinion and no doubt would have demonstrated resolve both to Hanoi and its great-power protectors, Washington's reluctance to take such a drastic step was comprehensible. Indeed, a declaration of war might have been an excessive response to Washington's Indochina problem. US policymakers tried to deflate artificially the importance of the war; conversely, declaring war on a minor communist power – especially after the precedent of the undeclared Korean War – would have focused extraordinary public attention on what was, ultimately, only a part of the overall effort to contain communist expansion.[50]

Ultimately, a declaration of war was not necessary for the United States to achieve its goals because such a formal resolution was *not prerequisite to vigorous warfighting in Indochina*. Simply conducting the war with a less constrained approach would have had a salutary effect on public opinion. In order to maintain public support over a long period, US leaders needed to demonstrate their commitment to the Vietnam enterprise. This required that the US government both explain in a coherent fashion why it was in Indochina and demonstrate its dedication to the Vietnam enterprise by conducting war in a resolute manner.

As we shall see, largely because of their concern about Beijing's possible intervention, US policymakers indirectly decided to fight in Vietnam in such a way that the war was bound to be long and therefore unpopular. Declining formally to declare war against North Vietnam was not necessarily one of Washington's errors but choosing to place excessive restrictions on overall US military efforts in Indochina was disastrous. This mistake, in turn, was linked directly to US overestimation of the dangers presented by Chinese intervention in Vietnam. Thus, US policymakers fought a highly constrained war that allowed North Vietnam to exercise a high degree of control over the intensity of the conflict. This was despite the fact that Washington possessed a vast advantage over Hanoi, at least in nominal military capabilities, and was free to 'construct' the expeditionary war in Vietnam according to its preference, using such tools and methods as it considered appropriate. North Vietnam did not enjoy such a luxury: that country could control its war only to the extent that the United States chose to permit.

NOTES

1. On the American public's reaction to the attack on Pearl Harbor, see John W. Dower, *War Without Mercy: Race and Power in the Pacific War* (New York: Pantheon, 1986), pp. 36–7.

2. As Kissinger points out, the United States could have chosen a less ambitious war aim, and might have forestalled Chinese intervention in the war. 'The best decision would have been to advance to the narrow neck of the Korean peninsula, a hundred miles short of the Chinese frontier. This would have been a defensible line which would have included 90 per cent of the population of the peninsula as well as the capital of North Korea, Pyongyang. And it would have achieved a major political success without challenging China.' (*Diplomacy* (New York: Simon & Schuster), p. 480.)

3. In his memoirs Truman asserts that his decision not to run in 1952 was actually made after he won the 1948 presidential election. Further, he writes that on 16 April 1950 he composed (and locked away for more than one year) a memorandum to himself; this memo stated his refusal to run for another term as president or to accept the nomination of the Democratic party for that office. See Truman, *Years of Trial and Hope: 1946–1953* (London: Hodder & Stoughton, 1956), pp. 517–32. However, as late as March 1952, Truman did consider running for re-election, although Alonzo L. Hamby argues that this may actually have been a result of Truman's unpopularity, which motivated him to seek vindication. *Man of the People: A Life of Harry S. Truman* (New York: Oxford University Press, 1995), p. 600. On Truman's last-minute contemplation of a re-election bid in 1952, see David McCullough, *Truman* (New York: Simon & Schuster, 1992), pp. 891–2.

4. One author even estimates 'that the Korean War had a large, significant independent negative impact on President Truman's popularity of 18 percentage points, but that the Vietnam War had no independent impact on President Johnson's popularity'. (John E. Mueller, *War, Presidents, and Public Opinion* (New York: John Wiley & Sons, 1973), p. 240.)

5. Some policymakers even argued that the United States benefited from certain advantages in the Korean War that it did not enjoy in Vietnam. In a memorandum to President Johnson, Vice-President Humphrey, arguing against a war with North Vietnam, is pessimistic about likely public support for war. 'American wars have to be politically understandable by the American public. There has to be a cogent, convincing case if we are to have sustained public support. In World Wars I and II we had this. In Korea we were moving under UN auspices to defend South Korea against dramatic, across-the-border conventional aggression. Yet even with those advantages, we could not sustain American political support for fighting the Chinese in Korea in 1952. Today in Vietnam we lack the very advantages we had in Korea. The public is worried and confused. Our rationale for action has shifted away now even from the notion that we are there as advisors on request of a free government – to the simple argument of our "national interest". We have not succeeded in making this "national interest" interesting enough

at home or abroad to generate support.' ('Memorandum From Vice-President Humphrey to President Johnson', 17 February 1965, *FRUS, 1964–1968*, p. 2:310.)

6. There is some controversy as to whether in June 1965 Gen. Westmoreland led civilian policymakers to believe that he 'expected victory by the end of 1967' – the Pentagon Papers make such a claim, but Westmoreland asserts that he 'had no such expectation and made no prediction whatsoever as to terminal date'. See William C. Westmoreland, *A Soldier Reports* (New York: Da Capo, 1989; originally published 1976), pp. 142–3.

7. See Harry G. Summers, Jr, *On Strategy: A Critical Analysis of the Vietnam War* (Novato, CA: Presidio, 1982), p. 35.

8. Westmoreland, *Soldier*, p. 12.

9. Eric F. Goldman, *The Tragedy of Lyndon Johnson* (New York: Alfred A. Knopf, 1969), pp. 415–16.

10. Summers writes of this general phenomenon: 'By its nature the media can be counted on to show the cost of war, and the antiwar movement, not surprisingly, will do everything in its power to magnify those costs. But "costs" only have meaning in relationship to value, and it is the responsibility of the government to set national objectives and in so doing establish the value of military operations ... [In the Vietnam War] the objective was never clear. Because the value was never fixed, the costs soon became exorbitant.' (*On Strategy II: A Critical Analysis of the Gulf War* (New York: Dell, 1992), p. 18.)

11. British counterinsurgency expert Sir Robert Thompson noted that, 'I have asked many Americans what the American aim is in Viet Nam and have never yet received the same reply. The replies have varied from containing China, preventing aggression and defeating the Viet Cong to giving the people of South Viet Nam a free choice.' ('Squaring the Error', *Foreign Affairs*, 46, 3 (April 1968), p. 448.) Also see Chester L. Cooper, 'The Complexities of Negotiation', *Foreign Affairs*, 46, 3 (April 1968), pp. 456–7.

12. As John E. Mueller notes, 'Compared to World War II, in particular, the enemy engaged in the Korean and Vietnam conflicts was less obviously "evil", and it was far more difficult to find convincing ideological or humanitarian reasons to justify the wars to the public ... Both were "dirty little wars". Furthermore, because of their limited faraway nature, it was more difficult to view the wars as necessary from the standpoint of direct American security, although the idea of "stopping the Communists" was related to this concern.' (*War, Presidents, and Public Opinion*, p. 34.)

13. See 'Memorandum for the Record', 3 August 1965, *FRUS, 1964–1968*, pp. 3:294-8.

14. See, for example, *Public Papers of the Presidents of the United States: Lyndon B. Johnson, 1963–64*, vol. 2 (Washington, DC: GPO, 1965), pp. 926–32.

15. In a meeting on 8 July 1965 the 'Wise Men' failed in an attempt to convince President Johnson 'that the administration must fully explain the military situation and the need for more troops to the American public'. (Robert S. McNamara, with Brian VanDeMark, *In Retrospect: The Tragedy and Lessons of Vietnam* (New York: Times Books, 1995), pp. 197–8.)

16. There was certainly latent public support for strong action in Vietnam, even well after the beginning of the war. A survey conducted from 27 October to 2 November 1967 asked the following question: 'We are now bombing North Vietnam, but we have not sent troops into North Vietnam. Would you favor or oppose extending the ground war into North Vietnam?' Even at this late date, 39 per cent of respondents favored such a move, 44 per cent opposed the invasion of the DRV, and 17 per cent indicated no opinion. (George H. Gallup, *The Gallup Poll, Public Opinion 1935–1971*, vol. 3, 1959–1971 (New York: Random House, 1971), p. 2094.)

17. Even the outcome of the 12 March 1968 New Hampshire primary, in which antiwar Senator Eugene McCarthy received 42.2 per cent of the Democratic vote, was more a result of opposition to the war as fought than it was to the war itself. 'Among the pro-

McCarthy voters, those who were dissatisfied with Johnson for not pushing a harder line in Vietnam outnumbered those who wanted a withdrawal by a margin of nearly three to one.' (Peter Braestrup, *Big Story: How the American Press and Television Reported and Interpreted the Crisis of Tet 1968 in Vietnam and Washington*, vol. 1, Westview Special Studies in Communication (Boulder, CO: Westview Press, 1977), p. 671.)

18. Mueller, *War, Presidents, and Public Opinion*, p. 107.

19. Although its most important long-term effect was on American public opinion, the Tet Offensive was mainly intended by the communists to affect the military situation on the ground in South Vietnam, not American public opinion. See James J. Wirtz, 'Deception and the Tet Offensive', *Journal of Strategic Studies*, 13, 2 (June 1990), pp. 82–98.

20. Table based on Mueller, *War, Presidents, and Public Opinion*, p. 107. Data from the Gallup Opinion Index.

21. Some observers disagree with the contention that the press is a powerful force shaping events and contend that government policymaking, even in a democracy such as the United States, is such a shadowy and perhaps corrupt process that it is little impacted by the press and other outside forces. For an expression of this view see Seymour Hersh, 'The Press and the Government: II', in Harrison E. Salisbury (ed.), *Vietnam Reconsidered: Lessons From a War* (New York: Harper & Row, 1984), pp. 140–1.

22. It is also notable that Vietnam was the first American 'television war' and that nightly television coverage graphically showed the effects of the war, including collateral damage, to a public not yet desensitized to televised graphic violence.

23. One author observes that '[t]he best-known journalist who ever went to Vietnam – in fact, he was not merely famous, he was a national figure – Walter Cronkite, could not conceivably have done the kind of reporting as a United Press man in World War II that he did in Vietnam. Cronkite was never what one could describe as 'antiestablishment', dovish, or even particularly probing in his questioning of the motives or the goals of leaders – but there he was in Vietnam one day, standing up and calling upon his government to get out.' (Peter Davis, 'The Effect of the Vietnam War on Broadcast Journalism: A Documentary Filmmaker's Perspective', in Salisbury (ed.), *Vietnam Reconsidered*, p. 98.) In a 27 February 1968 broadcast Cronkite claimed that the Tet Offensive was a defeat for the United States and called for negotiations. By one account, Cronkite had been briefed on American and South Vietnamese military successes by a senior US general but informed the general that he would not make use of the material presented to him, 'saying that he had been to Hue and seen the open graves of the South Vietnamese civilians murdered by the NVA troops and that he … had decided to do everything in his power to see that this war was brought to an end'. (Philip B. Davidson, *Vietnam at War: The History, 1946–1975* (Novato, CA: Presidio, 1988), p. 437.)

24. For a skeptical view on the media's ability to shape public opinion on Vietnam see Carlyle A. Thayer III, 'Vietnam: A Critical Analysis', *Small Wars and Insurgencies*, 2, 3 (December 1991), pp. 89–115.

25. In a memorandum to Johnson, McGeorge Bundy asserts that '[w]ith some exceptions, most *editorialists and columnists* support the President in his determination to keep Vietnam independent. This support for the broad objective is tempered by a noticeable strain of criticism over a "lack of frankness" on the part of the Administration in discussing the depth of the commitment.' ('Memorandum From the President's Special Assistant for National Security Affairs (Bundy) to President Johnson', 30 June 1965, *FRUS, 1964–1968*, p. 2:84. Emphasis in original.)

26. According to journalist Marguerite Higgins, when she solicited and quoted 'the views of the American mission, including General Paul Harkins, to the effect that "the Viet Cong was going to lose"' for a 1963 series of articles, she received a strong negative

reaction from the Saigon press corps. 'This was much criticized by the resident correspondents in Saigon, who felt that the US mission was lying and undeserving of being quoted.' (*Our Vietnam Nightmare* (New York: Harper & Row, 1965), p. 131.) However, it should be noted that, generally speaking, the relations between Higgins and other Saigon correspondents were poor. See William Prochnau, *Once Upon a Distant War: Young War Correspondents and the Early Vietnam Battles* (New York: Times, 1995), pp. 332–57.

27. Prochnau, *Once Upon a Distant War*, p. 354.

28. For an influential example of this trend see Harrison E. Salisbury, *Behind the Lines – Hanoi* (New York: Harper & Row, 1967).

29. President Nixon believed the press had a strong antiwar (and anti-Nixon) bias. 'In the presidential election of 1972, when I won with 61 per cent of the vote, my antiwar opponent received 81 per cent of the votes of the members of the national news media. Their antiwar views showed in their reporting. Equal credibility was granted to enemy propaganda and United States government statements; and while our statements were greeted with skepticism, North Vietnam's word was usually taken at face value. Secret documents were published whenever reporters could get their hands on them. Reporters considered it their duty to try to oppose government policy by whatever means were available. The Vietnam War started the tradition of "adversary journalism" that still poisons our national political climate today.' (Nixon, *No More Vietnams* (New York: Avon Books, 1985), pp. 161–2.) Many figures around Nixon, such as Walter Annenberg, the ambassador to Great Britain, also believed that the press had a strong bias against the administration. See George Lardner, Jr, 'Nixon Papers Portray Fear of News Plot', *Washington Post* online edn, 19 March 1998,<http://www.washingtonpost.com/wp-srv/digest/poll.htm>.

30. Tom Wells, *The War Within: America's Battle Over Vietnam* (New York: Henry Holt 1994), p. 557.

31. Kissinger argues convincingly that, 'Rightly or wrongly – I am still convinced rightly – we thought that capitulation or steps that amounted to it would usher in a period of disintegrating American credibility that would only accelerate the world's instability. The opposition was vocal, sometimes violent; it comprised a large minority of the college-educated; it certainly dominated the media and made full use of them. But in our [Nixon administration] view it was wrong. We could not give up our convictions, all the less so since the majority of the American people seemed to share our perception.' (*White House Years* (Boston: Little, Brown, 1979), pp. 292–3.)

32. The term 'silent majority' was used in the conclusion to the speech. Nixon utilized it in a conscious attempt 'to go over the heads of the antiwar opinion makers in the media in an appeal directly to the American people for unity: "And so tonight – to you, the great silent majority of my fellow Americans – I ask you for your support."' (Nixon, *No More Vietnams*, p. 114.)

33. In the opinion of erstwhile Kissinger aide and antiwar figure Roger Morris, the 3 November 1969 speech had a devastating effect on the peace movement. See Roger Morris, *Uncertain Greatness: Henry Kissinger and American Foreign Policy* (London: Quartet, 1977), pp. 170–1.

34. Some Vietnam-era figures have confirmed that the existence of the antiwar movement served to confirm the actions of policymakers. 'As Admiral Thomas Moorer ... asserted, "The reaction of the noisy radical groups was considered all the time. And it served to inhibit and restrain the decision makers."' (Wells, *The War Within*, p. 579.)

35. For an account of the October 1967 march on the Pentagon by a celebrity journalist/participant see Norman Mailer, *The Armies of the Night: History as a Novel, The Novel as History* (New York: Signet, 1968).

36. However, Melvin Small argues that the fashion in which the media reported on antiwar rallies actually harmed the movement. See *Covering Dissent: The Media and the Anti-Vietnam War Movement, Perspectives on the Sixties* (New Brunswick, NJ: Rutgers University Press, 1994).

37. One difficult and embarrassing issue for the decisionmakers was the question of whether to prosecute protesters who broke federal laws related to the draft. Although military desertion and 'draft dodging' were commonly punished, acts such as counseling young men to avoid the draft were generally ignored despite the fact that hundreds of men and women publicly committed this felonious act, sometimes with television news crews recording their actions. The most notable attempt by the federal government to enforce laws related to the Military Selective Service Act of 1967 was its attempt to convict the famous pediatrician Dr Benjamin Spock, Yale University chaplain the Revd Dr William Slone Coffin, Jr, and three other defendants on criminal conspiracy charges. Four of the defendants were convicted, but on appeal the convictions of Dr Spock and another defendant were reversed on grounds of insufficient evidence; Revd Slone and another defendant were held to be liable for retrial, but the government chose to drop their cases. See Daniel Lang, *Patriotism Without Flags* (New York: W.W. Norton, 1974), pp. 19–53 and 207.

38. Fulbright argues that under his chairmanship the Senate Foreign Relations Committee 'as a forum of debate and dissent, removed the stigma of disloyalty from the raising of questions about the war and from efforts to end war and the advocacy of peace'. (*The Price of Empire* (New York: Pantheon, 1989), p. 122.)

39. Braestrup, *Big Story*, vol. 1, p. 632.

40. Alexander Kendrick, *The Wound Within* (Boston, MA: Little, Brown, 1974), p. 282.

41. On the reaction of Robert Kennedy to media coverage of Tet 1968 and Kennedy's own public statements on Vietnam see Braestrup, *Big Story*, vol. 1, pp. 642–8.

42. Kissinger, *White House Years, passim*.

43. Richard Nixon, *RN: The Memoirs of Richard Nixon* (New York: Grosset & Dunlap, 1978), pp. 888–9.

44. This question is explored in greater depth in Chapter 5.

45. One author argues that '[the Johnson administration] was aware of the dangers inherent in arousing the population too much. Given that constraint, the creation of enthusiasm for a limited war that seemed endless by early 1968 was an enormous, maybe even impossible, task. As was suspected as early as the first escalatory moves in the late fall of 1965, a limited war, even without organized dissent, as was the case in Korea, is difficult to manage in a democracy with periodic elections.' (Melvin Small, *Johnson, Nixon, and the Doves* (New Brunswick, NJ: Rutgers University Press, 1989), p. 156.)

46. In the transcript of a 2 March 1964 conversation with Robert McNamara, President Johnson delineated three options for dealing with the Vietnam problem. 'We [the United States] could send our own divisions in there and our own marines in there and they could start attacking the Viet Cong ... We could come out of there and as soon as we get out they could swallow up South Vietnam. Or we can say this is the Vietnamese war and they've got 200,000 men, they're untrained, and we've got to bring their morale up and we can train them how to fight and the 200,000 ultimately will be able to take care of [the insurgency] and that, after considering all of these, it seems offers the best alternative to follow'. (Walter Pincus, 'Vietnam War Tapes Reveal a Wary Johnson', *International Herald Tribune*, 14 October 1996, p. 10.)

47. These questions even confused many antiwar protesters. W.W. Rostow writes that '[when speaking about the Vietnam War to antiwar youth] someone will ask: "If Southeast Asia is all that important to the United States, why didn't we use all our military power and get it over?" I have had that question put to me on a good many occasions

by the most orthodox of student dissidents: barefoot, beads, ragged jeans, peace symbols, and all.' (*The Diffusion of Power: An Essay in Recent History* (New York: Macmillan, 1972), p. 499.)

48. Ibid., p. 478.
49. Alternatively, opting for an enclave-based operational strategy should also have mitigated the government's public relations problem, because it would have increased considerably the control the United States exerted over its level of casualties. However, this strategy still would not have addressed the fundamental public opinion problems with which US policymakers grappled.
50. A declaration of war might also have resulted in calls to move US forces from Europe, Japan, and elsewhere to Vietnam. As Chapter 3 notes, it would have been desirable if the number of US troops in Vietnam had been somewhat greater, particularly in the early years of the conflict. However, stripping garrisons in Western Europe and Japan in order quickly to place a huge US force in Vietnam would have been detrimental to the overall containment policy of the United States.

3

Mission Impossible?
The Prosecution of the Ground
War in Vietnam

It would have been wise of civilian policymakers to create political–diplomatic conditions advantageous to Military Assistance Command, Vietnam (MACV), but they failed to do so; instead, Washington placed severe constraints on the conduct of military operations, and thereby undermined the military effort in Indochina. However, this fact does not excuse the US military leadership for its own errors in its guidance of the conflict. An exceptional performance by MACV might have made the marginal difference that would have created circumstances under which South Vietnam would have survived as an independent entity. Although choices made in Washington regarding the bombing campaign against the DRV, the attitude toward Laos and Cambodia, and so forth had the primary role in determining the American prospects of victory in Vietnam, there is a serious argument that MACV could have made good the errors of its civilian masters.

MACV's unhealthy preoccupation with statistical measures of success has been much-commented on, and certainly both military and civilian leaders tended to concentrate on quantitative measures of success, such as the 'body count' and seemingly precise statistics on the number of enemy weapons captured, village pacification, and other matters.[1] This was indeed deleterious,[2] but it was hardly the only – or even the most significant – of MACV's errors. Suspicious statistics misled policymakers, and encouraged them in error, but probably had little effect on the ultimate outcome of the war. Generally, statistics were used to rationalize courses of action toward which leaders were predisposed rather than determining the general course of the decision. Washington's decisions about how to operate in Laos, Cambodia, and North Vietnam were political, not statistical. In turn, given the limitations placed on MACV's war effort by civilian policymakers, Westmoreland saw an attrition-based strategy as the best way to address the military problem in Vietnam;[3] he mainly used statistics to gauge the success of his efforts and to undermine the arguments of those who endorsed alternative operational strategies.

The United States military made two broad errors in Vietnam. One, it failed to use its own forces efficiently – rotating personnel too quickly, shaping an extravagant logistical network that drained potential combat personnel away to supporting tasks,[4] and placing too much emphasis on the search for large unit engagements and too little on defense of the population. MACV was never able to shape an appropriate support-to-combat personnel ratio or strike a satisfactory balance between the necessity to control the activities of large communist units and provide security for the Vietnamese rural population.

Equally or even more damaging was MACV's second general error: until the latter years of US involvement it did not take reasonable steps to prepare South Vietnam for a future wherein that state would have to provide for its own defense with relatively little US assistance.[5] It did not take a prophetic gift to conclude that such an eventuality might occur; even before US troops entered the ground war, many policymakers questioned how long the United States would have the political will to remain in Vietnam. Yet for the first three years of the war, MACV neglected its supposed commitment to improve the ARVN.[6] After the Tet Offensive, military and civilian policymakers more fully recognized the vital role of the ARVN in the long-term struggle for Indochina,[7] but by early 1968 far too much time had been wasted: there had been a sizeable US combat force in Indochina for over two years, and a substantial US advisory effort had been ongoing for much longer.[8] By that point, the ARVN should have been a disciplined, highly skilled force capable of working smoothly with the United States and other allies but also rapidly maturing to the point where it could conduct South Vietnam's conventional and counterinsurgency defense without the assistance of foreign troops. Some ARVN units did display a high degree of professionalism during Tet (a surprise to many US advisors),[9] but ARVN quality was highly inconsistent and many structural problems – such as corruption within the ARVN officer corps – had not been meaningfully addressed. However, for reasons discussed below, speedy and dramatic improvement of the ARVN was probably only attainable if that organization were placed within the context of a unified forces command. Somewhat paradoxically, the ARVN needed outside assistance to purge itself of bad officers and practices, but – after a period of adjustment – the organization would then have been stronger and more capable of standing on its own.

MACV's role transformed over time from an advisory organization to a warfighting command and back again, but it was never able to create the conditions necessary for a political victory in Vietnam. In the period from its founding in February 1962 under General Paul Harkins (Westmoreland became commander of MACV (COMUSMACV) in June 1964) to the middle of 1965 MACV was chiefly an advisory organization. Although it increased vastly in size in the period from 1962 to 1965, it undertook relatively little preparation for the huge US military effort that would soon take place in Vietnam. MACV, however, was not responsible for this neglect: it was Washington that was remiss, drifting toward war without building the logistic network to support a vast US military presence in Vietnam (although the reluctance of MACV to lay the groundwork for a unified allied forces command in this period is notable).[10]

The period from mid-1965 to January 1967 was a time of transition, with the United States fighting numerous large-unit engagements and building its force levels. Westmoreland's strategy for big-unit operations in rural South Vietnam was implemented in this period, to the detriment of small-scale pacification operations and efforts to improve the ARVN. This might be called the 'era of searching and destroying'. Feeling that it lacked the forces to undertake serious pacification efforts while also attempting to destroy enemy main force formations, MACV essentially opted to do the latter and neglect the former. As a result, operations in this period, while often successful (for example, the November 1965 campaign in the Ia Drang valley),[11] were of relatively little long-term benefit to the allied forces.

In the next two years of the conflict, from early 1967 to March 1969, the number of US troops reached its maximum level and then began to decline. In many respects the allied ground war progressed greatly in this period: most importantly, the NLF was virtually destroyed (although, because the infiltration routes through Laos were not closed effectively, the North Vietnamese Army (NVA) was able to take an increasing combat role in South Vietnam), and, despite generally poor execution of pacification programs,[12] there was considerably progress in pacifying the countryside.[13]

MACV progressively resumed an advisory role in the last period of the Vietnam conflict. Under Westmoreland's successors, Abrams and Weyand, the Nixon program of Vietnamization (which is described in greater depth in Chapter 7) was implemented. MACV, which had largely ignored the ARVN during the critical era from mid-1965 to early 1969, was charged with preparing that force to take over sole responsibility for the defense of South Vietnam.[14] In March 1973, MACV was disbanded.

MACV's methods were too inefficient and its operational strategy insufficiently bold to meet effectively and promptly the difficult tasks it faced in Vietnam. Most importantly, MACV's efforts to improve the ARVN, comprehensively and permanently pacify the countryside, and confront the problem of infiltration through Laos were too little, too late. In a narrow sense, MACV was a capable military organization: overall, it discharged competently the military tasks on which it placed a priority – certainly, there was no equivalent of Dien Bien Phu or the 1975 debacle at Ban Me Thuot on Westmoreland's watch, and that is an accomplishment not to be underestimated. The problem was that for most of the war MACV misjudged how best to effect a long-term improvement in South Vietnam's military fortunes – it did the wrong things well.

UNSTABLE ARMY: US PERSONNEL ROTATION IN VIETNAM

The decision to rotate US military personnel rapidly through Vietnam was, for morale and other reasons, an understandable one. There was certainly substantial morale value in allowing troops (particularly those in combat units) a specific date on which they could expect to be transferred to easier and less hazardous duty. NVA soldiers infiltrated into South Vietnam generally remained in service 'for the duration', but it was not realistic or desirable that the US military impose a similar burden on its own troops. The US military, however, erred in the opposite direction – tours of duty (and, perhaps most importantly, tours of combat command duty) were unduly brief.

The standard Vietnam tour was one year, regardless of whether troops were in combat or rear-area assignments. While this rather short tour was good for morale in some respects,[15] it presented more problems than it solved. Most importantly, it meant that shortly after soldiers and Marines became skilled jungle fighters, they were rotated out of combat assignments and replaced by unskilled personnel who would have to learn the very skills that their predecessors had only recently acquired.[16] Moreover, 'short-timer's syndrome' was a major problem: a soldier's combat effectiveness usually dropped precipitously during the last one to three months of his tour.[17] Short-timers were often so distracted and/or overly cautious that they were moved from combat units to rear areas.[18]

Thus, the period of a combat soldier's optimum combat effectiveness was very short – perhaps three to six months, depending on the individual. This was particularly a problem with non-commissioned officers (NCOs). Because of the short officer command tours in Vietnam, the burden on NCOs to serve as leaders and to pass knowledge to their subordinates was even heavier than is usual in modern armies. Quick rotation, however, meant that NCOs were themselves on a 'learning curve' for much of their Vietnam tour.

The United States would have been wise to impose a slightly longer tour of duty – perhaps as long as 18 months – for NCOs and other enlisted personnel in Vietnam.[19] Decreasing the rapidity of personnel rotation would likely have reduced casualties and increased the efficacy of combat operations, because at any given time the percentage of 'green' troops who had been in Vietnam for less than a few months would have been much smaller and the percentage of highly knowledgable soldiers who possessed considerable combat experience much greater.

Six-month combat command tours for officers were instituted for several reasons.[20] Most importantly, these short tours were intended to increase the number of US military officers with combat command experience. Experience in combat command was, quite understandably, seen as a valuable asset for officers. Short tours were also rationalized as being necessary to prevent the 'burn-out' of overstressed commanders – but few officers who served in

Vietnam accepted this as a valid concern, and in oral history interviews many officers expressed the opinion that 'they had just begun to be fully proficient at their jobs only a month or two before their six months expired'.[21]

Moreover, the fact that officers generally served six months in combat while enlisted personnel served a full year understandably resulted in resentment of officers by those serving under their command.[22] This indignation was further fueled by the belief that soldiers in rear-echelon units enjoyed a far higher quality of life. These feelings, combined with the fact that quick rotation of officers meant that many unit commanders were less knowledgable about jungle warfare than most of their men (amateur officers could and did get their troops wounded and killed), encouraged the breakdown of discipline.

Overall, while there were small benefits to the six-month rotation of command assignments, this policy was seriously damaging to the US war effort;[23] in operational terms, the results of the rapid rotation system were poor. It would have been far better to assign officers to combat commands that lasted at least as long as the standard combat tour. Moreover, it would have been desirable for officers to have the option of extending their tour (with, of course, appropriate career rewards and financial bonuses for doing so).[24] Knowledgable officers and senior NCOs are vital to the success of any military effort. The United States should have made a particular effort to find competent leaders and keep them in positions of responsibility, particularly in the case of combat assignments; instead the US military pursued a rotation policy that damaged unit cohesion, encouraged officer amateurism, created resentment in the enlisted ranks, and resulted in unnecessary casualties.

THE TENSION BETWEEN THE BIG WAR AND THE SMALL WAR

Johnson administration decisionmaking on the effort in Vietnam tended to reflect short- to medium-term considerations and to display a dearth of serious, long-term strategic thinking. This was reflected both in the fashion in which Washington shaped the nature and parameters of the war – the bombing campaign against North Vietnam, US policy toward Laos and Cambodia, and the unwillingness of the United States to menace the territory of the DRV all provided substantial military–diplomatic benefits for Hanoi – and in the way in which it slowly increased its commitment to Vietnam without constructing clear goals or a credible theory of victory.

The ad hoc, 'minimal-commitment' approach to the Vietnam enterprise proved disastrous: the United States took far too long to build to its full commitment,[25] and by the time that it had done so enthusiasm for the Vietnam project had waned. In January 1969 the United States deployed 542,400 military personnel in Vietnam, its maximum contingent, but it soon began to reduce that number, and within two years there were only slightly more than 300,000 troops in Vietnam,[26] and the restrictions on the war in Laos, Cambodia, and North Vietnam assured that US troops in Vietnam were not used to best effect. Indeed, given the decades-long involvement of the United States in Vietnam, the US government entered the ground war in Vietnam with surprisingly little preparation. Although civilian policymakers had worried for several years about the possibility that the United States might be faced with the choice between direct military intervention in Vietnam and the collapse of the GVN, even in 1964–65 relatively little preparation had been made for the logistic support of a sizeable US expeditionary force.[27]

As COMUSMACV, General Westmoreland played a more important role than any other officer in shaping the US ground war in Vietnam. A competent but cautious officer, Westmoreland's role in the war is controversial; this is particularly true of his preference for 'search-and-destroy' missions primarily intended to destroy enemy main force units.[28] Westmoreland saw some value in 'ink-blot' strategies that created a zone of safety that would be gradually expanded outward to cover progressively more of the country, but believed that they were too slow for the purposes of the United States. He preferred to attempt to bring the enemy to battle in large-unit actions in the Vietnamese hinterland, an operational strategy that was agreeable to Secretary McNamara.[29]

While it would be unfair to single out Westmoreland for blame for the US defeat in Vietnam – certainly, Johnson, Kennedy, and McNamara bear a much greater responsibility, because they made the political decisions that set the operational parameters within which Westmoreland was forced to operate – his operational strategy was insufficiently creative to address in a timely fashion the problems that MACV confronted. While not an especially hidebound military leader,[30] his tendency to take the seemingly safer, more traditional (in American terms) course – seeking large-unit engagements, insisting on the construction and maintenance of a vast logistical network, and so forth – had significant disadvantages.[31]

In July 1965, Westmoreland attended a series of meetings in Saigon with McNamara, JCS Chairman Wheeler, and other policymakers. He explicitly described his concept for the US war in Indochina as being a three-phase endeavor.[32] In Phase I, the United States would put in place the forces necessary to prevent further degradation of the military situation in Vietnam. This would be accomplished by the end of 1965. In Phase II, the United States and its allies would take the offensive in '"high priority areas" to destroy enemy forces and reinstitute pacification' efforts.[33] There was no explicit time limit on Phase II. Finally, in Phase III, 'if the enemy persisted, he might be defeated and his forces and base areas destroyed during a period of a year to a year and half following Phase II'.[34]

Certainly, there was some merit in Westmoreland's approach. Large concentrations of enemy troops directly undermined government control in rural areas: a region could hardly be considered pacified if enemy battalions (many of them, even in the mid-1960s, composed of North Vietnamese troops rather than indigenous insurgents) were tramping through the countryside. At a minimum, enemy main force units had to be isolated from the bulk of the rural population. Large engagements in rural areas allowed the United States to bring its decisive advantage in firepower and mobility to bear against vulnerable enemy troops; Westmoreland also believed that use of heavy fire 'in remote regions would mean fewer civilian casualties and less damage to built-up areas'.[35] Furthermore, he was understandably concerned about the problems that might result from large numbers of US troops interacting with the Vietnamese civilian population, wanting Vietnamese civilians to deal mainly with their countrymen in the ARVN rather than with foreigners. Westmoreland feared that contact with US troops would provoke Vietnamese xenophobia and sometimes lead to 'unfortunate incidents'.[36]

US civilian and military policymakers had assumed that, if the United States was capable of inflicting a sufficient number of casualties on the communists, a crossover point would eventually be reached where communist units would be depleted more quickly than they could be replaced by the NVA. However, attempting to degrade enemy units without closing the avenues of North Vietnamese infiltration was an inherently flawed strategy. Unless serious efforts were made to prevent the DRV inserting NVA troops into South Vietnam – which would require either a permanent American presence in eastern Cambodia and Laos, preferably paired with a simultaneous air effort to cripple North Vietnam's ability to carry on the war, or an invasion of the North that would distract Hanoi from its Southern adventure – the United States could not expect to disable the enemy's main force units in a timely fashion. The communist forces often refused to expose themselves in large engagements and, even when the US military did engage communist main force units, this had comparatively little impact on the guerrilla war – many communist troops remained dispersed and concentrated on control of the population.

Westmoreland was aware of this conundrum but, in the early years of his command, he thought that it was more important to maximize the number of US troops in South Vietnam. Given the number of personnel required to cut the infiltration routes through Laos, Westmoreland believed that he 'would be unable for a long time to spare that many troops from the critical fight within South Vietnam'.[37] When, in 1968, Westmoreland was finally satisfied that the United States was sufficiently strong to move into Laos, President Johnson refused to allow such a move.[38] Thus, the cautious Westmoreland succeeded in his short-term goals of propping up the GVN, assuring that US units were not defeated in detail by communist forces, and creating a sound logistical base for future operations. Nevertheless, he failed in his larger goal of creating an environment in which the United States could take advantage of the potentially advantageous military circumstances that had developed by 1967–68.[39] Too much time had been consumed in setting the stage for victory; Congressional and public support for the war was dissipating even when the troop build-up in Vietnam was still continuing. Michael A. Hennessy aptly describes the dilemma facing the US military:

> In sustaining the big-unit war of attrition, US forces were placed within a vicious cycle of operations. Clear-and-hold operations were their only long-term solution to the insurgency, but they could not be very successful until search-and-destroy operations had split up and held off the enemy's main force units. On the other hand, search-and-destroy operations would never succeed until clear-and-hold operations severed the enemy's supply, intelligence, recruiting, and other relationships with the rural and urban populations. Conducting such operations in tandem to search-and-destroy missions yielded a solution, but the overall increase in enemy strength was now [in 1967] threatening to stretch US ground troop commitments to their limit. This in turn required mobilization of more American troops. With Saigon equally unprepared and ill-equipped to mobilize the necessary troops, the allied forces were stretched gossamer thin. The total US military forces in Vietnam surpassed 470,000 at the close of 1967, but only 74,000 men were in combat-maneuver battalions.[40]

MACV faced a critical dilemma. On the one hand, there was a clearly recognized need to insulate the population from the communists, and to protect the South Vietnamese citizenry from communist coercion.[41] But, on the other hand, there was a real threat of defeat in detail if military forces were dispersed into Vietnamese villages: small, isolated groups of Americans were vulnerable to large-unit communist actions. Even airmobile units could not guarantee that small pockets of US troops would not be overrun.[42]

This also points to the vital difference between the challenges presented by the NLF and the NVA in South Vietnam. Although the communist movement in the South was essentially controlled by Hanoi, the NLF consisted primarily of indigenous South Vietnamese. Most soldiers affiliated with the NLF fought primarily as guerrillas, and many NLF guerrillas were effectively 'part-time insurgents'.[43] Access to the population was vital to the guerrillas both for recruitment and supplies.[44] NVA forces in the South, on the other hand, relied heavily on logistic links with the DRV; although its troops often fought in an unconventional fashion, the NVA was a recognizably conventional army, not a group of insurgents.

Even though the NLF and the NVA were deeply interconnected, the two placed quite different defensive demands on the allied forces. Pacification – in the broadest sense of the term, including land reform and similar initiatives[45] – was central to the defeat of the NLF. Although cutting off the NLF from DRV support was also important, this alone would not have resulted in the comprehensive defeat of the guerrilla movement. The severing of North–South communications would have damaged morale, denied the NLF needed supplies, and so forth, but, even if the connection between the northern and southern communists was effectively severed, much work would have remained for allied forces acting in a counterinsurgency role.

For the NVA, however, the situation was reversed: successful pacification assisted US and South Vietnamese forces – for example, friendly villagers might give the location of NVA forces to allied units – but only by cutting the North–South connection could the NVA presence in South Vietnam be eliminated; pacification *per se* could not achieve this goal. One key oversight of the US policymakers was their refusal to acknowledge meaningfully that unless infiltration into the RVN were cut no pacification program could control the communist challenge to the GVN.

The US military never successfully resolved the tension between 'clearing and holding' and 'searching and destroying'. The effort against the NLF was largely successful, however, and pacification programs did show some effectiveness over the medium term. Operational errors on the part of the NLF (most notably, the Tet Offensive) also contributed vitally to erosion of the internal rebellion; over time, the NLF became an enormously less important part of the military equation in South Vietnam.[46] These successes were, however, undermined by US unwillingness to undertake a serious effort to control infiltration into the RVN: as the NLF withered, the NVA took responsibility for fighting the communist ground war in South Vietnam.[47]

The core dilemma within South Vietnam for the US military was beyond the control of Westmoreland: Washington was not willing to give MACV a sufficient number of troops to perform both anti-main force and counter-insurgency tasks comfortably. Nevertheless, the COMUSMACV did have discretion in his use of available personnel. The decision to concentrate against main force communist units within South Vietnam, and largely to ignore efforts to improve the ARVN, was Westmoreland's own. When this effort was combined with the previously mentioned overlarge US support network (mainly the result of MACV's refusal to contemplate changes to its preferred 'traditional' method of waging war), the result was a highly improvident use of personnel, an extravagance that MACV could not afford, given the very limited number of US troops available.[48]

The comparison between MACV's preoccupation with search-and-destroy operations and the preferred operational style experience of the United States Marine Corps (USMC) in Vietnam is instructive. Always much smaller than the Army and usually starved for resources, the Marines developed an institutional tradition very different from that of the larger service.[49] The USMC also had a strong twentieth-century counterinsurgency tradition, with substantial small-war experience in Central America that was reflected in a well-developed doctrine. In Vietnam, the Marine Corps displayed considerable creativity in its counterinsurgency methods and enjoyed a high degree of success with some of its experimental programs. Several key Marine officers – including Commandant Wallace M. Greene, Jr, Lt-General Victor Krulak, the commanding general of the Fleet Marine Force Pacific, and III Marine Amphibious Force commander Major (later Lt) General Lewis Walt – disapproved of Westmoreland's general strategy and wished to emphasize population protection.[50] Rather than seeking out large-unit engagements, the USMC preferred to concentrate on securing coastal enclaves and creating an ever-expanding zone of security for the population (an idea similar to counterinsurgency concepts utilized by the French in North Africa). While the Marine leadership was skeptical of Westmoreland's operational style,[51] the Marines did not avoid combat – USMC units of various sizes engaged vigorously in combat operations.[52]

The most noted of the Marine experiments was the combined action platoon (CAP) program.[53] Initiated in response to the Marine belief that the war for control of the population was of primary importance,[54] the CAPs, known as joint-action companies when the program was first initiated in 1965, combined small US units with Vietnamese popular forces (PF) militia units. The CAP program, although successful in many respects – Marines in CAPs even demonstrated generally higher morale than did most US troops in Vietnam[55] – was never expanded to any great size. At its height, no more than 2,500 men out of a US Marine contingent of more than 79,000 were assigned to the CAP program.[56]

Despite the potential benefits that counterinsurgency programs like CAPs offered and the minimal resources they required, however, there was hostility to such initiatives within MACV (including from Westmoreland himself) – which demonstrates how preoccupied the Saigon command was with search-and-destroy operations. This is not to argue that MACV should have abandoned altogether the 'American way of war' and fought the war strictly as a counter-insurgency, dispersing most US combat troops to the Vietnamese villages to command PF units and perform similar functions. That would have been excessive, and communist main force units would have cheerfully taken advantage of such folly. It was appropriate that only a moderate percentage of the total number of US troops should participate directly in village defense and similar efforts, but that percentage should nonetheless have been considerably higher than was actually the case. It was also to be expected that the United States would make use of artillery, airpower, and general technological superiority when appropriate;[57] refusing to apply its technological advantages would have been tactically unsound.[58]

It became increasingly clear over time that MACV's overall strategy for the war in the South was unsatisfactory. Moreover, despite the fact that the errors in his favored strategy became increasingly apparent with the passage of time, the COMUSMACV proved highly resistant to a shift toward a clear and hold strategy that would emphasize long-term, comprehensive population security. Even within the Army there were powerful figures – most notably, Chief of Staff

General Harold K. Johnson – who, along with many of the planners on the MACV planning staff, disagreed fundamentally with Westmoreland's operational concept and actually favored a shift away from large-unit operations,[59] but Westmoreland resisted pressure to adapt his general strategy.

Therefore, MACV never came to grips with military pacification, and rejected programs that would have increased security in the villages. In itself, this was probably not decisive in the outcome of the war; despite MACV's early neglect, the NLF infrastructure was eventually eroded, and the NLF played a relatively small role in the final years of the conflict. However, MACV's negligence of pacification did slow substantially the process of military–political stabilization in South Vietnam and left the ARVN with a problem that absorbed much of its institutional energies for years.

Although the internal security problem in the RVN was not the most important task for the United States in Indochina, it was a problem worthy of considerably greater attention than it was accorded by MACV. Furthermore, 'clear and hold' was a logical compliment to an American strategy centered on the prevention of communist infiltration into South Vietnam; the United States should have focused its efforts on preventing enemy troops from infiltrating into Vietnam or being recruited within the RVN rather than on battling existing main force units. If the two main sources of communist personnel had been cut off, communist incapability to form main force units would have followed inevitably.

FLAWED COMMAND STRUCTURES

The US command arrangement for Vietnam was eccentric. Westmoreland, as COMUSMACV, was in command of US ground forces in Vietnam, but not of the air war against the DRV – except for a small segment of the country north of the demilitarized zone (DMZ), which was technically within the purview of Admiral U.S. Grant Sharp, the Commander-in-Chief, Pacific (CINCPAC).[60] Sharp, however, did not actually enjoy unencumbered authority over the air war – as we shall see, President Johnson and his advisors made targeting decisions in Washington.

Moreover, the US ambassador to South Vietnam – a post held at various times during Westmoreland's tenure by Maxwell Taylor, Henry Cabot Lodge, and Ellsworth Bunker – also had technical authority over both the military and civilian aspects of the Vietnam effort.[61] However, the ambassador, understandably, did not in practice exert much control over the military effort and even civilian agencies such as the United States Information Agency (USIA), Agency for International Development (AID), and the Central Intelligence Agency (CIA) enjoyed considerable independence and employed much larger staffs than did the US embassy.[62]

This unworkable command structure should never have been instituted. It would have been much more rational for the commander of MACV to have wielded comprehensive authority over the entire war in Indochina – including the efforts in Laos, Cambodia, and North Vietnam – as well as coordinating military efforts with Thailand.[63] US policymakers discussed instituting alternative command arrangements,[64] and as late as 1967 the United States toyed with the idea of creating a unified comprehensive Southeast Asia Command (a notion that was, for obvious reasons, supported wholeheartedly by Westmoreland),[65] but major changes were never implemented.

The convoluted command arrangements in Indochina exemplified Washington's stubborn reluctance to recognize that Indochina was a unified theater of war and to acknowledge that by placing US combat units in Vietnam it had become a full belligerent in the ongoing conflict. A Southeast Asia unified command should have been created, with appropriate Pacific Command assets – specifically, the Seventh Fleet – placed under control of the Southeast Asia CINC.

In the interest of command unity the ambassador's role in South Vietnam should have been restricted or, alternatively, the US military commander in Vietnam could also have held the title of ambassador;[66] in either case, the commander of MACV should also have exerted full control over the pacification effort.[67] Attempting to create a civil–military distinction in the Vietnam context was injudicious: as many observers acknowledged, the pacification effort, political stability, land reform, and counterinsurgency progress were all related.

Even more important than issues related to unity of command within the US effort were issues of unity between the allied forces. Westmoreland, in keeping with his sensitivity toward Vietnamese pride, rejected the option of creating a unified command structure that would include officers from all the allied forces. While his decision was certainly defensible on nationalist grounds, its ultimate wisdom is arguable. Given the constraints on personnel under which he labored and the clear threat – foreseeable even in 1965–66 – that the United States might lack the will to conduct a long ground war in Vietnam, it would have been prudent for Westmoreland to conclude that the creation of a competent ARVN should be a primary task of the MACV, rather than a low-priority consideration.[68]

By refusing to create a unified command Westmoreland believed that he would prevent the delegitimization of the RVN government, but the presence of hundreds of thousands of US troops in South Vietnam had a far more powerful and detrimental effect on Saigon's legitimacy than did technical command structures. Under the circumstances, the creation of a unified command would probably have made a marginal difference. It is unlikely that there were very many Vietnamese who were willing to accept the presence of over a half-million foreign troops but who would have found a unified allied forces command utterly insulting.[69]

Those Vietnamese who were willing to tolerate a large foreign presence were likely to accept Americans sometimes exerting direct authority over ARVN troops. However, '[w]ith the exception of the CAP program, encadrement of ARVN forces by US personnel was rejected in every instance. Instead the Americans assigned advisors to ARVN.'[70] While the advisory program had certain merits, it also had disadvantages: US advisors lacked clear authority to root out corrupt officers, insure that the ARVN treated the Vietnamese civilian population with courtesy, or initiate beneficial reforms.[71] Lacking authority, the advisors could only dispense counsel that able ARVN officers might embrace, but that corrupt or incompetent ones were likely to reject; this seriously limited the effectiveness of the advisory program.[72]

Split command arrangements encouraged the US military to ignore the ARVN. US commanders found it inconvenient to coordinate operations with the ARVN (and they also, for valid reasons, worried about revealing operational plans to an organization that had been extensively penetrated by North Vietnamese intelligence).[73] This policy proved detrimental in later years, when the US military had to work frantically to improve the ARVN before the former's final withdrawal. By the time that US combat units were completely withdrawn from Vietnam, the ARVN was a reasonably good army – but it would have been a substantially better army if the United States had been vigorously 'Vietnamizing' since the early days of the conflict.

In short, the COMUSMACV should have functioned as *de facto* supreme commander of a unified allied command (although sensitivity to Vietnamese pride might have required that a Vietnamese officer – perhaps, for example, the Chief of the General Staff of the Vietnamese Armed Forces – function as titular chief of the war within the RVN).[74] The absence of a combined command meant that, even when US officers could identify corrupt or incompetent ARVN counterparts, there was nothing which they could do to remove them from their positions. The surest way to professionalize the troubled ARVN officer corps would have been to give a US-dominated unified allied forces command complete authority over command assignments.[75] Thus, South Vietnamese officers would generally obtain desirable commands on the basis of personal merit rather than for purely political reasons or, worse still, as a result of bribing corrupt superiors.

The deep politicization of the South Vietnamese military damaged both the ARVN and the South Vietnamese state. Effective political reform required the placement of a firewall between the army and RVN politics – one of the greatest hindrances to stability in Saigon was the machinations and intrigues that obsessed the highest echelons of the ARVN. Nevertheless, over time, the military did partially remove itself from politics. Thieu, although himself a military figure, was able to create a reasonably stable government which lasted from his election in September 1967 to his resignation in April 1975. The image of the GVN as victim of ongoing coups is a caricature – there was a succession of coups in Saigon after the death of Diem, but the Saigon political scene had calmed somewhat even before the election of Thieu to the presidency.

Under a joint command arrangement, the ARVN officer corps would not immediately have reached a high-quality level, but over the course of months and years, such an arrangement could have made a very real difference in the overall quality of the ARVN leadership. The notion that the ARVN was incapable of reform under any circumstances is specious. There were competent, patriotic individuals in the ARVN who wished to serve their country, but they found it difficult to thrive within an officer corps that, at least in the mid-1960s, was largely dominated by criminals and incompetents.[76] However, given the nature of Saigon politics, and (at least until the Thieu government stabilized) the relative shakiness of the South Vietnamese state, it was almost impossible for reform to come from within the ARVN organization.

Overall, a unified command structure was clearly preferable to parallel US, South Vietnamese, and other allied commands. While the construction of a joint command would create substantial temporary problems, it was the best device to build a professional, competent South Vietnamese military. The US military certainly had experience with unified commands, and the experience of the Korean War indicated how beneficial such arrangements could be, and it is probable that such organization of the allied forces would have substantially accelerated the pace of ARVN improvement.

CONCLUSION: MISGUIDED PRIORITIES

The US military effort in Vietnam was not by any means a complete disaster, and MACV's overall conduct of the war was certainly not incompetent – it was, however, generally uninspired. MACV could have performed its duties substantially better, and this might have made a difference in the ultimate outcome of the war. The US military suffered from a lack of creative leadership, and MACV adapted slowly to the circumstances of the Vietnam conflict. The generally adequate but lacklustre approach of MACV might have been sufficient if civilian policymakers had made the correct key strategic decisions about the conduct of the war; given the handicaps under which the US command in Saigon labored, however, there was little room for error.

Nevertheless, MACV displayed little capacity for rapid positive change; several poorly conceived experiments undertaken in Vietnam were continued long after their negative effects became obvious. For example, quick rotation of personnel, particularly six-month combat commands for officers, was deeply inappropriate in the circumstances of Vietnam and the attempts to make life comfortable for military personnel in the rear may have actually harmed the morale of fighting troops. In addition, the refusal of MACV to create a unified command in Vietnam, as existed during the Korean War, placed a nearly insuperable barrier between the ARVN and the US military, the two functioning as essentially separate entities even though they shared common war aims, and had the effect of hampering the development of the ARVN as a fighting force.

In hindsight, it would have been preferable for Westmoreland to take population-defense and ARVN-building more seriously, even at the cost of damaging the short-term fighting efficiency of the US military. While it is undeniable that this would have given the communists the initiative in large areas of the countryside for a considerable period of time, this was the most workable strategy for long-term operational success; it was vital that the ARVN be made a coherent and well-disciplined fighting force as rapidly as possible. Furthermore, a dramatically improved ARVN would solve the personnel dilemma facing MACV. Ultimately, and ironically, Westmoreland's emphasis on the conventional war against main force units cost the United States time that would have been better used in more intense pacification[77] and in the creation of a better, more confident ARVN.

In short, given the political constraints under which it operated, MACV misordered its priorities. The most important ground combat tasks of the United States in Indochina have already been discussed in detail above. If ground operations against North Vietnam were disallowed by civilian policy-makers, the cutting of the Ho Chi Minh and Sihanouk Trails should have been the primary combat mission of US ground forces in Indochina. Successfully cutting the trails would have isolated the local insurgents, leaving them vulnerable to long-term pacification. Allowing the routes through Laos and Cambodia to remain open, however, made pacification immensely more difficult and gave a hostile power free access to the territory of the RVN – a situation that should have been clearly unacceptable both to Washington and MACV. Westmoreland would have been wise to petition for permission to occupy sections of Laos in 1965–66 and, if his request were granted, do so as rapidly as possible, even at the expense of short-term progress in South Vietnam.

Also, it would have been desirable for Westmoreland to have presented the Johnson administration with a forthright evaluation of how the war in Vietnam should be waged and to make abundantly clear to civilian policymakers that, if the United States were to wage war in Indochina in an effective manner, a very large US force would be required as soon as possible. This, in turn, would have required the mobilization of the reserves.[78] Instead, the politically sensitive Westmoreland attempted to make moderate demands of administration policymakers – repeatedly asking for small increases of troops (at first, to prop up the deeply troubled GVN; later, to take advantage of the possibilities present in the post-Tet military environment). While the Joint Chiefs of Staff have properly absorbed the main blame for not assertively confronting civilian policymakers on this issue,[79] Westmoreland also cannot escape criticism. As the theater commander, he had an obligation to provide a frank estimate of the military situation in Vietnam, regardless of what his civilian superiors wished to hear.

Even if President Johnson allowed operations in Laos, and particularly if he did not, intelligent pacification programs such as CAPs and, even more importantly, efforts to improve the ARVN deserved a higher priority than they received. Distasteful though it was, MACV should have acknowledged the fact that communist main force activity in remote areas was a threat which would have to be accepted for several years. Pitting the bulk of US effort against communist main force units was futile for the simple reason that, without effective pacification and control of infiltration, the threat presented by the main force units could not be eliminated. So long as they had consistent access to replacement personnel, the communists could replace their combat losses.

Along with these measures, it would have been essential for the United States to work to improve the ARVN as rapidly as possible. While choking off the southern insurgents from northern support made it feasible for the United States to win the guerrilla war in the South in a tolerable time period, the GVN would still face a conventional threat from the DRV. Although it was not obvious in the mid-1960s that no permanent US presence would remain in South Vietnam, it was clear that the GVN faced a long-term conventional threat from the North and eventually would have to provide for its own defense with comparatively little outside assistance.

NOTES

1. See William C. Westmoreland, *A Soldier Reports* (New York: Da Capo, 1989 [1976]), p. 273.
2. For a critique of the use of body counts as a measure of progress see Gen. Colin L. Powell, with Joseph E. Persico, *A Soldier's Way: An Autobiography* (London: Hutchinson, 1995), pp. 146–7. It should also be noted that there were many contemporary observers who warned that it was difficult to accurately assess the progress of the effort in Vietnam. See, for example, Bryce F. Denno, 'Military Prospects in Vietnam', *Orbis*, 9, 2 (Summer 1965), p. 411.
3. See Westmoreland, *Soldier*, p. 153, and Bruce Palmer, Jr, 'Commentary', in John Schlight (ed.), *The Second Indochina War Symposium: Papers and Commentary* (Washington, DC: US Army Center of Military History, 1985), p. 155.
4. Vast numbers of personnel were required simply to sustain the network of PXs, officers' and enlisted clubs, and other support and recreational facilities that were built by the US military in Vietnam. Even base camps such as Cu Chi often sported facilities such as swimming pools and clubs – with soldiers serving as full-time lifeguards and bartenders. See Eric M. Bergerud, *Red Thunder, Tropic Lightning: The World of a Combat Division in Vietnam* (Boulder, CO: Westview Press, 1993), pp. 28–37. However, it is important to moderate criticism of the overlarge support network in Vietnam by noting that some vital non-combat functions – such as medical care – were performed with notable excellence. For a description of the US Army's highly competent medical system

see Neel Spurgeon, *Medical Support of the US Army in Vietnam, 1965–1970*, Vietnam Studies (Washington, DC: Department of the Army, 1991).

5. It should be noted that the US advisory effort of the 1950s onward concentrated on creating an ARVN geared toward conventional warfare, particularly to the task of repelling a North Vietnamese invasion. Sir Robert Thompson describes the ARVN of 1960 as 'a totally conventional army, suitable for meeting a North Korean-type invasion, not a North Vietnamese-directed insurgency'. (*Make for the Hills: Memories of Far Eastern Wars* (London: Leo Cooper, 1989), p. 128.) On Thompson's activities in the RVN see Ian F.W. Beckett, 'Robert Thompson and the British Advisory Mission to South Vietnam, 1961–65', *Small Wars and Insurgencies*, 8, 3 (Winter 1997), pp. 41–63. On the Military Assistance Advisory Group, Vietnam (MAAG-V) efforts to create ranger units and improve ARVN counterinsurgency training see Ronald H. Spector, *Advice and Support: The Early Years of the US Army in Vietnam, 1941–1960* (New York: Free Press, 1985), pp. 349–57.

6. MACV did of course make some efforts to improve the ARVN. For example, see 'Memorandum From the Commander, Military Assistance Command, Vietnam (Westmoreland) to the Ambassador in Vietnam (Taylor)', 6 September 1964, *FRUS, 1964–1968*, pp. 1:736-42, and 'Memorandum From William Leonhart of the White House Staff to President Johnson', 30 August 1966, *FRUS, 1964–1968* (Washington, DC: GPO, 1998), p. 4:610. However, these efforts were not sufficiently ambitious to promise a rapid improvement in the overall quality of the South Vietnamese military.

7. Ronald H. Spector, *After Tet: The Bloodiest Year in Vietnam* (New York: Free Press, 1993), pp. 92–3.

8. It is noteworthy that even before the Diem government came to power, the JCS – which was wary of involvement in Indochina – resisted a US advisory role in Vietnam. See Spector, *Advice and Support*, pp. 223–30.

9. Spector, *After Tet*, p. 92.

10. The United States did, of course, build and maintain some military infrastructure. However, Washington was extremely reluctant to build a comprehensive logistical infrastructure in Vietnam even after it became clear that US involvement in the war was highly likely. In summer 1964, Westmoreland unsuccessfully requested brigade-size logistical command and engineering groups. In response to a December 1964 request by Westmoreland, the Defense Department sent a team to survey MACV's logistical needs. Westmoreland writes that 'in keeping with guidance from Deputy Secretary [Cyrus] Vance, the team recommended only some ridiculously small augmentation, as I recall some thirty-nine people to be added to a tiny US Army Support Command. I repeated the request early in February but again without success.' (*Soldier*, p. 127.)

11. On the Ia Drang campaign see Harold G. Moore and Joseph L. Galloway, *We Were Soldiers Once ... And Young: Ia Drang: The Battle that Changed the War in Vietnam* (Shrewsbury, UK: Airlife, 1994).

12. Bui Diem, who held numerous high-level posts in the GVN, vividly describes the confusion caused by overlapping authority in pacification. 'Vietnamese officials, often unsure of how their own duties were defined, were told by their superiors to coordinate their activities with the Americans. But which ones? So many American agencies were involved in the countryside: MACV, USAID, JUSPAO, CIA, DIA, to name just a few ... Pacification was everyone's business and no one's, and the results were predictably deplorable.' (*In the Jaws of History* (Boston, MA: Houghton Mifflin, 1987), p. 190.)

13. See Philip B. Davidson, *Vietnam at War: The History, 1946–1975* (Novato, CA: Presidio, 1988), p. 531.

14. For a thoughtful, and highly favorable, account of MACV's Vietnamization efforts in the latter part of the war, see Lewis Sorley, *A Better War: The Unexamined Victories and*

Final Tragedy of America's Last Years in Vietnam (New York: Harcourt, 1999), *passim*.

15. Westmoreland notes that this factor, along with other considerations such as general health and homefront support for the war, was important in his decision to continue one-year tours for advisors, a practice which was already in place when he arrived in Vietnam, and to institute the same policy for combat troops. See *Soldier*, pp. 294–5.

16. See Robert B. Asprey, *War in the Shadows* (rev. edn, Boston, MA: Little, Brown, 1994), p. 836.

17. See Spector, *After Tet*, pp. 63–5.

18. Ibid., p. 64, and James R. Ebert, *A Life in a Year: The American Infantryman in Vietnam, 1965–1972* (Novato, CA: Presidio, 1993), p. 320.

19. An army study conducted in 1970 concluded that an 18-month tour of duty would have been most expedient. See 'Memo for the Vice-Chief of Staff by Acting DCSPER, subj.: Study of the 12 Month Vietnam Tour', 29 June 1970, DCSPER-DRO, 570-0071. Copy in the Center for Military History, cited in Spector, *After Tet*, p. 67.

20. For Westmoreland's defense of this practice, see *Soldier*, pp. 296–7.

21. Spector, *After Tet*, pp. 66 and 333.

22. See 'Cincinnatus' [Cecil B. Currey], *Self-Destruction: The Disintegration and Decay of the United States Army During the Vietnam Era* (New York: W.W. Norton, 1981), p. 160.

23. Many observers recognized this fact while the war was still ongoing. For example, Herman Kahn includes 'longer tours of duty, at least for officers' as part of a list of reforms to revitalize the American military effort. ('If Negotiations Fail', *Foreign Affairs*, 46, 4 (July 1968), p. 639.)

24. It was often argued by proponents of six-month rotations that rapid turnover prevented the 'burn-out' of commanders. In a 1976 study of students with Vietnam experience at the Army Command and General Staff College, however, 61 per cent of respondents disagreed with the 'burn-out hypothesis'; only 8 per cent of students accepted it. Most officers also felt that the policy had a negative effect on discipline and morale. ('Cincinnatus', *Self-Destruction*, p. 158.)

25. In some respects, the reluctance of American civilian policymakers to increase the size of the force in Indochina was militarily understandable: the United States had important commitments elsewhere in the world that were potentially endangered by an overcommitment to Vietnam. For example, despite the slow nature of the troop build-up, the Vietnam effort had a disastrous effect on the combat readiness of the US Army in Europe. See Shelby L. Stanton, *The Rise and Fall of an American Army: US Ground Forces in Vietnam, 1965–1973* (Stevenage, UK: Spa, 1989), pp. 366–8. The only realistic solution for this dilemma was to initiate a large-scale call-up of US military reserve units, but the Johnson administration was of course unwilling to take this step.

26. Joseph M. Heiser, Jr, *Logistic Support*, Vietnam Studies (Washington, DC: Department of the Army, 1991 [1974]), p. 14.

27. See Dave Richard Palmer, *Summons of the Trumpet* (New York: Ballantine, 1984), pp. 104–5. In 1962, COMUSMACV Lt-Gen. Paul D. Harkins first suggested a centralized US logistical command in Vietnam, but such an organizational unit – the 1st Logistical Command – was not formed until 1965. Even then, the US logistics network in Vietnam remained unsatisfactory in many respects. See Heiser, *Logistic Support*, pp. 8–36. Also, it should be noted that well before US combat entry into the conflict, the US Army and Air Force cited South Vietnam's lack of infrastructure as a reason not to intervene in the Indochina conflict.

28. For an influential and highly unfavorable analysis of Westmoreland's strategy see Andrew F. Krepinevich, Jr, *The Army and Vietnam* (Baltimore, MD: Johns Hopkins University Press, 1986), *passim*.

29. See Michael A. Hennessy, *Strategy in Vietnam: The Marines and Revolutionary Warfare*

in I Corps, 1965–1972, Praeger Studies in Diplomacy and Strategic Thought (Westport, CT: Praeger, 1997), pp. 74–7, and Victor H. Krulak, *First to Fight: An Inside View of the US Marine Corps* (Annapolis, MD: Naval Institute Press, 1984), p. 186.

30. As Deborah D. Avant points out, the creation of an airmobile helicopter division and its use in Vietnam was a clear example of military innovation. (*Political Institutions and Military Change: Lessons from Peripheral Wars*, Cornell Studies in Security Affairs (Ithaca, NY: Cornell University Press, 1994), pp. 66–9.) Westmoreland was an enthusiastic supporter of this initiative.

31. In an interview, Adm. Elmo Zumwalt, Jr, made the intriguing argument that that if Abrams had been COMUSMACV at the beginning of the war 'he would have been able to participate in policymaking with the civilian authority that would have led to better decisions earlier'. (Interview with author, 4 September 1997, Rosslyn, VA.)

32. Westmoreland, *Soldier*, pp. 141–3.

33. Ibid., p. 142.

34. Ibid.

35. Ibid., p. 146.

36. Ibid. However, it should be noted that ARVN troops often failed to endear themselves to the population or to carry out pacification in an efficient manner. For an analysis that unfavorably compares ARVN pacification efforts to those of the Korean Army in Vietnam, see Eun Ho Lee and Yong Soon Yim, *Politics of Military Civic Action: The Case of South Korean and South Vietnamese Forces in the Vietnam War*, Asian Studies Monograph Series (Hong Kong: Asian Research Service, 1980).

37. Westmoreland, *Soldier*, p. 148.

38. Westmoreland saw the eventual blockade of the infiltration routes as an important part of his strategy, and warned Johnson that blocking the routes was essential to the success of attrition. See Palmer, 'Commentary', in Schlight (ed.), *Second Indochina War Symposium*, p. 155.

39. However, it should be noted that Westmoreland was not without successes. For example, operations *Cedar Falls* and *Junction City*, conducted in January and February 1967, were arguably significant operational victories. See Adm. U.S.G. Sharp, United States Navy (USN) and Gen. William C. Westmoreland, *Report on the War in Vietnam* (Washington, DC: US Government Printing Office, 1968), pp. 137–8, and Davidson, *Vietnam at War*, pp. 383–5; for a differing view, see Stanton, *Rise and Fall of an American Army*, pp. 134–5.

40. Hennessy, *Strategy in Vietnam*, p. 127.

41. See John R.D. Cleland, 'Principle of the Objective and Vietnam', *Military Review*, 46, 7 (July 1966), p. 83. It is important to note, however, that as the war continued South Vietnam was simultaneously undergoing a rapid process of urbanization – a trend that presented many problems to the communists, who generally found it very difficult to control the population of urban areas. See Samuel P. Huntington, 'The Bases of Accommodation', *Foreign Affairs*, 46, 4 (July 1968), pp. 642–56. Furthermore, much of the NLF infrastructure in the cities was destroyed during and after the Tet Offensive, a setback which made urban population control even more difficult for the communists.

42. Sudden attack by overwhelming enemy forces was a significant threat for the small Marine CAP platoons. See Hennessy, *Strategy in Vietnam*, p. 157.

43. The dubious status of sympathizers and similar issues provoked debate within MACV and the CIA, with numbers of supposed guerrillas varying wildly. See Sam Adams, *War of Numbers: An Intelligence Memoir* (South Royalton, VT: Steerforth, 1994), *passim*.

44. Andrew F. Krepinevich, Jr, goes so far as to describe 'the people' as 'the only target the Viet Cong could be forced to fight for'. ('Recovery from Defeat: The Army and Vietnam', in George J. Andreopoulos and Harold E. Selesky (eds), *The Aftermath of Defeat: Societies, Armed Forces and the Challenge of Recovery* (New Haven, CT: Yale University

Press, 1994), p. 132.) Robert Asprey makes a similar point in arguing that '[h]ad the pacification process developed in a qualitative, orderly, and intelligent manner, the enemy probably would have attacked in force and been flattened by unquestionably superior firepower'. (*War in the Shadows*, p. 949.)

45. Bernard Fall argues in a 1966 article that 'a genuinely "peasant-oriented" land reform, including a freeze on land holdings already distributed by the Viet Cong, would do more to change the allegiance of the peasantry than probably any other single counter-insurgency measure'. ('Vietnam in the Balance', *Foreign Affairs*, 45, 1 (October 1966), p. 5.) On the impact of land reform see MacDonald Slater, 'The Broadening Base of Land Reform in South Vietnam', *Asian Survey*, 10, 8 (August 1970), pp. 724–37; William Bredo, 'Agrarian Reform in Vietnam: Vietcong and Government of Vietnam Strategies in Conflict', *Asian Survey*, 10, 8 (August 1970), pp. 738–50; and Roy L. Prosferman, 'Land-to-the-Tiller in South Vietnam: The Tables Turn', *Asian Survey*, 10, 8 (August 1970), pp. 751–64.

46. See Chalmers Johnson, *Autopsy on People's War* (Berkeley, CA: University of California Press, 1973), pp. 47–9.

47. In an interview, Harry G. Summers, Jr, pointed out that '[t]he North Vietnamese never wavered in their strategic objective, but they constantly changed the means to achieve that objective ... They began with internal pressure on the Diem regime ... then they activated their guerrillas in the South and waged a counterinsurgency war. Then ... [the North Vietnamese] sending their regular forces South. Then the last seven years of the war are almost totally the North Vietnamese regular army. The perception in [the United States], especially among academics, is that this was purely a counterinsurgency/ revolutionary war. Well, that was true for a very short period of time, but it certainly wasn't true for the last seven years ...' (Interview with author, 9 September 1997, Bowie, MD.)

48. In a 1966 memorandum, Special Assistant to the President Robert Komer states his belief that in 1967–68 the United States would have the opportunity to accelerate positive military–political trends in Vietnam. However, he warns that '[t]he key [to success] is better orchestration and management of our Vietnam effort – both in Washington and Saigon. To me, the most important ingredient of [a positive] outcome is less another 200,000 troops, or stepped-up bombing, or a $2 billion civil aid program – than it is more effective use of the assets we already have.' Komer argues that '[o]ur *most underutilized asset is the RVNAF*. Getting greater efficiency out the 700,000 men we're already supporting and financing is the cheapest and soundest way to get results in pacification.' ('Memorandum From the President's Special Assistant (Komer) to Secretary of Defense McNamara', 29 November 1966, *FRUS, 1964–68*, p. 4:872. Emphasis in original.)

49. An overview of the USMC's institutional ethos is provided in Krulak, *First to Fight, passim*.

50. See Hennessy, *Strategy in Vietnam*, pp. 77–81, and Jack Shulimson, 'The Marine War: III MAF in Vietnam, 1965–71', paper delivered at the 18–20 April 1996 Vietnam Symposium at the Texas Tech University Center for the Study of the Vietnam Conflict, <http://www.ttu.edu/~vietnam/96papers/marwar.htm>.

51. On the strife between Westmoreland and the Marines over operational concepts see Michael E. Peterson, *The Combined Action Platoons: The US Marines' Other War in Vietnam* (New York: Praeger, 1989), pp. 21–3.

52. On small-scale Marine combat operations, see Francis J. West, Jr, *Small Unit Action in Vietnam, Summer 1966* (Washington, DC: History and Museums Division; Head-quarters, USMC, 1977; originally published 1967).

53. For a detailed history of the CAP program see Peterson, *Combined Action Platoons, passim*.

54. On Marine civic action efforts and the USMC's attitude toward relations with villagers see Russel H. Stolfi, *US Marine Corps Civic Action Efforts in Vietnam, March 1965–March 1966* (Historical Branch, G-3 Division, Headquarters, USMC, 1968), and Peter Brush, 'Civic Action: The Marine Corps Experience in Vietnam', *Vietnam Generation Journal* online, 5, 1-4 (March 1994), <http://jefferson.village.virginia.edu/sixties/HTML_docs/Texts/Scholarly/Brush_CAP_01.html>.
55. See Peterson, *Combined Action Platoons*, p. 26.
56. Ibid., p. 123.
57. On the American use of artillery and aircraft in Vietnam, see Robert H. Scales, Jr, *Firepower in Limited War* (rev. edn, Novato, CA: Presidio, 1995), pp. 63–154.
58. Indeed, the communists themselves conducted a 'poor man's war' against the United States out of necessity, not preference – there was simply no realistic way for the NVA or NLF to stand toe-to-toe against the US military in the air, on the sea, or in large armored engagements. North Vietnam's invasions of the RVN in 1972 and 1975 demonstrated that the NVA was perfectly willing to undertake armored operations when it perceived itself as having an advantage over its opponent. On US military and ARVN use of armor in Vietnam see Gen. Donn A. Starry, *Mounted Combat in Vietnam*, Vietnam Studies (Washington, DC: Department of the Army, 1978).
59. Lewis Sorley, 'To Change a War: General Harold K. Johnson and the PROVN Study', *Parameters*, 28, 1 (Spring 1998), *passim*.
60. See Westmoreland, *Soldier*, p. 76. Also, because MACV was a subordinate command to the unified Pacific command, CINCPAC was nominally COMUSMACV's superior; in practice, however, this made little difference.
61. As originally implemented in 1962, the COMUSMACV would have command of all military matters, and the ambassador would have no real authority over the COMUSMACV. However, then-Ambassador Nolting did not wish to see military and civilian authority divided, and was partially successful in exerting ambassadorial authority over military issues. See Fredrick Nolting, *From Trust to Tragedy: The Political Memoirs of Fredrick Nolting, Kennedy's Ambassador to Diem's Vietnam* (New York: Praeger, 1988), pp. 50–3.
62. Richard A. Hunt, *Pacification: The American Struggle for Vietnam's Hearts and Minds* (Boulder, CO: Westview Press, 1995), p. 64. The CIA also directed some small-scale military operations, particularly in Laos, and controlled Air America, an airline corporation active in several countries. On the CIA's efforts in North Vietnam see Richard H. Schultz, Jr, *The Secret War Against Hanoi: The Untold Story of Spies, Saboteurs, and Covert Warriors in North Vietnmam* (New York: Perennial, 1999), *passim*.
63. For a time the head of MACV also commanded the US Military Assistance Group in Thailand, but in 1965 this authority was revoked 'on Ambassador Martin's theory that it was distasteful to the Thais to have military advisors in their country subject to a headquarters in another Asian country'. (Westmoreland, *Soldier*, p. 77.)
64. For instance, questions about the 'pros and cons' of '[o]rganizing a Southeast Asia theater' and 'assuming direct command of South Vietnamese forces' are included in a typed list of questions for McNamara to ask on his May 1964 trip to Honolulu and Saigon. ('Questions for Honolulu and Saigon', Papers of Robert S. McNamara, RG 200, Box 63, United States National Archives, NN3-2000-092-001 HM 92-93.)
65. See ibid. Slightly different claims, however, are made in Davidson, *Vietnam at War*, pp. 356–7. The formation of a unified theater command was also endorsed in the PROVN study ('A Program for the Pacification and Long-term Development of Vietnam') – a recommendation that was not appreciated by Adm. U.S. Grant Sharp, whose Pacific Command would have been removed from the Vietnam chain of command. (Sorley, 'To Change a War', p. 102.)

66. For a time in 1967, President Johnson considered appointing Westmoreland ambassador to South Vietnam, and the latter requested that if he were given the position he also be officially named the commander in chief of US forces in Vietnam and given full control over the entire war effort in South Vietnam. In turn, he would have three deputies – 'one for political affairs, one for economic and national planning matters, and one for military operations, the latter to have the title of COMUSMACV and bear responsibility for all field operations'. (Westmoreland, *Soldier*, p. 213.)

67. This is not to imply that the pacification notions of the ambassadors were inferior simply because they were civilians. In a November 1966 memo, for example, Ambassador Lodge – probably wisely – called for an increase in the placement of small numbers of US troops in South Vietnamese units and US–ARVN cooperation in the destruction of the NLF infrastructure. ('Letter From the Ambassador to Vietnam (Lodge) to President Johnson', 7 November 1966, *FRUS, 1964–1968*, pp. 4:805-8.) A history of Lodge's tenure as ambassador is offered in Anne E. Blair, *Lodge in Vietnam: A Patriot Abroad* (New Haven, CT: Yale University Press, 1995).

68. By late 1967, the United States was placing greater emphasis on the improvement of the ARVN. For example, Johnson and Westmoreland agreed that Gen. Abrams, who was then the deputy commander of MACV, should expend much of his effort on this issue. See Lyndon B. Johnson, *The Vantage Point: Perspectives on the Presidency, 1963–1969* (New York: Popular Library, 1971), pp. 260–1.

69. This was not, however, the opinion of Ambassador Taylor, and there was some cause for concern. Regarding a report in the South Vietnamese press about the possibility of joint military command, which 'triggered many adverse comments both in public and in private', Taylor writes that '[a] joint command to the Vietnamese means one dominated by the US and such a subordination would be offensive to most Vietnamese'. ('Telegram From the Embassy in Vietnam to the Department of State', 5 May 1965, *FRUS, 1964–1968*, p. 2:619.) This opinion – and Westmoreland's views – were not, however, necessarily shared by everyone in military policymaking circles. On 20 May 1965, the JCS ordered the CINCPAC to prepare a plan for the creation of a combined coordinating staff in South Vietnam that would be jointly commanded by the COMUSMACV and the Commander in Chief of the Armed Forces of the Republic of Vietnam. 'The instruction indicated the Secretary of Defense had approved the establishment of the joint staff, and noted that the Joint Chiefs of Staff had informed the Secretary that COMUSMACV was preparing a plan for a more formal command authority to be implemented upon the introduction of a significant number of additional US combat troops.' Sharp and Taylor, however, opposed presenting such plans to the GVN at that time, and the State and Defense departments agreed that South Vietnam should not be approached on the question 'until it was politically feasible to do so'. ('Editorial Note', *FRUS, 1964–1968*, pp. 2:679-80.)

70. Hennessy, *Strategy in Vietnam*, p. 115.

71. See ibid., pp. 115–16.

72. For a telling memoir by a former advisor who implicitly questions the effectiveness of the advisory effort see Tobias Wolff, *In Pharaoh's Army: Memories of a Lost War* (London: Picador, 1994).

73. See Jeffrey Record, 'The Critics Were Right', *US Naval Institute Proceedings*, 122, 11 (November 1996), p. 66.

74. For a description of how the United States and Saudi Arabia resolved a similar controversy concerning command arrangements for the Persian Gulf War, see H. Norman Schwarzkopf, with Peter Petre, *It Doesn't Take a Hero: The Autobiography* (New York: Bantam, 1993), pp. 434–5.

75. For a differing view, see Davidson, *Vietnam at War*, p. 358.

76. The complications that highly placed corrupt officers presented to the GVN are well illustrated in 'Memo From the Executive Secretary of the National Security Council (Smith) to President Johnson', 22 August 1966, *FRUS, 1964–1968*, pp. 4:589-90.

77. Also, as Guenter Lewy argues persuasively, attacking the guerrilla infrastructure would have done much to degrade the effectiveness of large communist units. 'Without the support of the VC infrastructure in the villages, the communist main force units were blind and incapable of prolonged action – they could not obtain intelligence and food or prepare the battlefield by prepositioning supplies.' ('Some Political–Military Lessons of the Vietnam War' in Lloyd J. Matthews and Dale E. Brown (eds), *Assessing the Vietnam War: A Collection from the Journal of the US Army War College* (Washington, DC: Pergamon-Brassey's, 1987), p. 146.)

78. Although Johnson was extremely reluctant to mobilize the reserves, McNamara was willing to contemplate the notion. Upon returning from a July 1965 trip to South Vietnam he pessimistically stated in a memorandum to Johnson that '[t]he situation in South Vietnam is worse than a year ago (when it was worse than a year before that)' and was willing to support both substantial increases in the Vietnam commitment and even the activation of 235,000 personnel in the National Guard and Reserve. ('Memorandum From Secretary of Defense McNamara to President Johnson', 20 July 1965, *FRUS, 1964–1968*, pp. 3:171-9; see also Robert S. McNamara, with Brian VanDeMark, *In Retrospect: The Tragedy and Lessons of Vietnam* (New York: Times, 1995), pp. 203–4.)

79. Most notably in H.R. McMaster, *Dereliction of Duty: Lyndon Johnson, Robert McNamara, the Joint Chiefs of Staff, and the Lies that Led to Vietnam* (New York: HarperCollins, 1997). Whether the chiefs should have actually resigned if President Johnson failed to heed their advice is, however, a difficult issue. While McMaster is a proponent of resignation, former Chief of Naval Operations Zumwalt offered the at least partially persuasive argument that military personnel 'are taught that you make your best case to your civilian authority and once they make the decision you carry it out', and that an officer has a different responsibility than 'a civilian cabinet member [who has] not only the right but the obligation to quit if he is not in sympathy with his boss's decision'. (Interview with author, 4 September 1997, Rosslyn, VA.)

4

A Theater Divided:
Laos, Cambodia, and Victory in Indochina

Military access to Laos and Cambodia was vital to the communist war effort in Vietnam: the Ho Chi Minh Trail, which ran through those countries, was the logistic enabler for North Vietnam's war in the RVN.[1] These two states did not willingly choose to ally themselves with Hanoi (even though various leaders, notably Prince Sihanouk of Cambodia, at times attempted to accommodate the communists), but both countries were so militarily and politically weak that they could not defend their own territory and neither wished to incur the wrath of the DRV.

The United States did not ever effectively grapple with the question of how one should treat a 'neutral' country that is not conquered *per se* but is brazenly used as a staging area for operations against US and allied troops.[2] In both Laos and Cambodia there existed political forces willing to contemplate an accommodation with the United States (and in both countries there were also indigenous communist forces). It is conceivable that the United States could have undertaken a military commitment to those countries during the Kennedy years. There were significant political problems with this course, particularly in the case of Cambodia, but they might have been overcome. Laotian and Cambodian neutralists were largely motivated by the fear that North Vietnam would be the eventual victor in the Vietnamese struggle and that Hanoi would proceed to exercise hegemony over the two weaker and less populous countries of Indochina (certainly, in retrospect, a justifiable concern). If the United States had convincingly demonstrated its commitment to eliminating the communist rebellions in Laos and Cambodia, the attitude of non-communist leaders in those countries likely would have been highly cooperative, as the besieged governments of Phnom Penh and Vientiane would have benefited greatly from large-scale US economic and military assistance.

The reluctance of US policymakers to deal with the issue of communist use of Laos was understandable, if unwise. Any assertive position on Laos and Cambodia certainly would have been used by the communists for propaganda purposes. Furthermore, the military options in Laos were unappealing and the enormous future importance of those two countries to the Vietnamese communists was not entirely clear in the early 1960s; US policymakers did not realize how significantly the inability to isolate the South Vietnamese battlefield would handicap their war effort in South Vietnam.[3] Nevertheless, the actions of the Kennedy administration were imprudent and had substantial negative effects. The administration's policy made the eventual construction of the communist logistic network into South Vietnam possible, while, ironically, later communist propaganda about US activities in Laos and Cambodia was largely the result of an illusion of neutrality partly created by the United States.

The situation in Laos in the early 1960s resembled the contemporaneous predicament in South Vietnam in some respects – both countries had severe internal political problems and suffered from communist insurgencies that were supported by North Vietnam. However, there were also important differences that affected the actions of policymakers: it was difficult to project US power to a mountainous landlocked country lacking in infrastructure,[4] the small and impoverished country was of less obvious significance than South Vietnam, and the government of Laos was even less stable than Diem's government in South Vietnam (communist, neutralist, and right-wing elements all vied for control of the former). President Kennedy was personally reluctant to undertake unilateral action in Laos,[5] and he 'made the decision to go for a political compromise and military cease-fire in Laos rather than support the right-wing General Phoumi Nosavan, who had wrested control from the neutralist Prince Souvanna Phouma in December 1960'.[6] Elements within the administration toyed with the idea of making a major military stand in Laos,[7] but '[w]ith Britain and France clearly having no stomach for a Laos war, and with the problems of Cuba and Berlin pressing down hard on the White House, the newly inaugurated President Kennedy opted for the search for agreement'.[8] Kennedy wanted a diplomatic solution to the troublesome situation.[9]

THE QUIET LOSS OF LAOS

Well before the entry of US ground troops into South Vietnam, the United States made a series of decisions effectively granting military use of Laos to the North Vietnamese and surrendering its own right to intervene to stop communist military activities in that country. The 'Declaration on the Neutrality of Laos', or Laos Accords, negotiated at Geneva and signed on 23 July 1962, was clear in its purposes. The Laos Accords would neutralize the country, creating a coalition government around Prince Souvanna Phouma that would incorporate communist, anticommunist, and neutralist elements, and all foreign troops were to be withdrawn within 75 days after the signature of the Accords. Most of the communist troops in Laos were North Vietnamese, but the Soviet Union and China were the key communist participants in the Geneva negotiations.[10] Soviet Deputy Foreign Minister Georgiy Pushkin convinced the head of the US delegation, W. Averill Harriman, that the USSR would back the neutralization of Laos and ensure that North Vietnam and the Pathet Lao complied with the Accords.[11]

The aspiration of US policymakers to neutralize Laos was responsible, but unrealistic. If Laos had been neutralized and all foreign troops removed from Laotian soil, the US defense of South Vietnam would have been far easier. Most importantly, there could have been no Ho Chi Minh Trail or North Vietnamese use of Laotian sanctuaries.[12] It would have been much more desirable to prevent the creation of a supply route through Laos than to attempt to cut it once it was already in place. If the situation in Laos could have been totally localized and all foreign troops removed from that country, it would have been of immense military benefit to the United States.

The problem for Washington was that, although the Laos Accords promised such benefits, it delivered none of them and, in fact, created an enormous military–political problem. The 'cloak of neutrality' created by the 1962 Accords severely constrained US action in Laos, but had a minimal effect on the activities of North Vietnam. For example, in compliance with the Accords, the United States rapidly withdrew its advisors, while the DRV at first refused to acknowledge that there even were North Vietnamese troops in Laos. The United States and the Soviet Union withdrew all their military personnel from Laos; North Vietnam removed 40 soldiers through the approved exit checkpoints, leaving an estimated 5,000–7,000 troops behind.[13] The United States was aware of such violations, but the Kennedy administration turned a blind eye to North Vietnamese activities in Laos.[14]

US leaders were not altogether naive about the probability that the Accords would not enhance South Vietnamese security. Indeed, the Accords were personally endorsed by many policymakers, particularly Congressional leaders, primarily because they allowed the United States to evade otherwise-imminent military action in Laos,[15] not because it was believed that they would be effective. However, there was apparently an expectation on the part of some policymakers, notably Harriman, that the Accords would at least partially solve the long-term problem of North Vietnamese infiltration into Laos.[16] Most policymakers were reluctant to authorize US military operations in Laos, and the Geneva process was used to avoid difficult military–political decisions. In this respect, the Accords were successful: in Laos, unlike Vietnam, policymakers were able consistently to avoid difficult decisions and the problem faded from the political agenda. US leaders became accustomed to North Vietnam's use of eastern Laos, and came to accept it as a routine part of the war in Indochina.

From a military–strategic standpoint the Accords were a disaster. As feebly enforced by the International Control Commission, the Accords effectively ceded control of much of Laos to the communists in exchange for no significant security benefits for South Vietnam or the United States. The Soviet Union simply ignored its commitment to control the North Vietnamese, and the Kennedy and Johnson administrations never loudly demanded that the USSR restrain its North Vietnamese clients.

The United States later made some half-hearted efforts to cut the communist supply route through Laos.[17] This included air interdiction[18] and, in 1971, Lam Son 719, in which South Vietnamese troops supported by US air cover and artillery mounted an expedition into that country.[19] However, these operations demonstrated little long-term success.[20] This is not surprising: Lam Son 719 was too little, too late. In order to be effective over the long term, it would have been necessary to begin interdiction efforts early and to operate freely in Laotian territory on a long-term basis. The Laos Accords prevented this; therefore, the vital 'Battle of Laos' was effectively won by North Vietnam in 1962.[21]

US policymakers privately justified their unwillingness to do anything to correct the Laotian situation with the dubious claim that a 'tacit agreement' existed that allowed the communists to use Laos so long as they kept 'use of the routes [to South Vietnam] down to a level that was less than fully provocative'.[22] But in practice this formulation simply meant that the United States would tolerate reasonably discreet use of Laos by the communists, not that Laos would have minimal strategic importance for them.[23] If US policymakers were serious about enforcing the Accords any non-compliance would have been considered 'fully provocative'. Nonetheless, and in clear violation of the letter of the Laos Accords, the North Vietnamese greatly increased their presence in Laos in the mid-1960s, and communist forces became increasingly ambitious, both protecting the Ho Chi Minh Trail in the southeast and striving to gain permanent control of as much Laotian territory as possible.[24] Even China eventually dispatched large numbers of troops to Laos. After concluding an agreement with the Pathet Lao, Beijing sent a road-building contingent totaling approximately 20,000 troops to 'construct a road from Mohan, Yunnan province, to Muong Sai in northern Laos'.[25]

It was strategically unwise for the United States to allow North Vietnam to use Laos as a sanctuary and logistical connection to the South. Allowing North Vietnamese troops to operate freely in Laos virtually guaranteed that the 'internal rebellion' of the Viet Cong could not be defeated; the supply line to the South offered communist forces in South Vietnam weapons, supplies, and men.

The 'tacit agreement' arguably did protect the neutralist Laotian government based in the northwestern portion of the country, but that part of Laos was not vital to the defense of South Vietnam. The southeastern portion of Laos, however, was critical to the communist supply line into the RVN.[26] With the benefit of hindsight, it almost certainly would have been preferable for the United States to fight in Laos – despite all the military and political difficulties that entailed – rather than simply to surrender logistical use of that country to the communists.[27]

Cambodia also presented a political and strategic problem for the United States. Like Laos, it was ostensibly neutral, but throughout the Johnson and Nixon years much of the eastern part of the country was under communist control. As in Laos, Cambodian politics were in a state of turmoil; attempts to deal with the unreliable Prince Sihanouk often proved frustrating for the Americans. Poor relations and border disputes between Cambodia and its neighbors further complicated American efforts in Cambodia.[28] Although policymakers agreed on the importance of denying use of Cambodia to the communists, they felt constrained by that country's titular neutrality; the communists, however, felt free to use Cambodia as a staging and supply area.[29] In 1970, US intelligence indicated that 80 per cent of the supplies shipped to communist forces in Cambodia and the southern half of South Vietnam moved through the port of Sihanoukville.[30]

As early as 1965, MACV was aware of at least seven major bases in Cambodia and of other indications that Cambodia was a major asset to the communists;[31] however, despite the recommendations of General Westmoreland and the Joint Chiefs of Staff that substantive action be taken against the Cambodian base structure, President Johnson only granted highly limited authority to US forces to operate in Cambodia.[32] Westmoreland was not even allowed to mention publicly communist use of Cambodia until late 1967.[33]

The Johnson administration simply did not address the Cambodian problem in any substantive way; only during the Nixon years was energetic action taken to deny use of the country to the communists. The 'secret' bombing of Cambodia was ordered by Nixon in an effort to disrupt the Ho Chi Minh Trail; ground and air attacks were also made against communist bases in Cambodia. These efforts were useful insofar as they disrupted local communist operations. However, like US efforts in Laos, they were an irritant and temporary setback to the communists but were both too meager and too late to have a substantial effect on the outcome of the war.

CONTROL OF INFILTRATION AND THE WAR FOR SOUTH VIETNAM

Conducting a defensive war in Laos and Cambodia would have been difficult, but not impossible, for the United States. The primary demands of such a war would have been to cut the Ho Chi Minh Trail through Laos and the Sihanouk Trail through Cambodia.

The latter task would have been the less demanding: simply denying the communists use of the port of Sihanoukville would have largely prevented communist military supplies from passing through Cambodia without first passing through Laos. However, procurement of rice and other goods by Vietnamese communist forces would still have constituted a problem,[34] as would communist use of Cambodia as a sanctuary. Similarly, in order to deny the communists use of Cambodia (and destroy the local communist movement),[35] it would have been necessary for US and allied troops to operate freely in Cambodia on a long-term basis.

Laos presented a more difficult, and more vital, case. For the reasons cited above, control of Laos was potentially decisive and a sound US strategy would have acknowledged this fact. It was strategically prudent to defend Laos from communist infiltration, even though such an effort would have required a substantial commitment of US military power. Westmoreland's assumption 'that blocking the [Ho Chi Minh Trail] would have required at least a corps-sized force of three divisions' was sound,[36] and cutting the Trail might even have required a more extensive campaign.[37]

Stationing a substantial portion of US forces in Laos of course would have been controversial, because it would have decreased the number of US troops available for duty in the RVN. The argument that US troops were needed chiefly in South Vietnam itself was not unreasonable. Particularly during the early years of the war, the ARVN was weak and its officer corps corrupt; the South Vietnamese were unable skillfully to perform counterinsurgency tasks during this period. Placing a large percentage of US forces in Laos would have meant that substantial areas of South Vietnam would, for the time being, have been ceded to the communists. US troops in Laos would do little directly to solve South Vietnam's internal stability problems and to put the population under the control of the GVN. As many US policymakers believed that the South Vietnamese revolution was fundamentally an internal problem that was only supported and partially controlled by Hanoi, it seemed logical to them to attack South Vietnam's problems directly through nation-building and internal policing.

Nonetheless, a 'Laos first' strategy had great merit.[38] As was increasingly demonstrated over the course of the war, the revolution in South Vietnam was ultimately reliant on North Vietnamese support. So long as the United States provided minimal moral and physical support to the Saigon government, the Viet Cong was a serious but not fatal problem. The Viet Cong could harass the GVN and exercise control over large swathes of the countryside but lacked the mass to overwhelm South Vietnam militarily. When the United States initially deployed combat units to South Vietnam, the purpose was partly to protect US facilities and partly psychological: the presence of US soldiers was a demonstration of support by a protecting superpower for a tormented client. Placing a limited number of US personnel (including some combat troops, as well as headquarters personnel, advisors, troops to protect US facilities, and logisticians overseeing the flow of equipment through ports and airports) in South Vietnam while also putting troops in Laos would have demonstrated a commitment to the former, as well as to the entire Indochina theater. Moreover, it would have displayed to all of Southeast Asia (including, perhaps most importantly, North Vietnam) that the United States favored a holistic solution to the problem of communism in the region and that a communist take-over anywhere in the area – even in the hinterlands of an inland country – was unacceptable.[39]

AN EFFECTIVE WAR OF ATTRITION

Many authors have commented on the Viet Cong's minimal reliance on northern supplies and personnel during the early years of the Vietnam conflict. However, although the quantity of supplies brought southward was relatively low initially, the north–south logistical network was ultimately crucial to the communist war effort. In the later years of the war, the Ho Chi Minh Trail became a well-established highway and by 1967 portions of the Trail 'consisted of four highways, each about twenty-five feet wide, down which trucks roared in a steady stream'.[40] By 1968, North Vietnam was even sending tanks down the Trail.[41] The Ho Chi Minh Trail and the related Sihanouk Trail made it possible for the DRV to conduct a large expeditionary war in South Vietnam.[42]

The NLF's vulnerability to attrition was displayed in the wake of the 1968 Tet Offensive. Because of its effect on the American home front, the offensive was ultimately a strategic success for the North Vietnamese; however, it was a tactical disaster for the NLF, who 'lost the best of a generation of resistance fighters'.[43] After the losses incurred in the Tet operations, 'increasing numbers of North Vietnamese had to be sent south to fill the ranks'.[44] The burden of maintaining the 'internal rebellion' in South Vietnam increasingly fell on North Vietnamese soldiers and the surest road south led through Laos.[45]

Because the infiltration routes between North and South Vietnam had not been severed, it was possible to send a constant stream of thousands of NVA troops to replenish the communist army in the RVN; effective interdiction in Laos and northern South Vietnam would have made this impossible. It is certainly true that no defensive system is perfect, and that mountainous and jungle terrain aids guerrillas; even the conveniently narrow demilitarized zone between North and South Vietnam was not an excellent defensive glacis.[46] Nonetheless, post-Tet North Vietnamese strategy required that *large numbers* of troops go south. If the odd small unit slipped through the US dragnet in Laos, it would have made little difference to the outcome of the war.

Without consistent replenishment, the communists would have been unable to menace most of the countryside or assemble into larger units. The latter capability was critical to communist strategy – the more the allied forces, particularly the ARVN, were liberated from the threat of defeat in detail, the greater their ability to concentrate on local village defense and to deny the communists access to the population. This, in turn, would have negatively affected communist collection of food supplies and recruitment of soldiers and spies. As the communists increasingly appeared to be the failing side, ever-fewer South Vietnamese youth would have felt inclined to tie their fates to the revolutionary movement;[47] furthermore, the ability of the communists to press-gang 'volunteers' would have been eroded as they lost control of the countryside. Although there is little doubt that the NLF could have survived for years, perhaps decades, even if denied consistent access to northern supplies and personnel, it would have progressively dissipated as the ARVN improved and the GVN took control of an increasing percentage of the countryside.

In order for the United States to achieve its main strategic goals in Vietnam, it was not necessary that the Viet Cong be completely wiped out. It was merely necessary to prevent the fall of South Vietnam and create a political environment that would encourage political stability (and, preferably, democracy) over the long term. Personnel pressures on the communists would have undermined their political–military position, and allowed South Vietnam to conduct its process of state-building more effectively.

Most importantly, time would have been on the side of the South Vietnamese. It is often the case that, if guerrillas work for the complete overthrow of a government (as opposed to a more limited goal), the guerrilla movement tends to lose momentum and weaken if it cannot perpetually threaten the survival of that government. The guerrilla war in Malaya provides obvious parallels but one could also look to El Salvador, the Philippines, Peru, and elsewhere for examples of ambitious guerrilla movements that troubled states for years but failed to accomplish their goals. In South Vietnam, however, the guerrilla movement was frequently weakened but always allowed to revive itself and continue to threaten the GVN's control of the countryside. Truly 'winning hearts and minds' in South Vietnam required more than simply making the GVN more popular than its communist competitors. The United States and South Vietnam needed to establish clear long-term supremacy over the guerrilla movement, demonstrate to the population that cooperation with the guerrillas was a path offering probable punishment and little possibility of reward, and protect the people from coercion by the guerrillas.

CONCLUSION: NEGOTIATED DISADVANTAGE

To secure the South Vietnamese countryside, it was necessary to cut the communists off from the north and grind them down. There are strong reasons to believe that the United States could have performed the former task in Laos and the northern RVN and that, given time, the ARVN (supported by South

Korea, the United States, and other allies) would have been adequate to the latter task. The competent performance of basic counterinsurgency tasks does not require tactical brilliance so much as discipline and experience. Furthermore, ultimately it was preferable that the ARVN, rather than foreigners, interact with Vietnamese civilians whenever possible; by demonstrating that the GVN was capable of controlling its territory, this would have tended to enhance the legitimacy of the Saigon government in the eyes of the populace.

Indochina was a unified theater of war. The leadership in Hanoi was entirely cognizant of this fact and North Vietnam formed a cogent warfighting strategy that involved operations in all four of the countries of Indochina. US policymakers preferred not to dwell on the strategic unity of the theater, and sustained an intellectual fiction – the neutrality of Cambodia and Laos – even though that fiction was enormously damaging to their war effort and even though they were well aware that enemy troops were operating in both of those countries.[48] The Laos Accords allowed US policymakers to evade one series of difficult decisions, but at the cost of positioning the United States for later defeat. By signing the Accords, the United States placed a handicap upon itself that made victory on the ground far more difficult; the opportunity costs the Accords imposed on the United States were immense.

NOTES

1. Communist forces in South Vietnam did partly rely on seaborne supplies infiltrated into the Mekong Delta; in response the United States initiated Operation Market Time in 1965. Because of Market Time and other interdiction operations, seaborne logistical support was too hazardous for Hanoi to rely on primarily to support the war in the South. See Jonathan S. Wiarda, 'The US Coast Guard in Vietnam: Achieving Success in a Difficult War', *Naval War College Review*, 51, 2 (Spring 1998), pp. 43–4.

2. However, the laws of war would have allowed for a considerable amount of American activity in Laos and Cambodia. See Guenter Lewy, *America in Vietnam* (New York: Oxford University Press, 1980), p. 174. It would arguably have been legal to undertake 'hot pursuit' of enemy troops, attacks on known enemy positions, and similar operations even without the permission of the Cambodian and Laotian governments. Furthermore, the areas in which North Vietnamese and Viet Cong troops were operating were thinly populated; while there is no international ban on military operations in populous areas, it is obviously desirable that as few civilians as possible are harmed by military operations.

3. However, policymakers were certainly concerned about the possible effect of losing Laos to the communists. On the early 1961 debate over Laos, see John M. Newman, *JFK and Vietnam: Deception, Intrigue, and the Struggle for Power* (New York: Warner, 1992), pp. 9–23.

4. One of the earliest reports on Laos for Kennedy administration policymakers was produced by a State–Defense–CIA task force and included a long list of 'Current Adverse Factors' that were damaging to US efforts in Laos. The problem of Laotian geography was well summarized, and included 'its isolation and lack of access to the sea, its mountainous-jungle terrain, absence of railroad, inadequate roads and airstrips. The

conclusion that 'Laos would be a most undesirable place in which to commit US forces to ground action' was reasonable. ('Report Prepared by the Inter-Agency Task Force on Laos', 23 January 1961, *FRUS, 1961–1963*, vol. 24 (Washington, DC: GPO, 1994), p. 24:28.)

5. 'The President expressed concern at the weakness of the local situation in Laos coupled with the weakness of allied support for our position. He proposed that, if the British and French aren't going to do anything about the security of Southeast Asia, we tell them we aren't going to do it alone. They have as much or more to lose in the area than we have.' ('Memorandum From the Assistant Secretary of Defense for International Security Affairs (Nitze) to Secretary of Defense McNamara', 23 January 1961, *FRUS, 1961–1963*, pp. 24:26-7.)

6. Paul H. Nitze, with Anne M. Smith and Stephen L. Rearden, *From Hiroshima to Glasnost: At the Center of Decision – A Memoir* (New York: Grove Weidenfeld, 1989), p. 255. For a detailed analysis of Kennedy's thinking on Laos, see David Kaiser, *American Tragedy: Kennedy, Johnson, and the Origins of the Vietnam War* (Cambridge, MA: Belknap Press/Harvard University Press, 2000), pp. 36–57.

7. Roger Hilsman claims: '[I]t had become apparent [in a series of meetings in early May 1962] that Secretary McNamara had moved over to side with the dominant view among the military opposing the limited use of force for political purposes. The proposal was that if force had to be used, the first step should be a large-scale movement of troops to occupy the whole of the panhandle of Laos, right on over to North Vietnam ... The advocates of this view, however, warned that the two hundred miles of mountains and jungles bordering North Vietnam would be impossible to defend. They recommended that unless the Communists, including the guerrillas in southern Laos, surrendered immediately, the next step should be an all-out attack on North Vietnam itself – land, sea, and air. What the United States would do if the Chinese Communists intervened was not spelled out, but the general impression was that the recommendation would be to retaliate on the mainland with nuclear weapons.' (*To Move a Nation: The Politics of Foreign Policy in the Administration of John F. Kennedy* (New York: Delta, 1967 [1964]), p. 147.) McNamara's memoirs do not directly address Hilsman's claim, but McNamara portrays himself as being very cautious about any involvement in Laos. See *In Retrospect: The Tragedy and Lessons of Vietnam* (New York: Times Books, 1995), pp. 37–8.

8. Stanley G. Langland, 'The Laos Factor in a Vietnam Equation', *International Affairs*, 45, 4 (October 1969), p. 633.

9. See President Kennedy's brief reference to Laos in his second State of the Union address of 11 January 1962. (John F. Kennedy, in Allan Nevins (ed.), *The Burden and the Glory* (London: Hamish Hamilton, 1964), p. 15.)

10. An enlightening discussion of China's role in the neutralization of Laos is offered in Qiang Zhai, *China and the Vietnam Wars, 1950–1975* (Chapel Hill, NC: University of North Carolina Press, 2000), pp. 92–111.

11. Norman B. Hannah, *The Key to Failure: Laos and the Vietnam War* (Lanham, MD: Madison, 1987), pp. 37–8.

12. As one author observes: 'The concept of neutralization of Laos had pulled everything together. There would be no need to send forces into Laos. The problem of South Vietnam could be handled internally as Harriman had recommended – i.e., within the framework of the new doctrine of counterinsurgency. If it should become necessary to deploy US forces, they would only be deployed to Vietnam – not to Laos – *behind* the protective screen provided by the Accords on Laos ... Harriman had found the "political route" between abandonment and war or, to put it in his words, he had "transferred the problem from the military to the political arena".' (Ibid., p. 40. Emphasis in original.)

13. Roger Warner, *Back Fire: The CIA's Secret War in Laos and Its Link to the War in Vietnam*

(New York: Simon & Schuster, 1995), p. 84.

14. Langland, 'The Laos Factor', p. 638.

15. 'Congress accepted the 1962 Laos settlement with little open dissent, partly because of deference to the Executive, but primarily because few Members wanted to see the [United States] become more actively involved, especially militarily, in Laos. At the same time, many if not most Members were privately if not publicly skeptical that the settlement had "settled" anything, and there was considerable concern, especially among those who favored a strong stand by the US in Southeast Asia, that it would work in the Communists' favor.' (William Conrad Gibbons, *The US Government and the Vietnam War: Executive and Legislative Roles and Relationships*, Part II: 1961–1964 (Princeton, NJ: Princeton University Press, 1986), p. 119.)

16. This confidence in the value of Soviet assurances is displayed in an 'eyes only' telegram from Harriman to President Kennedy: 'Pushkin has told me that when [the Laos] agreement is effective, corridor traffic through Laos to SVN will not be permitted. He has not admitted, but has not denied, that corridor traffic exists today. Incidentially, [*sic*] Souvanna Phouma has also agreed to do all he can to stop the traffic. This gives us extraordinarily direct and early opportunity to judge Soviet good faith after agreement goes into effect.' ('Telegram From the Delegation to the Conference on Laos to the Department of State', *FRUS, 1961–1963*, p. 24:497; also see Hilsman, *To Move a Nation*, p. 151.) In a 6 December 1993 letter to William Conrad Gibbons, Gen. Bruce Palmer contends that Westmoreland 'from the beginning had considered operations in the Laotian Panhandle and against enemy bases along the Cambodian border', but that 'any serious consideration of such a course of action' was prevented by the 'unalterable opposition of Averell Harriman ... [who] would never admit that the Accords were essentially a fraud'. (Letter cited in Gibbons, *US Government and the Vietnam War*, vol. 4, pp. 533–4.)

17. The United States used a variety of techniques in its attempts to interrupt the Ho Chi Minh Trail. Among other efforts, the military conducted Studies and Observation Group (SOG) operations in Laos that were intended to gather intelligence, find enemy installations, 'harass traffic along the Ho Chi Minh Trail', and so forth. There were even attempts by the Air Force to slow down traffic on the Trail by seeding the 'clouds above the Laotian panhandle, but there was no appreciable increase in rain'. (William C. Westmoreland, *A Soldier Reports* (New York: Da Capo, 1989 [1976]), pp. 107 and 281.) Also, there were attempts to expose the Ho Chi Minh Trail by expanding Operation Ranch Hand, the spraying of chemical defoliants, into Laos. See Wilber H. Morrison, *The Elephant and the Tiger: The Full Story of the Vietnam War* (New York: Hippocrene, 1990), p. 208.

18. Some of the US air operations in Laos are evaluated in Perry L. Lamy, *Barrel Roll 1968–73: An Air Campaign in Support of National Policy* (Maxwell Air Base, AL: Air University Press, 1996).

19. See Richard Nixon, *RN: The Memoirs of Richard Nixon* (New York: Grosset & Dunlap, 1978), pp. 498–9. For a detailed account of Lam Son 719 see Keith William Nolan, *Into Laos: The Story of Dewey Canyon II/Lam Son 719, Vietnam 1971* (New York: Dell, 1986). On the airmobile aspect of the operation see John J. Tolson, *Airmobility in Vietnam: Helicopter Warfare in Southeast Asia* (New York: Arno, 1981), pp. 235–52.

20. Despite Lam Son 719, 'the North Vietnamese [subsequently] expanded their presence in the Laotian panhandle'. (Timothy N. Castle, *At War in the Shadow of Vietnam: US Military Aid to the Royal Lao Government, 1955–75* (New York: Columbia University Press, 1993), p. 109.)

21. Evaluating three plans developed by MACV to deny use of Laos to the North Vietnamese, Westmoreland states that he is 'convinced that two and probably the third

would have succeeded, would have eliminated the enemy's steady flow of men and supplies through the Laotian panhandle, and would have materially shortened the American involvement in the war'. (*Soldier*, p. 271.)

22. See Hilsman, *To Move a Nation*, pp. 151–5.
23. Hannah, *Key to Failure*, p. 68.
24. Robert Shaplen, 'Our Involvement in Laos', *Foreign Affairs*, 48, 3 (April 1970), pp. 481–2.
25. Qiang Zhai, *China and the Vietnam Wars*, p. 180.
26. 'The [area] in the southeast [of Laos] was an indispensable tool for Hanoi's campaign to conquer South Vietnam. But the one in the northwest – while requiring strong US assistance – made no effective contribution to the salvation of South Vietnam. Accordingly, our ultimate failure in Indochina was virtually assured as long as we persisted in waging our effort within the asymmetrical parameters of the "tacit agreement".' (Hannah, *Key to Failure*, p. 73.)
27. Kissinger observes that there were even some military advantages for the United States in Laos. 'If Indochina were indeed the keystone of American security in the Pacific, as the leaders in Washington had claimed for over a decade, Laos was a better place to defend it than Vietnam; indeed, it was perhaps the only place to defend Indochina. Even though Laos was a remote and landlocked country, the North Vietnamese, as feared and hated foreigners, could not have waged a guerrilla war on its soil. America could have fought there the sort of conventional war for which its army had been trained, and Thai troops would almost certainly have supported American efforts. Faced with such prospects, Hanoi might well have pulled back to await a more propitious moment for full-scale war.' (Henry Kissinger, *Diplomacy* (New York: Simon & Schuster, 1994), p. 647.)
28. One message from the US embassy states that '[w]e have been proceeding on assumption that essential objective US seeks in Cambodia is denial this country to Communist control, either by takeover or through voluntary entry into Communist camp. At least as long as US is involved in SVN struggle against Communists, denial Cambodia to Communists must be overriding US consideration ... Greatest obstacle US faces in effort achieve its objective is relations between Cambodia and its neighbors, US allies Thailand and SVN.' ('Telegram From the Embassy in Cambodia to the Department of State', 20 November 1962, *FRUS, 1961–1963*, pp. 23:217-18.)
29. Westmoreland argues that 'Sihanouk had decided in March 1965 to side with the Communists, and in 1966 he made a deal with the Chinese Communists for delivery through Cambodia of supplies for the Viet Cong, although the man who subsequently headed the successor government, Lon Nol, allegedly arranged without Sihanouk's knowledge for a 10 per cent cut for the Cambodian Army. From 1966 through 1969 the VC received 21,600 metric tons of military supplies such as arms and ammunition, including almost 600 metric tons of Soviet rockets, and over 5,000 metric tons of nonmilitary supplies such as food, clothing, and medicine, all of which was transshipped in Cambodian commercial trucks to VC bases along the Cambodian–South Vietnamese border'. (*Soldier*, p. 182.)
30. Frank Snepp, *Decent Interval: An Insider's Account of Saigon's Indecent End Told by the CIA's Chief Strategy Analyst in Vietnam* (New York: Vintage, 1978), p. 20. There was earlier dissension in the intelligence community about the importance of Sihanoukville, and John Lehman writes that he 'participated in briefings in 1969 and 1970 in which the American intelligence community insisted that there were no North Vietnamese supplies coming in by sea through the Cambodian ports, only over land' and that only the Navy (correctly) dissented from this view. (John Lehman, *Making War: The 200-Year-Old Battle Between the President and Congress Over How America Goes to War* (New York: Charles Scribner's Sons, 1992), p. 84.)

31. Adm. Elmo Zumwalt, Jr, who commanded the US Navy in Vietnam from late 1968 to early 1970, stated that Sihanoukville was 'the single most important reason why the enemy were very tough to deal with in the Delta … that sustained their effort until we moved a thousand boats up along the border with Cambodia and knocked off that infiltration … once we did that we were able to pacify the Delta'. (Interview with author, 4 September 1997, Rosslyn, VA.)
32. See Westmoreland, *Soldier*, pp. 180–3.
33. See ibid., p. 183.
34. Cambodia was a very important source of rice for the communists. '[In the mid-1960s] Cambodia was selling the North Vietnamese, for transmittal to the VC, 55,000 tons of rice annually, a major portion of the VC requirements, and the VC were buying almost double that amount direct from Cambodian farmers'. (Ibid., p. 180.)
35. Considering what eventually happened in Cambodia, destroying the Khmer Rouge would have been, by any civilized standard, morally desirable in itself. Edward Luttwak observes that 'those who held that a suspension of war would self-evidently improve the circumstances of the Cambodian people have now had full opportunity to appreciate the oceanic depth of their error'. (*On the Meaning of Victory: Essays on Strategy* (New York: Simon & Schuster, 1986), p. 54.)
36. Westmoreland, *Soldier*, p. 148.
37. For a description of a possible US strategy for Indochina focused chiefly on Laos, see George and Meredith Friedman, *The Future of War: Power, Technology, and American World Dominance in the 21st Century* (New York: Crown, 1996), p. 235.
38. For a cogent argument against a US ground presence in Laos see Gregory T. Banner, 'The War for the Ho Chi Minh Trail' (master's thesis, US Army Command and General Staff College, 1993).
39. In addition, the negative impact of US support on Vietnamese and world perceptions of the legitimacy of the GVN would have been lessened. In American war reporting and anti-Saigon propaganda there was considerable comment about the allegedly disastrous effects of the US presence on traditional Vietnamese culture and morality. (There was no doubt some validity to such concerns: hundreds of thousands of foreign troops inevitably disrupt a small society.)
40. Geoffrey Perret, *A Country Made by War: From the Revolution to Vietnam – The Story of America's Rise to Global Power* (New York: Random House, 1989), p. 523.
41. Ibid.
42. At a 1995 event, retired North Vietnamese Col. Bui Tin underlined the strategic importance of the Ho Chi Minh Trail. When asked if there was any way in which the United States could have prevented a DRV victory, he replied that if President 'Johnson had granted General Westmoreland's request to enter Laos and block the Ho Chi Minh Trail, Hanoi could not have won the war'. He explained that '[i]t was the only way "to bring sufficient military power to bear on the fighting in the South. Building and maintaining the [Trail] was a huge effort, involving tens of thousands of soldiers, drivers, repair teams, medical stations, and communications units". If it had been cut, Hanoi could not have intensified the fighting with NVA regulars, as it did in 1965.' (Richard H. Shultz, Jr, *The Secret War Against Hanoi: The Untold Story of Spies, Saboteurs, and Covert Warriors in North Vietnam* (New York: Perennial, 1999), pp. 205–6.)
43. Dan Oberdorfer, *Tet!* (New York: Da Capo, 1984 [1971]), p. 329.
44. Ibid.
45. However, Spector points out that reliance on NVA troops presented significant problems for the communists. North Vietnamese lacked 'the experience, organization, and local knowledge provided by the Viet Cong'. The United States 'responded [to this weakness] with a determined attempt to win control of the countryside for Saigon and

smash the remaining large enemy units', and enjoyed 'considerable success, although that would not be evident until late 1969 or 1970'. (*After Tet: The Bloodiest Year in Vietnam* (New York: Free Press, 1993), p. 312.)

46. Westmoreland writes that 'a line through the Hai Van Pass' would have been more easily defensible than the DMZ, but he was, understandably, unwilling to surrender the two northernmost RVN provinces to communist control. (*Soldier*, p. 168.)

47. Also, the revolutionaries in the south had a deep psychological dependence on the north: the communist government led and supplied the revolutionary movement in the south, and the military–political link between North Vietnam and the Viet Cong was constantly reinforced by the Ho Chi Minh Trail. Physically cutting off the southern revolution from its northern leadership would have had a (possibly devastating) impact on communist morale.

48. Kissinger notes the prevalence of strategic stubbornness in the Johnson administration. '[T]he strategy which America in fact adopted [could not work]: the mirage of establishing 100 per cent security in 100 per cent of the country, and seeking to wear down the guerrillas by search-and-destroy operations. No matter how large the expeditionary force, it could never prove sufficient against an enemy whose supply lines lay outside of Vietnam and who possessed extensive sanctuaries and a ferocious will ... Johnson resolutely rejected any "expansion" of the war. Washington had convinced itself that the four Indochinese states were separate entities, even though the communists had been treating them as a single theater for two decades and were conducting a coordinated strategy with respect to all of them.' (*Diplomacy*, p. 660.)

5

Enter the Dragon:
China, the United States, and the
Conflict in Vietnam

The ominous precedent of the Korean War guided the Vietnam decision-making process: the fear of military intervention by the People's Republic of China (PRC) was a major ingredient shaping US policy in the conflict. Worries about possible intervention by China impacted many aspects of US warmaking in Vietnam, and fear of the communist giant played an important part in all decisions on escalation. In their effort to avoid provoking the PRC, US policymakers conducted the war in Vietnam in a fashion so unsound militarily that the US effort in that country was fundamentally undermined. Concerns about the provocation of China affected US bombing strategy, policy relating to Laos and Cambodia, and, especially, the debate over direct military action against North Vietnam.

The caution exercised by US decisionmakers was, however, self-defeating. As is demonstrated below, the leadership of the PRC wished to avoid war with the United States and would probably have intervened in Vietnam only in a case of perceived self-defense. Even very energetic action against North Vietnam might not have brought China into the war, although there certainly would have been a substantial possibility of this outcome. Furthermore, and of primary importance, Chinese intervention most likely would not have prevented a positive outcome of the Vietnam situation for the United States.[1]

Given the constraints placed on the US government by public opinion, the limitations on the conduct of the war had the effect of severely undermining the Vietnam undertaking. US policymakers could not fight a counter-insurgency campaign with nebulous goals in South Vietnam and perpetually maintain public support, yet they felt compelled to do so because they were unwilling to accept the hazards incidental to escalation of the conflict. Thus, the PRC, merely by maintaining its reputation as a bellicose power and credible protector of the DRV, was able to impair grievously the US effort in Vietnam and prevent policymakers from even considering options that might have secured a military victory over the Indochinese communists.

For policymakers in the Kennedy and Johnson administrations, the Korean War was a recent event that 'was still fresh in nearly every mind in Washington'.[2] In 1950, China had convincingly confirmed its willingness to intervene on behalf of a neighboring communist power when the latter's survival was in doubt.[3] Indeed, China's bold intervention in Korea occurred despite numerous problems and disadvantages for the PRC. For instance, the communists had only recently seized control of the mainland and ended a decades-long period of warfare; there was an enormous disparity between the war potential of the US and Chinese economies and the general quality of their respective military forces; the United States possessed nuclear weapons and China did not; and, even though the PRC and the Soviet Union were functional allies, neither power fully trusted the other.[4] The PRC even accepted the risk that the United States would use nuclear weapons against Chinese soil and/or accept no outcome to the conflict short of unconditional victory; the Chinese had no way of assuring that the United States would not escalate the conflict and, although it quickly became clear that President Truman wished strictly to limit Sino–American hostilities, Mao had taken a mighty risk by attacking US forces.

It is unsurprising that the perceived recklessness of China impressed Kennedy and Johnson administration policymakers. There were obvious parallels between the situations in Korea and Vietnam and the US concern about Chinese intervention was justifiable – it would have been irresponsible for decisionmakers not to consider the possibility that China would intervene on North Vietnam's behalf. Indeed, while many US policymakers over-estimated the degree of direct Chinese control over the DRV,[5] their belief that Chinese leaders would view an invasion of North Vietnam as a possible threat to China itself was essentially correct.

Yet, despite the importance of Indochina to the PRC, domestic and inter-national circumstances would likely have served to constrain Chinese responses to US actions against North Vietnam. In the 1960s China wished to avoid a war with the United States,[6] and US policymakers erred too far on the side of caution in their effort to avoid a military confrontation with the PRC. The perceived need to 'avoid another Korea' blinded key decisionmakers, most notably President Johnson and Secretary McNamara, to two key details. First, the geographical, political–diplomatic, military, and other circumstances of the Vietnam conflict were substantially different from those which resulted in the Chinese intervention in Korea. Overall, these differing circumstances had the effect of discouraging Chinese intervention in Vietnam. Second, even if China had intervened in Vietnam with the maximum force that it could immediately bring to bear, it is unlikely that it would have been decisive on the outcome of the war.

FROM THE YALU TO THE MEKONG

On 27 November 1950, Chinese troops (supposedly 'volunteers') launched a surprise offensive against US/UN forces; having moved stealthily southward from Manchuria, the PLA scored early victories against the US Eighth Army and threw most US Army units in the northern Democratic People's Republic of Korea (DPRK) into flight. Compared to US forces the People's Liberation Army (PLA) was grossly underequipped and undermechanized, but it successfully took advantage of the American belief that a massive assault was unlikely at that time (even though a small Chinese expedition into North Korea, probably intended as a warning, had already occurred in October–early November) and successfully 'divided [UN commander Gen. of the Army Douglas] MacArthur's overextended forces, and precipitated the greatest American military retreat in history'.[7] For a brief time, the PLA was able to use 'surprise, night fighting, and speed to overcome a professionally trained, well-equipped, and technologically superior enemy'.[8]

Even at the height of Chinese fortune in the war, however, Maj. Gen. Oliver P. Smith's First Marine Division, along with some US Army and Republic of Korea (ROK) units, conducted an extraordinary fighting withdrawal from the Chosin reservoir and inflicted severe casualties on the PLA despite an overwhelming Chinese advantage in numbers.[9] Shortly thereafter, under the guidance of Lt-Gen. Matthew Ridgeway, the reorganized Eighth Army was shaped into a highly effective fighting force. Ridgeway 'turned [the] Eighth Army into a huge killing machine' that he called 'the Meat Grinder'.[10] The grisly nickname was appropriate. The PRC suffered enormous causalities – more than one million Chinese may have died in the war (including Mao Anying, one of Mao Zedong's sons)[11] – but was nonetheless unable to eject the Americans from the Korean peninsula. This reversal of fortune was accomplished despite Washington's unwillingness to place the American economy on a full wartime footing, commit a mammoth field army to Korea, attack targets in mainland China, or use nuclear weapons. The United States fought a highly constrained war but achieved its key goal, the preservation of South Korean independence, and did so notwithstanding the fact that as the war continued (unnecessarily, since the PRC refused until July 1953 to settle for peace terms that it could have obtained much earlier) it became very unpopular in the United States.

The Chinese leadership had little reason to see the US presence in Vietnam as being a threat comparable to that presented by the United States in Korea. The Korean peninsula was a convenient base for large-scale operations against China (including the capital and key industrial centers in Manchuria), and Mao clearly believed that a unified Korea containing US troops posed a danger to the Chinese communist regime.[12] In fact, Mao probably even believed that a US invasion of China was imminent;[13] in February 1972, Zhou Enlai informed

Alexander Haig that the PRC had not merely attempted to prevent a US victory in Korea. For understandable reasons, Mao feared for the survival of his government:

> [Zhou Enlai] told [Haig] that the Chinese had entered the war because they believed, in the wake of MacArthur's shattering victory, that they were confronted by a pincers movement in which the American armies would advance on Beijing from Korea while Chiang Kai-shek's re-equipped and retrained Nationalist forces would invade the mainland across the Strait of Formosa under the protection of the US Seventh Fleet and strike for the capital ... Geographically and militarily, an operation of this kind was by no means impossible: Beijing is only four hundred air miles from the North Korean frontier, less than the distance from Pusan to the Yalu River. The United States certainly possessed the power to carry out a successful attack from Korea; Chiang had half a million troops, recently rearmed and retrained by the Americans, on Formosa; and, as a result of the very first order issued by President Truman after the North Korean invasion of the South, the Seventh Fleet was on station in the Formosa Strait. To the Communist regime in Beijing, which had been in power for less than nine months, these factors may very well have added up to something that looked like a mortal threat.[14]

Chinese concern about the US position in Korea was not irrational: the United States was hostile to the Chinese Communist Party (CCP) and, as Haig observes, the situation in Korea clearly offered the United States and the Republic of China in Taiwan (ROC) an opportunity to return control of the mainland to Chiang Kai-shek. Mao had no way of reliably knowing that Truman believed ground war with China to be totally unacceptable; the PRC's analysis of the situation was, although obviously flawed, logical if not entirely reasonable.[15] In retrospect, it is quite unsurprising that the circumstances of late 1950 agitated Mao, who was extremely suspicious of the United States and confident of his personal military prowess (a volatile combination of attitudes).[16] Also, a formal alliance between the PRC and the USSR had been signed shortly before. This secured China's northern flank and provided a basis for hope that, if complete Chinese failure in the war was imminent, the Soviet Union might intervene on behalf of its ally.

The US involvement in Vietnam presented China with very different problems than did the war in Korea and there were few sensible reasons for Mao to believe that Vietnam would be the base for a US invasion of China. By the 1960s, the communist government was well-established on the Chinese mainland; long-term military–political factors had shifted in the PRC's favor and it was deeply improbable that Chiang Kai-shek's dream of reconquering the mainland would ever be realized;[17] the 'road to Beijing' was secure and a revived and heavily armed DPRK stood between US forces on the Korean peninsula and the PRC; despite tensions during and after Korea, the United States had never attempted to overthrow the CCP regime by force; and the Sino–Soviet relationship had degenerated to the point that some Chinese leaders undoubtedly saw the USSR, rather than the United States, as posing the greatest threat to the territorial integrity of the PRC. Moreover, Indochina was not a desirable region from which to launch an invasion of the PRC, even if the United States were so inclined: there was no critical military–political 'center of gravity' to attack in the part of China directly north of Vietnam.[18] The capital city, industrial core areas, most military bases, and virtually everything else valued by the Chinese regime were located far from the Sino–Vietnamese border. This was the opposite of the case during the Korean War, where Mao's army was underarmed and China's capital and industrial core were vulnerable to a pincers movement formed by the US and Nationalist Chinese armies.[19]

PRC worries about US aggression were deeply misguided,[20] but such fears nevertheless appear to have been genuine;[21] Chinese actions during this period provide persuasive evidence that the Chinese leadership feared an attack by the United States. Certainly, efforts such as the Third Front development program, which 'was premised on the assumption that in the event of war with the United States, China's established industrial center along the coasts would be destroyed or occupied in the early stages of the conflict', indicated that China feared attack by the United States.[22] In 1964, as China still struggled to overcome the effects of the 'Great Leap Forward', Mao initiated the costly 'Third Front' development program, which was intended to increase industrial production in the interior of the PRC. The Third Front diverted scarce government development funds away from urban coastal regions to (commonly rugged) rural areas. This vastly increased the cost of development projects and, because resources were distributed inefficiently and often used unwisely, the overall process of industrialization in China was slowed.[23] Although not a terrible catastrophe like the Great Leap Forward – it did succeed in rapidly increasing the level of heavy industry in the Chinese hinterlands – the Third Front was exceedingly expensive. (Nevertheless, the program continued until 1971, a measure of the regime's devotion to its goals.) Even though it was nominally an industrial development program, the Third Front's primary benefits were largely intended to be military: by industrializing the interior, the PRC would be prepared for a long war of resistance that would oblige a would-be aggressor to fight a difficult war in China's vast spaces. Along with other evidence, the Third Front strongly indicated a primarily defensive mentality on the part of Mao and indicated that Chinese worries about military vulnerability were quite strong.

It is difficult to provide a wholly satisfying explanation for Chinese concerns in the 1960s, but much of the answer is probably to be found in the political culture of the PRC. The antipathy of the United States was assumed, and

Chinese policymakers (wrongly, but not irrationally) believed that Washington would act to destroy the PRC if it were given the opportunity.[24] The Chinese error was to misunderstand fundamentally the attitudes of the Kennedy and Johnson administrations and the general political culture of the United States. PRC policymakers simply did not believe that an unprovoked major offensive against China was impossible, even though that was in fact the case.[25]

Not all Chinese leaders, however, shared the same vision of how best to cope with the perceived threat from the United States. Many Chinese policymakers no doubt were willing to conduct an extremely high-risk strategy of confrontation with the United States and, despite the obvious risks, some probably wanted to commit PLA ground units to battle. Such an attitude, however, did not guide the actions of Mao and his immediate circle. Indeed, Mao – who, despite challenges to his authority, remained the pre-eminent Chinese decisionmaker throughout the 1960s – was apparently inclined to avoid unnecessary confrontation with the United States. Nevertheless, given Mao's backing of the effort to create a 'Third Front' within China and other evidence, it appears that he believed Nationalist China, the United States, and the Soviet Union presented clear long-term threats.[26] He did, however, feel sufficiently confident in China's short-term safety to concentrate on domestic issues and launch the Cultural Revolution.

In retrospect, it is probable that Mao was attempting to strike a difficult course: avoiding the appearance of weakness in the face of the United States, which would create internal political problems (and, he probably assumed, encourage US aggression), simultaneously avoiding unduly provocative actions that would bring about a war, and making prudent preparations for a possible conflict with the United States. Judging from China's half-hearted actions in this period, the PRC's general preference was to avoid war with the United States, but its attitude toward the Vietnam situation was still in flux when the Cultural Revolution descended on China.

A TORMENTED GIANT

The United States enjoyed more and greater military advantages over China in Vietnam in the mid-1960s than it did in Korea in the early 1950s.[27] Although the Chinese army of the 1960s was somewhat better equipped than the very light Chinese infantry units that were common in Korea, the PLA was damaged acutely by the Great Leap Forward, and hunger and disaffection among its troops were major problems in the early-to-mid 1960s.[28] Also, unlike the experienced combat troops that struck the Americans early in the Korean War, the PLA of the period was mainly composed of conscripts who had never seen combat. Furthermore, the good order and discipline of the PLA – already weakened by the Great Leap Forward – was deeply damaged by a series of

Maoist political initiatives. 'Professionalism' and hierarchical discipline were attacked, guerrilla doctrine enjoyed a resurgence in influence, and the need to apply Maoist principles to the PLA was emphasized. As a result, the PLA of the mid-1960s was a profoundly troubled institution.

> With the purge of [Peng Dehuai] in 1959, Lin [Biao] became minister of defense and moved the PLA sharply in the Maoist ideological, non-professional direction. In June 1965, the abolition of ranks within the PLA was the final step in its 'democratization' and thus deprofessionalization, precisely when United States military involvement in Vietnam significantly intensified. This entire process was accompanied by the gradual dismissal of almost all the highest officers who ever had directed the PLA in its purely military capacity.[29]

As a result of the victory over India in the 1962 Indo–Chinese border war, Marshal Lin 'could claim that the bringing of politics into the Army had in no way affected its ability to wage war, but had actually increased its morale and fighting spirit'.[30] This was a dangerous delusion: India was a weak opponent and the Indo–Chinese conflict was very brief and constrained;[31] the 1962 clash offered few useful lessons for a war against either the United States or the Soviet Union.

The 'professionals' (anti-Maoists) within the PLA were concerned by the politicization of the military, and these worries increased as the US involvement in Vietnam deepened and China made contingency plans for intervention in the war.[32] Their concerns were well justified. First, the PLA was grossly ill-prepared for a high-tempo modern war against a first-class power, and sizeable, direct Chinese intervention in the Vietnam War would have been costly in human terms and logistically near-impossible.[33] US troops, well-trained and thoroughly supplied with excellent equipment, were formidable. Second, in Vietnam the PRC would suffer from major disadvantages that it had not experienced in the Korean War. Most notably, in the 1960s the PRC was growing increasingly concerned about the Soviet Union. Sino–Soviet relations were fairly amicable in the early years after Mao's victory over the Nationalists, but progressively soured; by 1964, the level of Sino–Soviet trust was very low and Chinese leaders could not be confident that their northern border was secure (and were no doubt concerned that the United States and Soviet Union might even cooperate militarily against China). Third, North Vietnam's ports could be easily closed by the United States and the Chinese land logistic network into Vietnam was inadequate to the task of supporting large expeditionary forces and vulnerable to US airpower.

Finally, and perhaps most importantly, China was undergoing a long-term domestic political and economic crisis. The disastrous Great Leap Forward, initiated in the late 1950s, had grievously damaged the economy, and resulted in enormous declines in industrial and agricultural production.[34] Mao's ill-conceived (and sometimes bizarre) policies created one of the worst famines in human history: approximately 30–60 million Chinese died,[35] and PRC agricultural and industrial progress was set back by years, or even decades. The Soviet Union's decision to discontinue aid and assistance programs to China in summer 1960 further damaged Chinese industry,[36] and did conspicuous damage to the PLA.

Rather than granting the PRC an opportunity to recuperate from the economic troubles of the late 1950s to mid-1960s and stabilize politically, Mao initiated the Great Proletarian Cultural Revolution. The Cultural Revolution and its aftershocks threw Chinese society and government into acute crisis from 1966 until the end of the decade.[37] The instability in China was reflected in the politically divided PLA and viciously self-destructive Chinese leadership: Red Guard factions battled each other and the PLA, the political leadership suffered instability and denunciation, and the Chinese Communist Party was shattered.

It is probable that the Cultural Revolution so weakened the Chinese government that it was unfeasible for the PRC to undertake any substantial military action in Vietnam from late 1966 onward. The Cultural Revolution was a period of virtual civil war; at a time when riots and military engagements were occurring in China itself the actions of the Americans in Vietnam must have seemed comparatively unimportant to most Chinese decisionmakers. Indeed, the majority of CPP leaders undoubtedly expended most of their energy on the problems of preserving their own careers and avoiding 're-education' or worse at the hands of fanatical youths.[38] Severe domestic crisis tends to act as a constraint on foreign policymaking. (Internal troubles certainly affected the policymaking process in Washington, even though domestic problems in the United States were minuscule compared to those in the PRC.) China was a state on the verge of starvation in the early 1960s and of implosion in the late 1960s, and these crises impaired the PRC's ability to craft an effective foreign policy and, particularly, to enforce that policy through force of arms.[39]

China's most important interests regarding the US effort in Vietnam were concerns about the territorial integrity of the PRC itself. The DRV was mainly (and merely) a buffer state and unreliable client regime and, although Chinese leaders publicly stated that Hanoi was the legitimate government of all of Vietnam, making this claim a reality was certainly not central to China's overall national interests. The primary reason for China to offer protection to the DRV was to assure that the conflict in Vietnam did not result in a US invasion of the PRC. North Vietnam was not itself valuable enough to warrant a major war with the United States, and, even though China was seeking to expand its influence in Indochina, its key short-term concerns were defensive.

All other considerations were secondary to China's territorial integrity, and this created a perceived dilemma for Chinese policymakers that was, ironically, not unlike that experienced by US leaders. The PRC believed that it had to deter the United States from offensive action against China, but did not know precisely the limits of American tolerance – insufficient responses to supposed provocations could conceivably cause the United States to believe that China was weak and thus encourage aggression, while overly energetic action might cause US policymakers to overreact violently and invade China.

US decisionmakers worried that China would intervene in Vietnam while Chinese leaders were concerned about the possibility that the United States would invade China. Both sides were fundamentally misguided: it was unlikely that China would intervene in Vietnam in a fashion that would change the ultimate outcome of the war or vastly increase US casualties, and the United States had no desire whatsoever to fight the PRC (least of all on the home territory of the latter). The United States was deeply disadvantaged by its misconceptions. The belief that the PRC was on the verge of war deterred US decisionmakers from invading North Vietnam, the action that offered the best chance of allowing a speedy and favorable settlement of the Vietnam situation, or even undertaking several lesser options. For example, the fear of China played a major role in the Kennedy administration decision to seek the neutralization of Laos and the Johnson administration's tendency to pursue a 'slow squeeze' bombing strategy rather than an intense bombing offensive.[40] The erroneous estimation of China's military power and willingness to enter the war contributed mightily to the US loss in Vietnam. If US policymakers had made a less cautious estimate of Chinese intentions and military capabilities, the intellectual environment in Washington would have been very different.

The PRC, on the hand, successfully deterred the United States from invading North Vietnam or undertaking other strong military actions, even though that was only a secondary goal for China. The perceived need to stand up to the United States resulted in Chinese actions that demonstrated to US leaders like Johnson and McNamara what they were predisposed to believe – that the PRC was a power willing to go to war with the United States and that any US military action in North Vietnam would automatically result in a 'Korea II', a large-scale war in Indochina in which hundreds of thousands of PLA troops would overwhelm US forces.

China's deterrence of the United States would not have been possible if US decisionmakers had not been highly risk-averse. The PRC was an available bogeyman that reassured Johnson, McNamara, and other US policymakers who were reluctant to take robust action in Vietnam that their course was the only prudent one. Civilian policymakers consistently chose to ignore the advice of the Joint Chiefs of Staff and others who argued that China's ability to project military power effectively into Vietnam was minimal. US leaders usually preferred to be highly cautious and assume that the PRC possessed enormous military capabilities and the will to fight a costly war in Indochina. They had overlearned from the experience in Korea, and did not give sufficient weight to the PRC's many known military–political problems or realistically consider the problems that the PLA would have in projecting power into Indochina.

THE YEARS OF GREATEST DANGER

In the mid-1960s, the US military commitment to Vietnam increased exponentially; meanwhile, China was undergoing a breathing period between the Great Leap Forward and the Cultural Revolution. The period of relative domestic calm in China between 1962 and 1965 would have been the most convenient time for the PRC to intervene in Vietnam, and was also a time when the fear of the United States was high in PRC policymaking circles.[41] (It is also notable that on 16 October 1964 the PRC detonated its first atomic device, an event that may have bolstered China's confidence while at the same time confirming the Johnson administration view that China was a powerful foe.)

Throughout the 1960s, the Chinese government hinted that it would intervene militarily in Vietnam if the United States invaded the DRV.[42] After US air attacks on the DRV, Premier Zhou Enlai warned the United States that the PRC might not idly stand by while the United States committed 'aggression' and Foreign Minister Chen Yi indicated that China would fight if the United States invaded North Vietnam.[43] China also, however, tended to qualify some of its more aggressive rhetoric with vague indications that a Sino–American war would only occur if the United States attacked China or gave that country good reason to believe that an attack on its territory was imminent.[44] Chinese leaders avoided explicitly stating that an attack on only the southern portion of the DRV would not result in PRC military action, because this would indirectly have given the United States license to invade China's client, but Chinese statements about the PRC's commitment to North Vietnam tended to be somewhat tepid and reflected China's own concern about encirclement and a possible US invasion of the PRC.[45] Even strong Chinese statements tended to avoid specific commitments, instead keeping the level of Chinese tolerance deliberately vague while nonetheless implying that the PRC might take action in Vietnam.

In addition to public statements, the PRC did take many concrete actions to assist the DRV militarily. Most importantly, China supplied North Vietnam with military hardware, even at the cost of denying the PLA equipment.[46] The DRV would have been unable to carry on the fight in South Vietnam effectively without the multitude of rifles, artillery shells, bullets, and other supplies supplied by the PRC over the course of the war.[47] Until Sino–Vietnamese relations deteriorated substantially in the late 1960s, China also performed construction work and anti-aircraft defense for North Vietnam.

Official Chinese estimates indicate that 1,707 US aircraft were shot down and 1,608 others damaged by the PLA,[48] but these numbers are exaggerated –

they substantially surpass the American figure for the total number of US aircraft shot down (1,096) during the war. Nonetheless, the Chinese commitment to North Vietnam's air defense was impressive, and reportedly '[f]rom August 1965 to March 1969, a total of 63 divisions (63 regiments) of Chinese anti-aircraft artillery units, with a total strength of over 150,000, engaged in operations in Vietnam'.[49] The PRC was responsible for air defense for its own construction troops, as well as defense of certain strategic targets, such as railroads, in the northern portion of the DRV.

Chinese construction troops assisted Hanoi mainly by constructing and repairing rail lines, roads, bridges, telephone lines, and defense works. Most construction activity in Vietnam occurred from 1965 to 1968 (although some went on until 1970); work generally took place north of Hanoi, and apparently never below the twentieth parallel.[50] These projects were nevertheless sizeable, and the PLA built well over 1,000 kilometers of roads, as well as hundreds of bridges, in North Vietnam.

The total Chinese contribution to the North Vietnamese war effort was, in personnel terms alone, substantial: PRC figures indicate that from 1965 to 1969 about 320,000 troops served in Vietnam, with 170,000 there at the peak of the Chinese commitment.[51] By performing air defense and mundane construction tasks, the PRC enabled the North Vietnamese to send troops into other parts of Indochina that otherwise would have been tied down at home. Perhaps even more importantly, the Chinese commitment gave the DRV confidence that it had a reliable great-power protector. The North Vietnamese leadership was thus energized to continue with its national unification project in the difficult years of the late 1960s, when war costs were high, victory uncertain, and US–RVN progress in counterinsurgency was considerable. China convincingly promised to protect the one thing that the North Vietnamese leadership truly valued: the survival of its regime. So long as the PRC acted as guarantor of the national survival of North Vietnam and (along with the USSR) provided the means to carry out the war, the DRV was willing to pay the human costs of the conflict.

China was, however, uneasy with its role as protector of the DRV, despite the fact that Washington policymakers, who did not want to inflame Sino–American tensions, rarely mentioned Chinese involvement in the Vietnam War (and very much avoided publicly dwelling on the fact that the PLA was responsible for the capture or death of a large number of US pilots). There was 'a growing feeling of isolation and [siege] in Beijing, just as the United States began to increase substantially its involvement in Vietnam, posing the possibility of a direct attack on southern China in the near future'.[52] In April 1965, 'the CCP Central Committee issued "Instructions for Strengthening the Preparations for Future Wars", a set of directives which would ultimately be relayed to every part of Chinese society and become one of the most important guiding documents in China's political and social life for the rest of the 1960s'.[53] The Instructions noted that US aircraft were entering the airspace of the DRV, stated that the PRC needed to improve its readiness for a war with the United States, and made it clear that support for the DRV was considered a vital part of China's foreign policy.

In June 1965, North Vietnamese leader Van Tien Dung visited Beijing (Ho Chi Minh had visited China a short time before, in May–June) and the Chinese privately undertook potentially very serious obligations. PRC leaders agreed that, if the United States used its sea and airpower to support a South Vietnamese invasion of the DRV, they would respond with China's own naval and air forces. Further, if US land forces actually invaded North Vietnam, then 'Chinese troops were to serve as Hanoi's strategic reserve, ready to assist in defense or to launch a counterattack to take back the strategic initiative'.[54]

In addition to making promises, the PRC took limited steps to prepare for a military confrontation with the United States. Notably, the PLA constructed a large base complex at Yen Bai in the northeast part of the DRV. The complex 'grew to nearly two hundred buildings and a large runway with attendant facilities' and, in the event that Hanoi and Haiphong were overrun, offered the North Vietnamese 'a viable refuge on home territory for continued resistance, in contrast with the plight of the North Korean regime after fleeing Pyongyang'.[55] Moreover, if the PRC decided to enter the war in force, the complex could also have served as a base camp for Chinese troops. In addition to Yen Bai and additional projects in North Vietnam, the PRC also undertook other measures, such as building new airfields immediately north of the DRV and undertaking 'a systemic reinforcement of its air power, both by increasing the number of aircraft and by concentrating its relatively few MIG-19s which had previously rotated between Northeast and East China', as well as conducting joint air exercises with North Vietnamese fighters.[56]

Overall, the substantial Chinese contribution to the DRV war effort and the willingness of the PRC to promise the North Vietnamese that it would act as guarantor of their sovereignty provides impressive evidence that, at least in the mid-1960s, China would have been willing to contemplate entry into the Vietnam War.[57] This evidence is, however, not sufficiently compelling to indicate that China would *certainly* have fought on behalf of North Vietnam. It is conceivable that China would have been willing to renege on its promises to Hanoi if it believed that the United States posed no threat to China. Importantly, the PRC might have made a distinction between actions merely harmful to North Vietnam and those endangering Chinese territory. For example, a US invasion with the clear (stated or unstated) intention of eliminating the DRV as an entity, like the United States/United Nations invasion of North Korea, probably would have goaded Beijing into attempting action at almost any time in the war. On the other hand, even in 1965 an invasion a few miles north of the DMZ with very limited and clearly stated goals might not have overly excited the Chinese leadership.

In any case, the middle part of the 1960s was for China clearly the period of greatest capacity and will to defend North Vietnam. The PRC's likely reactions to US actions in Vietnam varied over time and both the Chinese desire and capability to become involved in Indochina degraded rapidly from 1966 onward. For example, if in 1965 the United States had undertaken an invasion of the DRV and announced a limited but ambitious goal for its effort – such as occupation of the Red River Delta, including Hanoi and Haiphong but leaving the northernmost portion of the DRV in communist hands – the PRC would likely have attempted to fight in Vietnam. If, however, this had occurred in 1967, China's capability to intervene would have been degraded and Mao might have been inclined to seek a quick settlement of the war.[58]

The year 1965 was, in retrospect, pivotal to the Sino–American relationship. The United States decided to fight the Vietnam War mostly in South Vietnam and to utilize an operational style that did not fundamentally alter for the rest of the war; the Chinese, in turn, chose to tolerate a US war in Indochina waged on those terms and did not modify their policy for the remainder of the war. US decisionmakers chose to place avoidance of a war with China above all other considerations (except of course the complementary goal of averting war with the USSR, which was correctly believed to be far less likely), even victory in Indochina. This consideration remained primary for the remainder of the war, although this was less important to Nixon than to Johnson. Developments within China and the United States progressively made the principal forces constraining the US war effort domestic rather than international and it was prudent for policymakers to assume that actions such as the mining of Haiphong or the Linebacker bombing campaigns would not bring about a conflict with the PRC.

Placing a negative goal, such as war avoidance, above a positive goal, such as assisting an ally, is not necessarily undesirable. If the known (or likely) price of an objective is outrageous in relation to that objective's importance, it is rational to abandon the desired end. However, the negative goal of US policymakers was itself the result of pronounced timorousness on their part. Myths about China's military potential played a greater role in the formation of US policy than did rational considerations. It was obviously desirable for the United States to avoid war with China. *It would nevertheless have been acceptable and defensible to risk war with the PRC in preference to fighting in Indochina in a way that defied basic military logic.*

AN UNREADY FOE

There are abundant reasons to doubt that even in the mid-1960s the PRC was capable of successfully initiating and sustaining a major expeditionary war against the United States in Indochina. A March 1964 memorandum for the Secretary of Defense from the Joint Chiefs of Staff states:

An assessment of enemy reactions to [possible US military action against North Vietnam] indicates that the Chinese communists [CHICOMs] view Laos and South Vietnam as DRV problems. It is unlikely that the CHICOMs would introduce organized ground units in significant numbers into the DRV, Laos, or Cambodia except as part of an over-all campaign against all of Southeast Asia. They might offer the DRV fighter aircraft, AAA units, and volunteers. They would assume an increased readiness posture and CHICOM aircraft might be committed to the defense of North Vietnam. The Soviets would probably be highly concerned over possible expansion of the conflict. To the extent that Moscow believed the Hanoi and [Beijing] regimes in jeopardy, Sino–Soviet differences would tend to submerge. It is believed that Moscow would initiate no action which, in the Soviet judgment, would increase the likelihood of nuclear war.[59]

Thus, in the best judgment of the Joint Chiefs of Staff – who were, of course, the principal uniformed military advisors to the president – action against North Vietnam presented some risk of escalation, but minimal risk of catastrophic escalation (a major war with China or, even worse, a conventional or nuclear war with the Soviet Union).[60] The JCS allowed for the possibility that China might take military action against several countries – including South Korea, Taiwan, and several Southeast Asian states – but noted that 'logistic limitations severely restrict that ability to sustain a major land, sea, and air campaign in more than one area'.[61]

The JCS calculated that, as of the time of the memorandum, '[13] CHICOM infantry divisions, less heavy artillery and armor, plus nine DRV divisions could be logistically supported during the dry season (November–May) in initial moves against Southeast Asian countries'. In addition, it was estimated that the PRC 'could make available about 400 jet fighter and 125 jet light bombers for operations in Southeast Asia', and could also conduct minor naval operations, possibly including the use of a small number of submarines. However, it was also noted that during the rainy season there would be a great decrease in the potential size of Chinese offensive operations.

The JCS estimate of potential Chinese combat power indicates that, far from being overwhelming, the military force that China could immediately bring to bear in Indochina was modest.[62] Thirteen relatively light Chinese divisions could not possibly have delivered a crushing blow against US forces in Vietnam: such a force would lack the mass, firepower, mobility, and troop quality to defeat US forces quickly. In addition, the approximately 500 aircraft that the JCS estimated the PLA might use would have been insufficient in number and too low in quality to effectively threaten US air superiority.

The PLA depended on mass and surprise temporarily to rout the Americans in Korea; in Vietnam, it would not have enjoyed either advantage over the

United States to a significant degree. Repetition of the early Chinese victories in the Korean War would have been extremely unlikely in Vietnam, because this would have required US policymakers to ignore all the lessons of the Korean experience – invading North Vietnam while leaving no buffer zone in the northern portion of that country, ignoring Chinese troop movements, and making other extraordinarily gross errors of judgment.

In the event of a US invasion, the defense of the North Vietnamese territory would have been very challenging for the PLA, and it would have been difficult for communist forces to retain control of strategically vital areas of North Vietnam. Command of the air and the sea would (probably quickly) have been secured by the United States. Even if the PRC had made a full effort to contest control of the sky, the quality of both NVA and PLA aircraft and pilots was too low to allow communist forces seriously to contest US land- and carrier-based airpower for very long. (The great majority of the aircraft losses that the United States suffered over the course of the war were the result of an anti-aircraft network constructed over the course of several years, during which time US policymakers often refused to destroy surface-to-air (SAM) sites that were under construction in North Vietnam.)

Ability to command the air, in turn, was a vital component of the overall US advantage in firepower. Various combinations of modern artillery, tactical and strategic aircraft, naval gunnery, and armor gave the United States the capability to deliver an enormous quantity of accurate fire on strategic and tactical targets. Both the PRC and the PLA lacked the technical–industrial capability to match US firepower, a disadvantage that would severely hamper any communist attempt to launch a counteroffensive and regain the initiative.

The fact that the PRC and DRV share a common border would have been logistically convenient for the two communist governments, but would not have guaranteed that Chinese assets could be easily moved into Vietnam. Given the terrain, logistical issues, and the likely ease with which the United States could have attained command of the air, and hence been able to target traffic on major roads in the DRV, Chinese units would have generally operated at a marching pace. Given the high level of mechanization of the United States military, and the US tradition of logistical excellence, this would have meant a substantial advantage in road movement for US forces. Furthermore, the helicopter gave US forces the ability to move large numbers of fighting person-nel with extraordinary speed and flexibility (a vitally important capability the US Army had not possessed in Korea, where helicopters were primarily used for reconnaissance and transportation of casualties). Helicopters made isolated enemy units vulnerable, provided the United States with the capability to harass enemy logistics, and enabled US forces facing enemy pressure to receive support quickly.

In order to defend North Vietnamese territory effectively, Chinese com-manders would have been obliged to mass their forces and fight US forces in pitched battles in which their units would have been exposed to US artillery and airpower.[63] Guerrilla tactics that communist forces employed with success in the war in South Vietnam would be irrelevant to defensive operations. Communist forces could, of course, have been pulled back into a rump DRV (assuming such an entity existed) or into China itself and thereafter conducted raids and other small operations (perhaps while preparing for a large offensive intended to eject allied forces from the DRV). That, however, would have ceded control of the great majority of North Vietnam's population and industrial capacity to the RVN.

The aforementioned facts should have served to reassure President Johnson and Secretary McNamara that they could, with considerable confidence, escalate the war against North Vietnam, but it appears to have had little impact on them. President Johnson privately professed great concern about China. At one point he even stated that 'If one little general in shirtsleeves can take Saigon, think about two hundred million Chinese coming down those trails. No sir! I don't want to fight them.'[64] Leaving aside the obvious exaggeration in Johnson's statement, it summarizes Washington's attitude toward the PRC. Many US leaders were in awe of China's population, had respect for China's potential power, and found the idea of confronting such an enormous country deeply disconcerting. Nevertheless, Johnson and McNamara refused to acknowledge that, giant though it was, China cast only a small military shadow over Indochina.

CONCLUSION: A FATAL ERROR

The evidence as to how China would have reacted to assertive US action in Vietnam is ambiguous and indicative of a country without a consistent policy. China underwent severe domestic turmoil in the period coincident with the US war in Vietnam, and the probable Chinese reaction to particular US actions changed over the course of the conflict. The only US activity that would have been highly risky at any time in the 1960s would have been the complete conquest of North Vietnam, and even that might not have resulted in Chinese intervention. As time passed, an unspoken agreement as to the acceptable scope of US activity in Indochina developed between Washington and Beijing; Nixon eventually went beyond these limits, but by that time there was a relatively high degree of trust between the two countries and the US withdrawal from Indochina was clearly imminent.

Political–military logic would indicate that the most auspicious times for the United States to have intervened in Indochina in an assertive fashion were during the Laos Crisis of the early 1960s, in 1964 (in the wake of the Gulf of Tonkin incident), or in 1965 (after the choice was made to commit ground units to Vietnam). Within these key decision points there were, of course, numerous sub-options, such as whether to occupy part or all of Laos, whether to invade the DRV, and so forth.

Firm US military action at any of these three points could have changed the course of the conflict in Indochina. Nevertheless, it is important to note that these were not the only times at which the United States could have altered its policy. It would be mistaken, for example, to assume that because the United States effectively agreed to a 'hands off North Vietnam' policy, it was locked permanently into such a position. Decisionmaking is a fluid process, and US leaders continually made the choice (albeit a negative one) to continue with their current policy. It is true that Mao did not 'unleash the Red Guards' until after the United States government had more-or-less formally notified the PRC in November 1965, at the Warsaw discussions between the countries, that there would be no invasion of North Vietnam,[65] and there certainly may have been a causal relationship between the two events. However, the United States was free to back away from its 'understanding' with China at any time. Mao could have let the Red Guards run amok in China and then been confronted with an altered US strategy in Vietnam. China did not trap US policymakers – because of their extreme risk aversion, those leaders trapped themselves. It does not reflect well on US leaders, particularly Johnson and McNamara, that even as it became increasingly obvious that their strategy in Indochina was deeply flawed and that China was undergoing a period of internal turmoil and probable military vulnerability, there was a complete unwillingness to contemplate a change in that strategy.

Beyond the intransigence of US decisionmakers is the more vital point that the United States so feared a war with the PRC that it was willing to comprehensively warp its effort in Vietnam in order to stay within the perceived limits of Chinese tolerance. US leaders hoped that by carefully constraining their effort in Vietnam they would have the best of both worlds: they would be able to protect South Vietnam while simultaneously minimizing the risk of war with the PRC. This was a prescription for ineffective warfighting and, given the constraints placed on policymakers by American domestic opinion, for ultimate failure. Policymakers achieved their key goal of avoiding war with China, but ultimately failed as guarantors of South Vietnamese independence.

The myth of Chinese military invincibility was shallow, and had already been largely discredited before US ground combat units were even deployed to Vietnam. As was discussed above, the United States could have fought and won a conflict with China in Indochina. When Chinese capabilities and disadvantages are weighed dispassionately, it is even imaginable that, if the United States had invaded North Vietnam and been met with PLA resistance, the resulting US casualties would have been fewer than occurred in the drawn-out war that actually did take place in Vietnam.[66]

Ultimately, the key error of US policymakers was not the unwillingness to change a flawed policy; it was the decision to make major concessions to

Chinese desires in the first place. Small accommodations to China were understandable and desirable; few policymakers, however hawkish, would have objected substantially to public and private professions of US intent to respect Chinese sovereignty. It would probably have been wise, even if the decision had been made to invade and occupy much of North Vietnam, to leave the northernmost portion of that country independent. *If, however, the United States was not willing to run a serious risk of war with China it should never have entered into a protective relationship with South Vietnam.*[67]

US policymakers believed, rightly, that the DRV essentially controlled the communist revolution in South Vietnam. Furthermore, they understood that China was North Vietnam's most credible protecting power. Therefore, part of the 'price of doing business' as South Vietnam's protector was the acceptance of a fairly high risk of war with the PRC. If war with Beijing was absolutely unacceptable, as the Kennedy and Johnson administrations believed it to be, the United States should never have become seriously involved in the war in Indochina. Having decided to become the RVN's protector, the United States should logically have accepted the risks that came with that position, including a possible clash with the PRC in Indochina (and even the unlikely proposition that the conflict with China would have continued for years, with the PRC government resisting a settlement).[68] The ongoing attempt to navigate a middle course that would allow them to coerce North Vietnam while not provoking China was a central error of US policymakers, and enormously damaged the US effort in Indochina. If US policymakers wished to act as the RVN's protectors, their only judicious course would have been to accept that limited war with the PRC was possible (if not probable), to be militarily ready for that eventuality and factor it into operational planning, and, if necessary, to defeat the PLA as promptly and thoroughly as prudence allowed. From a militarily favorable position, US leaders could have sought a settlement with Beijing that would allow the United States to achieve its goals in Indochina. Simply attempting to avoid a war with the PRC while simultaneously attempting to coerce its client was a poor approach, and the ultimate result was not surprising: the United States so distorted its war effort in order to appease North Vietnam's patron that it was unable to coerce the DRV itself effectively.

NOTES

1. A March 1966 poll indicated that American citizens were dedicated to the Vietnam enterprise even if China intervened in the war. Respondents were asked: 'If Red China decides to send a great many troops, should we continue to fight in Vietnam, or should we withdraw our troops?' Only 8 per cent wished to withdraw under those circumstances, 19 per cent had no opinion, and 73 per cent favored continuing the war. (Survey cited in John E. Mueller, *War, Presidents, and Public Opinion* (New York: John Wiley & Sons, 1973), p. 86.)

2. Alexander M. Haig, Jr, with Charles McCarry, *Inner Circles: How America Changed the World: A Memoir* (New York: Warner, 1992), p. 133. It also should be noted that Korea had a formative influence on American thinking about limited war and 'flexible response'.

3. In an interview, Harry G. Summers argued persuasively that Chinese intervention was a 'great shock' to Dean Rusk and that this affected his Vietnam decisionmaking, inclining him toward caution on the question of whether to invade North Vietnam. (Interview with author, 9 September 1997, Bowie, MD.)

4. For a study of Sino–Soviet relations in the Korean War era see Sergei N. Goncharov, John W. Lewis, and Xue Litai, *Uncertain Partners: Stalin, Mao, and the Korean War* (Stanford, CA: Stanford University Press, 1993).

5. However, China certainly had influence over Hanoi's warmaking decisions. See Xiaoming Zhang, 'The Vietnam War, 1964–1969: A Chinese Perspective', *Journal of Military History*, 60, 4 (October 1996), pp. 736–9.

6. See Robert Garson, 'Lyndon B. Johnson and the China Enigma', *Journal of Contemporary History*, 32, 1 (January 1997), p. 79.

7. David Allan Mayers, *Cracking the Monolith: US Policy Against the Sino–Soviet Alliance* (Baton Rouge, LA: Louisiana State University Press, 1986), p. 92.

8. Rosemary Foot, *The Practice of Power: US Relations with China Since 1949* (Oxford: Clarendon Press, 1995), p. 145.

9. See Eliot A. Cohen and John Gooch, *Military Misfortunes: The Anatomy of Failure in War* (New York: Free Press, 1990), pp. 186–90.

10. Geoffrey Perret, *A Country Made By War: From the Revolution to Vietnam – The Story of America's Rise to Power* (New York: Random House, 1989), p. 464.

11. Stanley Karnow, *Vietnam: A History* (New York: Penguin Books, 1984), p. 329.

12. See Li Zhisui, trans. Tai Hung-chao, *The Private Life of Chairman Mao* (New York: Random House, 1994), p. 117.

13. See Richard H. Bernstein and Ross H. Munro, *The Coming Conflict with China* (New York: Alfred A. Knopf, 1997), p. 78.

14. Haig, *Inner Circles*, pp. 48–9.

15. For a study that emphasizes factors in Beijing's Korean War decisionmaking other than China's fear of invasion, particularly its goals as a revolutionary power, see Chen Jian, *China's Road to the Korean War: The Making of the Sino–American Confrontation*, The US and Pacific Asia: Studies in Social, Economic, and Political Interaction (New York: Columbia University Press, 1994).

16. Mao may have been virtually alone among the CCP leadership in favoring intervention in Korea, but his authority at the time was so great that he nevertheless prevailed over more timid decisionmakers. See John W. Garver, 'Little Chance', *Diplomatic History*, 21, 1 (Winter 1997), p. 88; Goncharov, Lewis, and Xue, *Uncertain Partners*, pp. 176–83; and Chen, *China's Road to the Korean War*, pp. 218–19.

17. Nevertheless, in April 1964, Chiang speculated to Secretary of State Rusk about a possible ROC invasion of the mainland. ('Summary Record of the 528th Meeting of the National Security Council, Washington, April 22, 1964, 4:45 p.m.', *FRUS, 1964–1968*, p. 1:258.)

18. The greatest Chinese worry in the early 1960s was of a US–ROC threat to the coast of the PRC. In a 1962 speech wherein the term 'Third Front' was first publicly used, Lin Biao warned that Nationalist forces 'might take advantage of the post-Great Leap Forward crisis to launch an attack on mainland cities, and suggested that such an attack could not be successfully resisted in the coastal cities, especially if Kuomintang forces were backed by American naval power'. (Barry Naughton, 'The Third Front: Defense Industrialization in the Chinese Interior', *China Quarterly*, 115 (June 1988), p. 352.)

19. In contrast to the area north of the DRV, South Manchuria was 'China's principal industrial base, [consuming] one-third of its power supply; Shenyang's 2,000 plants accounted for the bulk of its machine-building capability; Anshan and Benxi produced 80 per cent of its steel; and Fushan was the site of its largest coal mine. All these industrial centers were less than 200 kilometers from the Yalu. Furthermore, the Suiho Hydro-electric Station, the largest of its kind in Asia, and other smaller stations were on the south bank of the river.' (Goncharov, Lewis, and Xue, *Uncertain Partners*, pp. 183–4.)

20. Not only Beijing was concerned about the possibility of a US campaign against China. Hans J. Morgenthau warned that war with China was possible and, indeed, that the logic of the US position in Vietnam might lead the United States to initiate it. 'The extension of war into North Vietnam can be interpreted as an attempt to create in Hanoi the psychological precondition for a negotiated settlement. But it can also be interpreted as an attempt to change the fortunes of war in South Vietnam by rupturing the assumed causal nexus between the policies of Hanoi and the victories of the Viet Cong. This causal nexus is a delusion, which has been given the very flimsy appearance of fact through the White Paper of 28 February. A policy derived from such a delusion is bound to fail. Yet when it has failed and when failure approaches catastrophe, it would be consistent in terms of that delusionary logic to extend the war still farther. Today, we are holding Hanoi responsible for the Viet Cong; tomorrow we might hold Peking responsible for Hanoi.' ('War with China?', *Survival*, 7, 4 (July 1965), pp. 155–9.) It should be noted that Morgenthau's belief that the NLF was not controlled by the DRV, which is central to his logic, is false. See R.B. Smith, *An International History of the Vietnam War*, vol. 2, *The Struggle for South-East Asia* (London: Macmillan, 1985), p. 37.

21. A 1966 CIA estimate indicated that Mao and those close to him believed that, if there were a substantial number of troops on the Chinese border, the United States would choose to join the ROC in an effort to overthrow the communists. See Bevin Alexander, *The Stranger Connection: US Intervention in China, 1944–1972*, Contributions to the Study of World History, 34 (New York: Greenwood, 1992), pp. 198–9.

22. John W. Garver, 'The Chinese Threat in the Vietnam War', *Parameters*, 22, 1 (Spring 1992), p. 79.

23. See Naughton, 'The Third Front', pp. 375–81.

24. There was also great disagreement in Western political and academic circles during the 1960s about the PRC's military capabilities and intentions. See for example, Henry Brandon, 'The Dilemma of SE Asia', *Survival*, 7, 1 (January–February 1965), pp. 38–40; Donald S. Zagoria, 'Communism in Asia', *Commentary*, 39, 2 (February 1965), pp. 53–8; George Lichtheim, 'Vietnam and China', *Commentary*, 39, 5 (May 1965), pp. 56–9; Benjamin Schwartz, 'Chinese Visions and American Policies', *Commentary*, 41, 4 (April 1966), pp. 53–9; Kenneth T. Young, 'American Dealings with Peking', *Foreign Affairs*, 45, 1 (October 1966), pp. 77–87; Roderick MacFarquhar, 'Mao's Last Revolution', *Foreign Affairs*, 45, 1 (October 1966), pp. 112–24; Lucian W. Pye, 'China in Context', *Foreign Affairs*, 45, 2 (January 1967), pp. 229–45; Stefan T. Possony, 'Mao's Strategic Initiative of 1965 and the US Response', *Orbis*, 11, 1 (Spring 1967), pp. 149–81; Alexander Woodside, 'Peking and Hanoi: Anatomy of a Revolutionary Partnership', *International Journal*, 24, 1 (Winter 1968/9), pp. 65–85; Bernard Fall et al., 'Containing China: A Round-Table Discussion', *Commentary*, 41, 5 (May 1966), pp. 23–41.

25. It is possible Mao believed in the late 1950s that the United States feared war with China but that his personal outlook concerning China's strategic environment darkened in the early 1960s and he came to consider a joint Soviet–American attack on China to be conceivable. See He Di, 'The Most Respected Enemy: Mao Zedong's Perception of the United States, *China Quarterly*, 137 (March 1994), pp. 152–4.

26. Interestingly, however, in 1969 Mao supposedly presented his personal physician with

a geopolitical riddle: 'Think about this ... [w]e have the Soviet Union to the north and the west, India to the south, and Japan to the east. If all our enemies were to unite, attacking us from the north, south, east, and west, what do you think we should do?' The next day the physician was unable to answer, and Mao explained that 'Beyond Japan is the United States. Didn't our ancestors counsel negotiating with faraway countries while fighting with those that are near?' (Li, *The Private Life of Chairman Mao*, p. 514.)

27. While the PRC tested its first nuclear weapon in 1964, it is extremely unlikely that Beijing would have judged nuclear usage in Vietnam to be to its advantage. Chinese use of nuclear weapons would have invited US retaliation in Vietnam (if not against China itself) – and the United States possessed a vastly larger and more advanced nuclear arsenal.

28. Stanley Karnow, *Mao and China: From Revolution to Revolution* (New York: Viking, 1972), pp. 108–9.

29. C.W. Cassinelli, *Total Revolution: A Comparative Study of Germany Under Hitler, the Soviet Union Under Stalin, and China Under Mao* (Santa Barbara, CA: Clio, 1976), p. 216.

30. Gerald H. Corr, *The Chinese Red Army: Campaigns and Politics Since 1949* (New York: Schocken, 1974), p. 149.

31. For an analysis of the Sino–Indian clash see Allen S. Whiting, *The Chinese Calculus of Deterrence: India and Indochina* (Ann Arbor, MI: University of Michigan Press, 1975), pp. 1–169.

32. Corr, *The Chinese Red Army*, p. 149.

33. For an analysis of the logistic difficulties facing the PRC, see Herman Kahn, 'On Establishing a Context for Debate', in Frank E. Armbruster *et al.*, *Can We Win in Vietnam?: The American Dilemma*, Hudson Institute Series on National Security and International Order, 2 (London: Pall Mall, 1968), pp. 56–7.

34. It is indicative of the poor quality of US intelligence on China during this period that a July 1959 National Intelligence Estimate stated that China's 'economy is rapidly expanding' and calculated 'that Communist China will be able to increase its GNP by about 12 to 15 per cent in 1959'. ('National Intelligence Estimate', 28 July 1959, *FRUS, 1958–1960* (Washington, DC: GPO), pp. 19:577-8.) In reality, the Chinese economy was on the verge of total collapse in 1959.

35. Arthur Waldron, '"Eat People" – A Chinese Reckoning', *Commentary*, 104, 1 (July 1997), p. 29. As Waldron recounts, the famine was so severe that it resulted in widespread cannibalism in the Chinese countryside.

36. Karnow, *Mao and China*, p. 103.

37. On the turmoil within China see Simon Leys, trans. Carol Appleyard and Patrick Goode, *The Emperor's New Clothes: Mao and the Cultural Revolution* (London: Allison & Busby, 1977).

38. In 1967, radical violence was so prevalent in the provinces that 'a number of provincial and municipal officials were brought to Beijing so that their physical safety could be ensured'. (Harry Harding, 'The Chinese State in Crisis, 1966–9', in Roderick MacFarquhar (ed.), *The Politics of China: The Eras of Mao and Deng* (2nd edn, Cambridge: Cambridge University Press, 1997), p. 211.)

39. It can be argued that Mao's decision to launch the Cultural Revolution should not necessarily be taken as evidence that he believed that war with the United States was unlikely in the short term. 'Just as Stalin believed that elimination of internal opposition dovetailed with the forced industrialization of the Five Year Plans to prepare the Soviet Union for war, Mao may well have believed that the purge of revisionists from China's leadership prepared China for battle. Mao, like Stalin, may have been mistaken about the military efficacy of his purges. That, however, is another matter.' (Garver, 'The

Chinese Threat in the Vietnam War', p. 82.) Nonetheless, it seems very unlikely that Mao would have undertaken the Cultural Revolution if he believed that war with the United States was *imminent*; just as Stalin undertook his purges as part of a long-term strategy, Mao probably believed that the Cultural Revolution would unsettle China in the short term but strengthen it in the long term.

40. See Foot, *The Practice of Power*, pp. 158–9.

41. This was also apparently a period (particularly in 1965) when powerful factions in China evidently wished to take an active part in the Vietnam ground war. See Karnow, *Mao and China*, pp. 147–53.

42. See Foster Rhea Dulles, *American Foreign Policy Toward Communist China, 1949–1969* (New York: Thomas Y. Crowell, 1972), pp. 214–15.

43. Ibid., p. 215.

44. Kissinger notes that Defense Minister Lin Biao's September 1965 article 'Long Live the Victory of People's War!' was interpreted as a warning by the Johnson administration not to invade North Vietnam, but they ignored 'Lin's subtext, which stressed the need for self-reliance among revolutionaries. Reinforced by Mao's comment that Chinese armies did not go abroad, it was meant as well to provide a strong hint that China did not intend to become involved again in communist wars of liberation.' (*Diplomacy* (New York: Simon & Schuster, 1994), p. 645.)

45. See Whiting, *The Chinese Calculus of Deterrence*, pp. 189–94.

46. Zhang, 'A Chinese Perspective', p. 737.

47. This generous supply continued despite the progressive widening of the Sino–Vietnamese breach, and even after Richard Nixon's visit to China. See Chen Jian, 'China's Involvement in the Vietnam War, 1964–68', *China Quarterly*, 141 (June 1995), p. 379.

48. Zhang, 'A Chinese Perspective', p. 759.

49. Chen, 'China's Involvement', p. 376.

50. Ibid., p. 375.

51. Zhang, 'A Chinese Perspective', p. 759.

52. Kenneth Leiberthal, 'The Great Leap Forward and the Split in the Yan'an Leadership, 1958–65', in MacFarquhar, *The Politics of China*, p. 129.

53. Chen, 'China's Involvement', p. 367.

54. Zhang, 'A Chinese Perspective', p. 750. Also see Qiang Zhai, *China and the Vietnam Wars, 1950–1975* (Chapel Hill, NC: University of North Carolina Press, 2000), p. 131.

55. Whiting, *The Chinese Calculus of Deterrence*, p. 188.

56. Ibid., pp. 176–7.

57. See Zhai, *China and the Vietnam Wars*, pp. 155–6.

58. On the US military's assessment of the probability of Chinese intervention, Adm. Zumwalt stated: 'The military view was that … the Chinese would not come in, because we had in essence defeated them in Korea. We stopped their invasion, and slowly moved them back, and got the truce … [S]ince then we had by a double order of magnitude improved our armed forces equipment and technology, whereas the Chinese had not, so the Chinese would know that we were better by far than we were in Korea, and we were better than they were in Korea. Second, if we were wrong, and they came, we could whip them … [T]he military view always was that we could seize Haiphong and Hanoi, not go out any further north, and put the war out at the heart, instead of dealing with the fingertips in the jungles of South Vietnam. (Interview with author, 4 September 1997, Rosslyn, VA.)

59. 'Memorandum for the Secretary of Defense', 2 March 1964, Papers of Robert S. McNamara, RG 200, Box 82, United States National Archives, NN3-2000-092-001 HM 92-93.

60. It is now clear that most US policymakers were correct in their presumption that the

Soviet Union genuinely wished to avoid a violent confrontation with the United States over Vietnam. See Ilya V. Gaiduk, *The Soviet Union and the Vietnam War* (Chicago, IL: Ivan R. Dee, 1996), *passim*.

61. 'Memorandum for the Secretary of Defense', 2 March 1964, Papers of Robert S. McNamara.

62. Other estimates of Chinese combat power, conducted both before and after 1964, tended to be skeptical of the PRC's overall capabilities. See Foot, *The Practice of Power*, pp. 150–66.

63. It should be borne in mind that the climate and prevalent terrain in Vietnam is as alien to most Chinese as it is to most Americans. There was no more reason for a soldier from Beijing to feel at home in the Vietnamese hinterlands than there was for a soldier from New York City to feel at home in a Florida swamp. Jungle fighting was not a particular speciality of the People's Liberation Army and disease and discomfort would likely have hampered the fighting efficiency of Chinese forces.

64. Karnow, *Mao and China*, p. 406.

65. Garver, 'The Chinese Threat', p. 82.

66. Adm. Zumwalt estimated that if the United States had seized Hanoi and Haiphong early in the conflict, the United States 'would have lost on the order of five thousand dead and had a war [in Vietnam] that lasted a year'. While this bold assessment may presume that Beijing would not become involved in the war, Zumwalt was in any case dismissive of the Chinese ability to project power into Indochina. (Interview with author, 4 September 1997, Rosslyn, VA.)

67. For a differing view, see Michael Lind, *Vietnam: The Necessary War: A Reinterpretation of America's Most Disastrous Military Conflict* (New York: Free Press, 1999), *passim*.

68. Garver argues that '[t]o stop and roll back a Chinese invasion of Southeast Asia, the United States would probably have used nuclear weapons, either against Chinese forces in Southeast Asia or against military and industrial centers in China itself'. ('The Chinese Threat', p. 83.) However, this is extremely unlikely, not only because of Soviet and, depending on the year, Chinese nuclear deterrence, but because nuclear usage would doubtless have been militarily unnecessary. It is very probable that US forces could have stopped a maximum Chinese effort in Southeast Asia using conventional means – a judgment readily reachable at the time.

6

Fettered Eagles:
The Use and Misuse of US
Airpower in Indochina

The intellectual poverty of the US theory of victory in Indochina was clearly demonstrated by the bombing campaign against North Vietnam. The bombing of the DRV could potentially have been an important component of an ultimately successful US military strategy, but the United States did not use airpower in an appropriate manner until 1972, eight years after the initial bombing of North Vietnam. The decision gradually to escalate the bombing and to use force frugally against the DRV, and the resulting inadequate air campaign against that country, was a key error of the United States.

The disappointing effect of the air campaign was the result of a critical strategic error made by US policymakers before it was first initiated – the decision to use bombing against the North primarily as a tool of diplomatic persuasion rather than as a instrument to undermine Hanoi's warmaking capability. As argued below, the strategy of graduated pressure[1] adopted by the United States was too parsimonious in its use of force: strategic airpower is a blunt instrument that can be effective when applied robustly, but, when used with great restraint, its efficacy is sharply reduced. The notion that targets in North Vietnam (particularly in Hanoi, Haiphong, and their environs) had to be preserved (so that the United States would retain negotiating leverage) undermined the effectiveness of the entire air war. Attempting to apply a precise amount of damage to the DRV so as to elicit a particular response was impractical and this assured that the DRV would have time to become accustomed to strategic bombing and to minimize the effects thereof by dispersing or hiding valuable facilities, setting up an excellent air defense network, and otherwise acting to neutralize the US airpower advantage.

THE FLAWED CÒNCEPT OF GRADUATED PRESSURE

During the Second World War and, insofar as practicable given that attacks on the PRC and use of nuclear weapons were not allowed, the Korean War, US airpower was applied robustly with the intent of both damaging the enemy's ability to conduct operations and breaking his will to continue the war. With relatively minor exceptions, such as the debate over whether it was wiser to immediately use the two atomic devices then possessed by the United States on Japanese cities or to save them for use against military targets, there was little perceived contradiction between the two objectives of impeding military operations and destroying the enemy's resolution.

The pursuit of these objectives in tandem was neither new nor unique to airpower; centuries before the development of aircraft, it was commonly accepted that there was a causal relationship between the degradation of an enemy's military capabilities and the will to resist. As military capabilities are debased, the probability of victory is lessened, leading to morale problems within the armed forces, a shattering of the confidence of policymakers, and other ill effects. This, in turn, encourages leaders to seek an acceptable peace in which losses are minimized rather than an optimum victory in which gains are maximized.

In Vietnam, however, US civilian policymakers saw a strong tension between effective warfighting and the creation of conditions likely to lead to a satis-factory diplomatic settlement. The experience of the Cuban missile crisis, belief in the value of quantitative analysis, the conviction that traditional ideas about the use of military force were not relevant to current strategic problems, and other factors led Secretary McNamara and his advisors to devise the concept of 'graduated pressure'.[2] The use of graduated pressure would supposedly allow the United States to show determination and thereby convince an enemy to modify his conduct.[3] Underpinning this idea was the false assumption that the pain threshold of the North Vietnamese leadership could be estimated within an acceptable margin of error (in truth, guessed: although much was known about the Hanoi regime in general, there apparently was little specific, meaningful information from which to extrapolate likely outcomes). This assumption, in turn, rested on the belief that Hanoi placed a very high value on the civil and military infrastructure of the DRV and, to a lesser degree, the population. This belief was, however, essentially speculation based on the belief that the negative goal of preventing damage to the North Vietnamese homeland would ultimately outweigh the positive goal of Vietnamese unification in the minds of the communist leadership.

The application of graduated pressure to the air war had a perverse effect. In order 'correctly' to coerce North Vietnam, that country's most lucrative targets had to be protected from US bombing. Targets which have previously been destroyed cannot be menaced,[4] so civilian policymakers were concerned that striking Hanoi's industrial capabilities too vigorously would devastate North Vietnam's industrial capacity, leaving the United States with no prospective targets to threaten.[5] In addition, there were other considerations that affected the targeting preferences of civilian policymakers, such as concerns over Chinese reaction to the destruction of targets near the DRV–PRC border.

The target approval process was tortuous. Targeting selections moved from in-theater targeteers to CINCPAC to the Joint Chiefs of Staff to the State Department, again to the JCS, and finally to the White House, at which time President Johnson and several of his advisors (often, but not always, including JCS Chairman Wheeler) would make the final targeting selections at Tuesday lunch meetings.[6] Unsurprisingly, the military disapproved of the White House's top-down decisionmaking process, which it correctly believed led to an uncoordinated sequence of attacks and targets being 'approved randomly, even illogically',[7] but it was powerless to alter President Johnson's decision to conduct the air war personally.

This lengthy and highly politicized process was almost the precise opposite of a militarily sound system for selecting targets. Furthermore, conserving targets so as to increase slowly the diplomatic–political tension on North Vietnam was militarily counterproductive. By constructing and then attempting to implement the seemingly elegant theory of graduated pressure, US policymakers outsmarted themselves – the combination of the overly complex targeting selection process and the policy of not attacking the most desirable North Vietnamese targets had the effect of hamstringing the air war against North Vietnam.

The tendency by the United States to increase only grudgingly the level of force applied to Vietnam was of course not only apparent in the air war over the DRV. Washington's reluctance to increase the US troop levels in Vietnam or to allow the military to operate freely outside of South Vietnam were also indicative of the desire to win the war 'on the cheap' and with minimal risk of Soviet or Chinese intervention, an understandable aspiration that nevertheless resulted in many militarily injudicious decisions. Nonetheless, the decision to gradually increase the level of force used in the strategic bombing campaign was an extraordinarily misguided use of a military tool. Even though the United States refused to treat Indochina as a unified theater of war and the accepted concept of how best to win the ground war was flawed, US ground forces were still able to conduct a partially effective ground campaign in South Vietnam. Simply by being on the ground in force the US military prevented Hanoi from toppling Saigon and, despite Washington's errors, the United States made substantial progress in its war against the guerrillas. In contrast, an aerial bombing campaign is (leaving aside questions of how enemy morale is affected) only as militarily productive as its targets allow: if worthwhile targets are not attacked, the effectiveness of the campaign is undermined. US tonnage over North Vietnam was often expended on minor targets and secondary missions.

The commonly cited statistic that more US bomb tonnage was dropped in Indochina than by all sides during the entire of the Second World War proves nothing. The most lucrative targets in North Vietnam – including the seat of government, most of the industrial infrastructure, the port of Haiphong, many bridges and railheads, and anything in the northernmost portion of the country – were intentionally left undisturbed by the Johnson administration. The actual amount of tonnage dropped is a secondary consideration – what those munitions are dropped on, and how much damage they do to their intended targets, are much more vital questions. It was only with the Linebacker bombing programs of 1972 that airpower was allowed to demonstrate convincingly even part of its potential value to the US effort in Indochina. Robert Osgood, an influential theorist of limited war, nicely summarizes the theory of graduated pressure as applied in Vietnam:

> In the spring of 1965 the American government, frustrated and provoked by Hanoi's incursions in the South and anxious to strike back with its preferred weapons, put into effect a version of controlled escalation ... Through highly selective and gradually intensified bombing of targets on lists authorized by the President ... the United States hoped to convince Hanoi that it would have to pay an increasing price for aggression in the South. By the graduated application of violence, the government hoped through tacit 'signaling' and 'bargaining' to bring Hanoi to reasonable terms. But Hanoi, alas, did not play the game.[8]

The final sentence is key: the DRV simply refused to accept calculations of its national interest which US policymakers regarded as rational. The North Vietnamese leadership placed a high enough value on national unification that, by Washington's standards, they were behaving irrationally. US calculations of North Vietnam's national interest were grossly dissimilar from those of the Hanoi leadership.[9]

A strategy based on graduated pressure contains an intrinsic defect that appears any time it is applied against a government possessed of an unexpectedly strong will: a highly dedicated foe can choose not to submit when threatened by 'sufficient' force – he will choose not to be 'rational'.[10] Such an opponent might be persuaded by terrible, unrelenting pressure (or he might not) but the untrammeled use of force is precisely what the proponents of graduated pressure wished to avoid in Vietnam.

A policymaker who accepts the premises behind graduated pressure will generally be reluctant to 'give up his hostages' by destroying the enemy's military–industrial complex. In turn, the dedicated foe, such as North Vietnam, is not under sufficient pressure to compel submission (assuming such a level of pressure exists), but the effectiveness of military action against the foe is artificially depressed below the level of damage inflicted by a traditional warfighting strategy. For such reasons, when graduated pressure failed in Indochina, it did so disastrously, minimizing damage to North Vietnam while increasing the price that the United States paid to inflict that damage (for example, with the loss of aircraft that would not have been shot down if the military had been allowed to repress comprehensively North Vietnam's air defense network).

The decision to pursue a strategy of slowly increasing pressure allowed Hanoi to retain a substantial degree of control over its military–political fortunes. North Vietnam was not stopped from carrying on its normal activities, because the bombing was merely intended to inconvenience its military effort, not make the ongoing effective conduct of the war against South Vietnam physically impossible. During the Johnson years, the United States purposefully did not disrupt substantially the daily life of North Vietnam. As closely as policymakers could approximate, North Vietnam remained a more-or-less normal underdeveloped country except for the fact that periodically it underwent limited aerial bombardment. The DRV was allowed to carry on its war against the RVN, and life continued in Hanoi and other major industrial–military areas in a relatively normal fashion. This was a critical error, and is discussed in greater detail below.

Colin Gray argues that airpower can do many things uniquely or well, and does other things less well, poorly, or not at all.[11] In Indochina, airpower was called upon to do many things, and generally performed appropriate functions, such as sustaining and supporting isolated units and denying the 'enemy ability to seize, hold, and exploit objectives' (as when it smashed the DRV invasion of South Vietnam in 1972), very well. However, airpower was often called upon to perform inappropriate functions and denied the opportunity to perform its strategic bombing mission effectively. As Gray argues, airpower is not good at 'occupying' territory from the air, sending clear diplomatic messages, grasping enemy forces continuously, '[applying] heavy pressure in low-intensity conflicts', or discriminating between civilians and combatants or friendly and unfriendly forces.[12] Nonetheless, over Indochina airpower commonly was called upon to perform these very functions, often with predictable ill effects.

BOMBING FRIENDS IS PROBLEMATIC

The level of effort expended on the air war was enormous: over 1.24 million fixed wing, and an incredible 37 million rotary wing, sorties were flown by the United States during the war; in the course of this effort 'over [14] million tons of bombs and shells' were dropped.[13] However, this enormous effort was not directed mainly against the North Vietnamese homeland or even against NVA activities in Laos and Cambodia; 71 per cent of high explosives were dropped within the RVN.[14] This was a unique, and ultimately unwise, use of airpower for the United States. Although the USAAF had extensively bombed occupied portions of friendly countries in World War II, and the USAF had done the same in South Korea, this was the only time that a large quantity of US aircraft were primarily dedicated to the task of fighting insurgents over a long time frame.[15] Most of the strikes were, of course, tactical rather than strategic,[16] but this does not alter the fact that when aircraft are used as delivery vehicles for munitions against populated areas collateral damage inevitably occurs. The US military is extraordinarily proficient at delivering massed fire, but this expertise in the delivery of munitions has the unintended, but unavoidable, side effect of endangering civilian lives and property.

There were several important practical reasons why the decision to use US airpower primarily in South Vietnam was dubious. Given the commonly accepted assumption that winning hearts and minds was a key to victory in Vietnam, the conduct of an ongoing mid-tempo military campaign in and around the homes of friendly, or at least potentially friendly, civilians was in many respects counterproductive. This is especially true of the heavy use of artillery and airpower, which are highly destructive and non-discriminate (but quintessentially American and often very effective) means of waging war. Accidental injury to civilians was notoriously common in rural South Vietnam. Even though the number of civilians killed has often been exaggerated, the fact that substantial collateral damage occurred is undeniable. Hearts and minds were not easily won under such circumstances.[17] In essence, the United States restricted the wrong part of the air war: the air campaign in the South should have been carefully circumscribed while the campaign in the North should have been nearly unrestricted.

The loss of hearts and minds was an inevitable result of the choices made by US policymakers, and airpower was far from the only component in this problem. By choosing to fight the US war primarily in the RVN, including in the very populous Mekong Delta, Washington made it inevitable that a sizeable number of South Vietnamese non-combatants would be killed by massed fire. This was not, however, the only way to conduct the effort in Indochina. Policymakers could of course have chosen to fight a conventional war against the DRV, using an invasion of the North and a conscious effort to force the communists onto the tactical defensive. Alternatively (and more plausibly), the United States could have opted for the previously described 'war of logistical control' in the sparsely populated eastern portions of Laos and Cambodia; if successful, this should have severed the Ho Chi Minh Trail and cut the lines of communication between the DRV and the insurgents in the south.

Over the long term, either of these strategies would have minimized the use of airpower against South Vietnamese civilians. Even more vitally, airpower would have been used for tasks at which it excels, particularly if it were used as an aid to the invasion of North Vietnam.

THE USE AND MISUSE OF US AIRPOWER AGAINST NORTH VIETNAM

The conventional wisdom that North Vietnam lacked an infrastructure worth bombing has little basis in fact. The DRV was of course not as asset/target-rich as were industrialized countries like Germany and Japan, but there were in fact many worthwhile military targets in that country. Indeed, the notion that a state can carry out a large expeditionary war without having a large number of military targets is absurd. The myth of the Vietnam conflict being won by guerrillas with little equipment and purloined weapons persists, but is essentially false: particularly during the later years of the war, the contest in the South was fought by North Vietnamese soldiers who were part of a very large and conventional military organization. A sizeable military–industrial complex existed within North Vietnam, which trained, armed, supplied, and transported a large army at war.

The claim that the DRV was underindustrialized and therefore immune to the effects of bombing also does not stand up to close scrutiny: indeed, the fact that the North Vietnamese were so reliant on foreign (mainly Soviet and Chinese) military supplies increased their vulnerability to airpower in some respects. In order to be efficiently transported, supplies must be moved by rail, water, or (less efficiently) truck. All of these, and particularly the first two, were highly vulnerable to US airpower: North Vietnam's ability to receive supplies through its oceanic ports could have been (and, indeed, briefly was) terminated easily, and railheads are always attractive targets. Road traffic is more difficult to interdict, but North Vietnamese roads were vulnerable to damage, and merely making a serious effort to destroy trucks greatly impeded the efficiency of the DRV's supply network, forcing truck drivers to operate at night and with circumspection. If more air assets had been dedicated consistently to the task of harassing road traffic, North Vietnamese logistics would have been placed under an even greater strain.

The interruption of port traffic alone would have virtually eliminated the Soviet Union's freedom to supply its client,[18] and that action, in addition to attacks on North Vietnamese railroads, highway networks, and the mining of inland waterways, would have severely constrained the PRC's ability to assist the DRV. Hanoi was deeply dependent on Soviet and Chinese supplies: without a constant supply of arms and other goods from its benefactors, North Vietnam could not even have properly equipped and supported its large army, and certainly could not have constructed one of the world's finest air defense networks. Contrary to the viewpoint of much of the Vietnam-related literature, the North Vietnamese lack of industrial infrastructure was *not* an advantage; rather, it was *a potentially severe liability that the United States failed to exploit properly.*

Besides railroads and port facilities, potentially worthwhile targets within the DRV included (but were not limited to): petroleum, oil, and lubricants (POL) storage facilities,[19] supply depots, factories producing war-related goods, bridges, locks and dams, the electrical grid, military bases and training facilities, airports, and government buildings. North Vietnam was a comparatively poor country, but it was a country at war, and possessed all the infrastructure necessary for sustaining organized violence on a mass scale. This provided ample targets for US pilots during the early stages of any comprehensive air campaign against North Vietnam. After the North Vietnamese infrastructure was shattered, airpower would then have been tasked with assuring that the DRV's warmaking capabilities were not rebuilt, that it was continually denied access to outside supplies, and that NVA operations were regularly harassed.

The Johnson administration compounded the error of graduated pressure by initiating 16 separate bombing halts. The precise circumstances surrounding each bombing halt were unique, but they were all intended to have a political effect both at home and abroad. Firstly, the Johnson White House hoped that it could maintain domestic support for the war by demonstrating to the American public that their government truly desired peace.[20] At the same time, it was hoped that Hanoi would be coaxed to the negotiating table by a display of moderation combined with the implicit threat that the bombing campaign would be restarted if Hanoi did not accept a reasonable settlement.

The bombing halts failed on both counts. The halts did not prevent the long-term erosion of public support and may even have speeded that process: they (rightly) made the United States appear irresolute and each time the bombing recommenced it appeared to many observers as though Washington was escalating the war. The effect on North Vietnam was even less desirable, and the halts confirmed to Hanoi that the United States was not serious about the prosecution of the war and was desperate to end its combat involvement in Indochina. In addition, they also had the immediate effect of providing rest periods for North Vietnam that could be used to military advantage: supplies could be moved without harassment, antiaircraft defenses improved, and so forth. In 1969, Johnson told Nixon 'that the sixteen bombing halts he had ordered in Vietnam had all been mistakes', and warned against a repetition of his error.[21] This belated judgment was correct: the bombing halts were counterproductive and prevented the few military–political gains that might have resulted from consistent low-level bombing pressure on the DRV.

One of the more obvious lessons of Vietnam is that airpower is not a dainty instrument: if bombing campaigns are to be effective, they must be conducted at a high level of intensity and with an absolute minimum of prohibited targets. While the decision to avoid terror bombing *per se* was wise – the American public was willing to accept a merciless campaign against civilian morale in the Second World War but would probably (and properly) have been appalled by a similar policy in Vietnam – legitimate military–industrial targets in Hanoi, Haiphong, and other areas should have been destroyed early in the war. The air campaign against North Vietnam was a failure primarily because of misguided restraint on the part of the United States.

While the pre-Linebacker bombing of the DRV certainly created problems for the NVA, Hanoi's losses were too scattershot and (deliberately) minor to warrant the human, political, and financial expense of the campaign. Moreover, the limitations on the bombing campaign and the bombing halts confirmed Hanoi's suspicion that the United States was not serious about the war. There were few things more likely to evoke the contempt of the North Vietnamese leadership – a group of serious, arguably even fanatical, nationalist communists who were willing to sacrifice the lives of hundreds of thousands of their compatriots in order to obtain their political goals – than the use of potentially overwhelming force in a casual, feckless manner. Hanoi respected implacability, not restraint: moderates do not fight decades-long wars of ideology against seemingly overwhelming odds.

LINEBACKER AND THE EFFECTIVE USE OF AIRPOWER

The 1972 mining of North Vietnamese harbors and the Linebacker campaigns represented the most assertive use of US airpower in the Vietnam conflict, and these events convincingly demonstrated airpower's military utility and its usefulness as an instrument of coercion. While Rolling Thunder had shown the deficiencies of airpower when applied in a severely restricted fashion, the Linebacker campaigns had established that less circumscribed uses of airpower could be of great benefit to the United States. Part of the success of the Linebacker offensives can be attributed to a generation of 'smart munitions' that were tested in the late 1960s and entering service in the early 1970s,[22] and to improved electronic countermeasures that minimized aircraft losses. Nevertheless, the main reason for Linebacker's success was political; the Nixon administration chose, to an unprecedented extent, to loosen the restraints on the US use of airpower. This was a politically risky approach, and resulted in severe and often-unfounded criticism of the administration,[23] but it paid substantial political–military dividends.

Initially, Linebacker I was both a part of the effort to halt the 1972 North Vietnamese 'Easter Offensive' (called the 'Nguyen Hue Campaign' by the DRV) against the RVN and an attempt to force Hanoi to negotiate a final peace with the United States. It is questionable whether Saigon would have survived the Easter Offensive without assistance from US airpower. The later experience of the 1975 Ho Chi Minh Offensive (as it was known to Hanoi) certainly provides compelling evidence that without US help the ARVN might not have been able to cope with the shock of a massive mechanized assault.

The offensive was launched on 30 March 1972, and was not unexpected: the United States had long anticipated that North Vietnam would eventually launch a full-scale conventional assault against the South. (Fear of vulnerability to such an offensive was one of the reasons why MACV and the ARVN were so reluctant to de-emphasize conventional warfare and move toward 'pure' counter-insurgency.) After the removal of the great majority of US units, the only question was precisely when the attack would occur. Indeed, '[t]he principal purpose of [the] Cambodian incursion of 1970 and Laotian dry-season offensive of 1971 had been to disrupt Hanoi's timetable' for invasion; the United States hoped that by forcing 'Hanoi to spend precious time each year rebuilding supply lines and replenishing stocks', time would be purchased for South Vietnam and the potency of North Vietnam's offensive would be weakened.[24]

In its first weeks, the 1972 offensive made substantial progress, and appeared to have momentum. Nevertheless, after making significant gains in early April the offensive lost its 'punch'.[25] The North Vietnamese were never able to co-ordinate their three-pronged offensive, which 'reflected the combined impact of the Cambodian and Laotian operations and of [US] air interdiction'.[26] Between the lavish use of US airpower and the combat proficiency of the ARVN the southward drive was halted and South Vietnam not only survived the offensive, but was also able to inflict severe damage on the exposed NVA units.

On 1 April, Nixon ordered the bombing of North Vietnamese territory within 25 miles north of the DRV–RVN border,[27] and '[o]n 12 April, B-52s bombed deep in the North for the first time since November 1967'.[28] This was, however, only the prelude to a major campaign against North Vietnam. In early May, while South Vietnam was still under threat from the Easter Offensive, President Nixon decided to launch a massive air counteroffensive against the DRV. Hundreds of B-52s and other aircraft were used to strike targets in North Vietnam, many of which had previously been off-limits; in addition, the long-discussed mining of Haiphong harbor was finally undertaken. The main short-term purpose of Linebacker I was 'to stem the flow of supplies into North Vietnam from its communist allies, to destroy existing stockpiles in North Vietnam, and to reduce markedly the flow of materials from Hanoi [to South Vietnam]'.[29] Nixon also intended to punish North Vietnam severely for its invasion, despite the warnings of many his more cautious advisors who were concerned about public reaction and the fate of the peace negotiations. In a complete reversal from the attitude of the Johnson White House, Nixon expressed displeasure with the timidity of the targeting plans devised by military planners. In a memo to Kissinger he complained:

> I cannot emphasize too strongly that I have determined that we should go for broke ... I think we have had too much of a tendency to talk big and act little. This was certainly the weakness of the Johnson adminis-tration. To an extent it may have been our weakness where we have warned the enemy time and time again and then have acted in a rather mild way when the enemy has tested us. He has now gone over the brink *and so*

have we. We have the power to destroy his war-making capacity. The only question is whether we have the *will* to use that power. What distinguishes me from Johnson is that I have the *will* in spades ... For once, I want the military and I want the NSC staff to come up with some ideas on their own which will recommend *action* which is very *strong, threatening,* and *effective*.[30]

Nixon's assumptions in 1972 about how to most effectively use airpower were fundamentally different from those that prevailed in the Johnson White House, and although his ideas were often expressed with outrageous machismo they were sounder than the graduated pressure concept. The latter was illustrative of one of the US government's most consistent errors in Vietnam: a tendency to reject traditional ideas about effective warmaking – distilled wisdom based on centuries of experience related to a frequent and much-studied human activity – and place confidence in the reliability of untested, but quasi-scientific, methods. Nixon's 1972 decision to use airpower to undermine North Vietnam's warmaking capability represented a much needed and long overdue revival of age-old thinking about the proper role of force in war.

The notion, implicit in the graduated pressure concept, that the United States could reliably send a message about US willingness to support its Saigon ally by selectively bombing secondary targets in North Vietnam, assumed too much about the ability of raw military force to communicate dependably complex ideas. The delivery of the proper message and, even more importantly, the desire to assure that the DRV's protectors would not misunderstand the missive, took priority over the military effect of the bombing. The message of the bombing effort was, however, ambiguous. US policymakers believed that the constrained use of airpower against selected targets in North Vietnam would demonstrate their steadfast resolution to support their ally while at the same time conveying the willingness of the United States to be reasonable and to negotiate a peace with North Vietnam that would not be altogether humiliating to Hanoi. Nonetheless, Hanoi could easily see the highly limited nature of the bombing as proof of uneasiness rather than as evidence of a steadfast US commitment to South Vietnam. Indeed, given the ideological bent of the North Vietnamese leadership and that government's public stance, it should have been obvious that Hanoi correctly would see limits on bombing as evidence of an unenthusiastic US commitment to Vietnam.[31]

Nixon's 1972 message,[32] unlike the Johnson administration's complex and muddled signals to Hanoi, was sufficiently simple that airpower (crude diplomatic messenger though it was) could deliver it reliably: that North Vietnam agree to negotiate a settlement of the war on terms acceptable to the United States or suffer grievous damage until it did so. Along with communicating that message, Nixon was consciously attempting to undermine the ability of North Vietnam to carry on the war in the RVN. Thus, even if North

Vietnamese policymakers were willing to accept virtually unlimited damage to their infrastructure, the United States would still succeed in substantially degrading the ability of the DRV to carry on the war. This had both important practical benefits and the advantageous side effect of reinforcing Nixon's main message. Excessive restraint undermined the Johnson administration's attempts to convey conviction and undermine North Vietnam's war in the South; in 1972, Nixon avoided this error and enhanced the strategic usefulness of airpower by using it convincingly and in a fashion that showed direct results on the battlefield.

Even in Linebacker I, however, the United States showed considerable caution. Nixon, like Johnson, chose to restrict the use of airpower to military targets;[33] deliberate terror bombing of civilian populations was never undertaken by the United States in Vietnam. Furthermore, '[t]here were bombing restrictions within a twenty-five to thirty-mile-deep buffer zone and within ten miles of Hanoi and five miles of Haiphong', although 'even within these areas, field commanders could hit certain types of targets – such as power plants, munitions dumps, and air bases – without approval from Washington'.[34]

Despite these restrictions, the air and naval campaign against North Vietnam was highly effective. A particularly notable event was the 8 May 1972 mining of Haiphong and other North Vietnamese ports, which reflected a strategic decision of considerable weight. The Johnson administration had always refused this tactically simple and inexpensive action, fearful that it might serve to bring the PRC or even the USSR into the war. Even Nixon, for most of his first term, had been reluctant to undertake an operation that was presumed to carry significant risks; there was also an understandable worry that mining North Vietnamese ports would undermine the administration's diplomatic initiatives toward the USSR and China.

At the time of the Easter Offensive, however, the risk of great-power intervention was seen by US policymakers as comparatively low. The Sino–American rapprochement had lately taken place; this event both decreased the perceived danger of the mining operation and reduced Nixon's dread that his overall diplomatic design would be catastrophically undermined by action against Haiphong. There was now essentially an understanding that China would not intervene in the war: during the February 1972 summit in China, Nixon warned that the United States 'would react violently if Hanoi launched another major offensive in 1972', while Premier Zhou Enlai indicated 'that China would not intervene militarily in Vietnam'.[35] After the mines were actually laid, both Beijing and Moscow reacted mildly – the latter was a particular surprise to US policymakers, most of whom believed it likely that the upcoming Soviet–American summit meeting would be canceled in retaliation for the mining.[36] Nixon had gambled intelligently and won, mining Haiphong and pressuring Hanoi without materially increasing tensions between the United States and the communist great powers.

The mining was a major military success. As expected, it had a significant effect on North Vietnam's ability to carry on the war in the RVN.[37] Like the bombing of the North, it had both an immediate practical rationale and the larger purpose of curtailing Hanoi's warfighting ability and therefore forcing North Vietnamese decisionmakers to settle the war. It clearly succeeded in the former purpose, and speculation that increased rail traffic would make up for the loss of the ability to transport by sea, and therefore that North Vietnam's flow of supplies would be virtually unimpeded, proved false. By early June it was reported that 'over 1,000 railroad cars were backed up on the Chinese side of the border [with the DRV] and that ammunition shortages were becoming acute. Hanoi's offensive had bogged down.'[38]

Nevertheless, the Linebacker I campaign did not immediately compel North Vietnamese policymakers to agree to US terms on ending the war. The air campaign continued well after the failure of the Easter Offensive, because Nixon and Kissinger wished to secure a peace treaty in a timely fashion and in the meantime wanted to keep North Vietnam under military pressure. In October 1972, Hanoi agreed to key US terms,[39] and a restriction on bombing north of the twentieth parallel was imposed. Subsequently, however, negotiations stalled, largely because of the RVN opposition to the nascent treaty. Nixon decided that another, exceptionally intense and hopefully final, period of bombing was necessary to reassure Theiu and push Hanoi to finalize the Paris Peace Agreement;[40] in December, he called for Linebacker II (often called the 'Christmas bombing'). This was to be the fiercest, and perhaps most effective, air campaign against North Vietnam.

Although Linebacker I loosened the constraints on US use of airpower, Linebacker II was the first time in the war that 'air power was employed strategically with the determination that had all along been advocated by US Air Force commanders'.[41] Although only a brief campaign (it lasted from 18 to 29 December 1972), effectively it incapacitated North Vietnam. The bombing, which included more than 700 B-52 sorties, rapidly dismantled the DRV's military capabilities. The main bombing efforts were 'concentrated on targets in the Hanoi–Haiphong complexes and included transportation terminals, rail yards, warehouses, power plants, airfields and the like'.[42] The Gia Lam railroad yard and repair facilities, the Bac Mai barracks, 80 per cent of North Vietnam's electrical power production, and 25 per cent of North Vietnam's petroleum stocks were all destroyed.[43]

Linebacker II was not, however, a simple, low-cost campaign for the United States. In the first three nights of the campaign, nine B-52s were lost,[44] which resulted in a shift in tactics in the days shortly before Christmas – but the United States nevertheless continued to lose aircraft. After a 36-hour Christmas standdown in the bombing (during which time the North Vietnamese restocked their SAM sites and the United States prepared for the next phase of the campaign),[45] the United States energetically attempted to destroy the DRV's air defense network. This was intended not only to protect US aircraft, but also to place 'North Vietnam totally at the mercy of the United States, thus allowing a strategic victory'.[46] On 26 December, the United States virtually destroyed the DRV's aerial defenses; on 27 December, two more B-52s were shot down, but no more were destroyed subsequently. By this point, '[t]he North Vietnamese had depleted their SAM supply, F-4s had wrecked their largest missile assembly facility, their command and control system was degraded, and the primary MiG bases were unusable'.[47] During the last two days of Linebacker II, 'all organized air defense in North Vietnam ceased', and 'surface-to-air missile firing became spasmodic and aimless and both the B-52s and fighter aircraft roamed over North Vietnam at will'.[48]

Bombing had been of very limited utility when applied with discretion and moderation, but, when used like a hammer to smash the enemy's military–industrial capabilities, it proved effective. Indeed, airpower succeeded in creating the circumstances for a face-saving US settlement, *despite the fact that the Nixon administration was under enormous pressure from Congress and the media to stop the bombing and end the war on almost any terms.* This was an enormous accomplishment, and an indication of the potential power of strategic bombing.

A TERRIBLE SWIFT SWORD: THE EFFECTIVE USE OF AIRPOWER IN INDOCHINA

A bombing program aimed at damaging the DRV's military–industrial and transportation capabilities would no doubt have hampered the North Vietnamese war effort. Such an effort could and should have been an integral part of the US effort to bring about a decisive outcome of the war. Nevertheless, this does not mean that airpower *alone* could have secured the independence of the RVN.

It is possible, for example, that intense bombing might have obliged North Vietnam to make a paper settlement of the war in the mid-1960s. Hanoi, however, was sufficiently obsessed with unification that it would unquestionably have continued with its attempts to control and supply the insurgents in the South. There were many opportunities to slip supplies through an air-only interdiction net: after 'settlement' of the war, the North Vietnamese transportation infrastructure would have been rebuilt, no doubt with substantial assistance from China, and even constant air patrols over Laos and Cambodia would not allow for the interdiction of all, or even most, of the supplies moving through those countries. The United States would perhaps then have punished North Vietnam's obvious treaty violations with a period of bombing, which would in turn have led to another agreement that would have quickly been ignored by the DRV. Eventually, US leaders – no doubt embarrassed at their inability to control the actions of North Vietnam – would probably have settled for an unofficial, 'acceptable' level of cheating, just as they did after the Laos Accords.

Airpower alone can conceivably coerce an enemy who is irresolute, unwilling to accept significant damage to his homeland, or unable to function militarily under conditions of harassment from the air. None of these criteria applied to North Vietnam except, to a degree, the third: US airpower could make the conventional military conquest of South Vietnam impossible for the DRV and could complicate everyday NVA operations. Hanoi, however, was probably willing to carry on a guerrilla war in the South for decades, waiting for either the internal collapse of the Saigon government or the disillusionment and withdrawal of the United States. Without a US ground commitment in Indochina, either of those conditions (most likely the latter) would have eventually occurred. Therefore, it is unlikely that massive use of airpower alone would have substantially altered the outcome of the war.[49]

Nevertheless, as part of an integrated strategy, airpower would have been enormously beneficial to the United States. The proper use of airpower would, however, depend on which overall course of action the United States chose to pursue in Indochina. The clearest military use of airpower would have been in the event of an invasion of North Vietnam. In that case, the purpose of action against the DRV would have been to cut the command and control links between Hanoi and NVA forces in the field; destroy North Vietnam's internal lines of supply; shut down the flow of supplies to North Vietnam by destroying the rail links to China and shutting down Haiphong and other ports; provide tactical assistance to allied ground forces; prevent the NVA from staging an orderly retreat northward; and to otherwise provide assistance to the invasion. In short, action in the air over North Vietnam would have primarily been in support of the ground war in that country.

If, on the other hand, the United States had opted for an interdiction-based strategy without an invasion, airpower could have assisted ground forces in a less spectacular, but nonetheless essential, fashion.[50] The combination of a large US expeditionary force in Laos and ongoing harassment of North Vietnam, including the closing of Haiphong,[51] would have formed an imposing obstacle to the effective conduct of an expeditionary war in the RVN. This 'active blockade' strategy would have made less extravagant demands on airpower than would an invasion of North Vietnam: after a brief but intense period of bombing, a moderate operational tempo (similar to the tempo of Linebacker I) would have prevented the DRV military–industrial and transportation infrastructure from functioning efficiently.

This would have had a substantial effect on the North Vietnamese war effort: fewer war-related products would have been produced by or imported into North Vietnam; in turn, because of loose bombing restrictions and ongoing damage to the transportation infrastructure, that material would have been distributed with less efficiency and more wastage. Moreover, there would have been further wastage in the movement of goods southward, whether through Laos or directly across the DMZ. The result would have been an insurgency in the South starved of resources and fresh NVA troops, a 'non-renewable' insurgency vulnerable over the long term to counterinsurgency work by the ARVN and its allies.

OVERACHIEVING: THE EXCESSIVE USE OF BOMBING

It would be erroneous to assume that the United States should have attempted to maximize damage to North Vietnam. There were conventional (in the sense of non-nuclear) methods that would have allowed the United States to inflict grievous damage on North Vietnam, such as fire-bombing North Vietnamese urban areas or using airpower to smash Hanoi's system of dams and dikes. Wisely, however, US policymakers rejected such options. The unrestrained bombing of the DRV's cities was correctly considered unacceptable in the political–diplomatic context of the Vietnam conflict.[52] Even supposed 'mad bombers' like LeMay did not ever propose the use of such methods against North Vietnam. Targeting dams, however, was given at least slight consideration and was supposed by a small number of policymakers to carry potentially great benefits.

The geography of the northern part of Vietnam is such that the country was and is vulnerable to flooding: in the mid-1960s fewer than one hundred key dams and dikes prevented natural disaster. Hanoi itself was vulnerable to catastrophic flooding. The destruction of many or most of the North Vietnamese dams would have presumably resulted in awful side effects such as the destruction of much of the DRV's rice crop (and hence the potential starvation of hundreds of thousands or even millions of civilians),[53] the creation of millions of refugees, and many thousands of deaths from drowning, disease, and the other troubles that would have accompanied such a disaster. As a result, North Vietnam would temporarily have been physically incapable of supporting the war in the South to any appreciable degree.

Nonetheless, there was little support within the government for any program to destroy North Vietnamese dams, even though similar bombing had been carried out in the Korean War with reasonable success and without appreciable public criticism. Instead of campaigning for attacks against the dikes, military leaders tended to emphasize the importance of the air campaign against the targets on the JCS list,[54] which were long on military–industrial targets in North Vietnam. The belief of Air Force leaders 'that industrial targets were the proper objective for an air campaign caused them to shun attacks on irrigation dams and the Red River dikes'.[55] Only eight of the DRV's locks and dams were on the JCS target list, targeted with the intent of disrupting traffic on the inland waterways,[56] and just two of those were struck; in addition, the bombing of inland waterways resulted in incidental damage to other dikes and locks.[57] In a January 1966 memo Assistant Secretary of Defense John McNaughton toyed with the possibility that such a bombing program might compel Hanoi to sign an agreement acceptable to the United States,[58] but he nevertheless did not provide strong backing for the idea.

The reluctance of policymakers to take on such a project was understandable: although arguably legal under international law (because the ostensible goal of the program would have been to reduce North Vietnam's military–economic ability to carry on its war in the RVN, not to kill civilians *per se*), such a bombing campaign would have troubled many Americans. Furthermore, a bombing program directed against the DRV's dikes and locks would have resulted in the public vilification of the United States by both communists and many non-communists; most US allies in Europe surely would have refused to support the bombing, and the US effort in Vietnam would have come under even more intense criticism than it already suffered.

Such problems might have been acceptable if bombing the dams had actually offered a quick and permanent solution to the problem of how to control Hanoi's behavior. However, it is probable that flooding North Vietnam ultimately would not have furthered Washington's military–political goals. Indeed, bombing the dams would probably have been counterproductive. Inherent in McNaughton's belief that the United States might be able to use North Vietnam's potential starvation for negotiating leverage is the assumption that the DRV would consent to surrender national unification under communism in exchange for aid. Considering Hanoi's willingness to sacrifice the lives of its subjects, this is by no means certain: North Vietnam might just have accepted the famine and used it for publicity purposes. This would have done enormous damage to the image of the United States. For justifiable reasons, a 'starvation policy' aimed at North Vietnam would have appeared barbarous to many observers throughout the world.

If the United States at some point abandoned its starvation policy and allowed other countries to provide humanitarian aid to North Vietnam, it would then have been impossible to cut the logistical link between the DRV and the communist great powers: if Hanoi was to receive food aid in quantity, it would have been necessary that Haiphong remain open, that the rail link with China be allowed to function, and so forth. Then the Soviet Union and PRC would surely not only have replaced most of the food shortfall resulting from the flooding; they would also have provided military aid unless their ships were searched. Given that there was no US declaration of war on North Vietnam, this would be legally problematic, and, in any case, it is extremely difficult to imagine the PRC and Soviet Union consenting to an American demand to search their vessels.[59]

In short, flooding the DRV would not have provided victory in Indochina:

one way or another, Hanoi would have simply rebuilt its infrastructure and continued its war against South Vietnam. If their dikes and dams were bombed in later years, North Vietnamese leaders would have repeated the process. Regardless of the level of casualties or the amount of damage to its infrastructure, Hanoi's will to continue the war would not have been broken before US determination to continue the grisly process collapsed. Ultimately, the massive flooding of North Vietnam would have been detrimental to the United States, discrediting the US effort and interfering with the vital business of severing the logistic connection between North Vietnam and its patrons. Moreover, a campaign to disable and break the will of North Vietnam through the manipulation of food supplies would have displayed an immense short-term effect, but at the cost of leaving Saigon's long-term security problem unsolved and, probably, hastening the speed of the eventual withdrawal of the United States from Indochina. Bombing military–industrial targets would have been effective as part of a larger, balanced military effort, but simply bombing dikes and dams would have done little to untangle the knot of political–military problems in Indochina.

CONCLUSION: MISPLACED PRIORITIES AND UNWELCOME OUTCOMES

The air campaign against North Vietnam was a disappointment because of the failure of US Vietnam policy. Airpower was a potentially beneficial instrument that was tasked with an overly ambitious primary mission – dissuading North Vietnam from harassing the RVN – and was asked to go about achieving that goal in the wrong way. Like seapower, airpower is an enabler; command of the air increases the likelihood of victory on land but it rarely, if ever, wins wars by itself.[60] The bombing of North Vietnam should have been part of a well-conceived overall US military strategy in Indochina, not the key component of an undependable 'quick-fix' effort to coerce Hanoi.

A vigorous air campaign against the DRV would have been a vital part of a proper US campaign to secure the independence of South Vietnam. Such an effort would have been based on one of two general strategies: either a campaign of interdiction aimed at choking off the insurgency in South Vietnam and allowing Saigon to stabilize and grow strong over the course of years, or a campaign intended to occupy most of North Vietnam, thereby leaving a communist government that was too weak to present a substantial long-term threat to South Vietnam. Pressuring Hanoi into abandoning its campaign was a legitimate objective of the bombing, but policymakers should have realized that the success of that mission was dependent on the American ability to deny Hanoi any reasonable expectation that it might achieve its long-term goals.

Because of the decision to accept the priorities inherent in the graduated pressure philosophy (and therefore to stress the diplomatic over the military use of bombing), the mission of ground forces was not well integrated with the goals of strategic bombing. The United States effectively chose to fight two wars: a counterinsurgency in South Vietnam, and a war of diplomatic pressure in North Vietnam. US policymakers did not maintain their focus on what was ultimately the key factor: the effect of the air campaign in the North on the military situation in South Vietnam, Laos, and Cambodia.

The graduated pressure hypothesis could not account for the persistence of North Vietnamese decisionmakers. US leaders assumed that the DRV had a fairly low pain threshold that the United States could discover and exploit. When Hanoi failed to flinch, it was necessary to raise the level of bombing pressure incrementally. Yet at the same time the imperative to avoid 'excessive damage' to North Vietnam remained. These were incompatible goals. Moreover, self-restraint in the bombing of military–industrial targets was counterproductive at the tactical level. Not destroying Hanoi's industrial complex or the DRV's rail network directly resulted in more personnel and arms being infiltrated into South Vietnam, and this undermined the US war in the South.[61] Therefore, *graduated pressure should have been rejected as an unusable hypothesis and never applied in Vietnam.* Instead of graduated pressure, established techniques for eliminating an enemy's ability to organize and bring force to bear at the decisive point of battle should have been applied in Vietnam. If a program of graduated pressure were nevertheless unwisely instituted, such a policy should have been abandoned when it failed to coerce North Vietnam in short order.

The institution of Rolling Thunder was a reflection of the reasonable, though misguided, search by US leaders for a swift low-risk solution to the Vietnam problem; the long continuation of the program was representative of a less easily forgiven refusal to learn from error. The 'airpower learning curve' of US policymakers was practically horizontal for close to eight years, an amazingly long period of intellectual dormancy.

NOTES

1. The concept behind the US bombing policy against North Vietnam is variously referred to by several terms, such as controlled escalation, graduated response, and gradualism; the terms are more-or-less synonymous in their general usage. 'Graduated pressure' is used herein so as to avoid confusion and because it accurately reflects the central ideas driving the bombing strategy.
2. H.R. McMaster, *Dereliction of Duty: Lyndon Johnson, Robert McNamara, the Joint Chiefs of Staff and the Lies that Led to Vietnam* (New York: HarperCollins, 1997), p. 62.
3. Ibid.
4. As one author notes, Johnson's advisors 'recognized that coercion based on the risk of

punishment imposed strict boundaries on the scale of the campaign. If the hostage were killed, the threat of future damage would be nullified ... the civilians' vision of coercive air power would work by threatening industrial assets, creating a powerful incentive for Hanoi to bargain away its support for the insurgency to ensure the survival of its nascent industrial economy'. (Robert A. Pape, *Bombing to Win: Air Power and Coercion in War*, Cornell Studies in Security Affairs (Ithaca, NY: Cornell University Press, 1996), pp. 179–80.)

5. Earl J. Tilford, Jr, *Crosswinds: The Air Force's Setup in Vietnam*, Texas A&M University Military History Series (College Station, TX: Texas A&M University Press, 1993), p. 73.
6. Ibid.
7. Ibid.
8. Robert E. Osgood, 'The Reappraisal of Limited War', in 'Problems of Modern Strategy: Part One', *Adelphi Papers*, 54 (February 1969), p. 50.
9. Westmoreland argues persuasively that 'The will and toughness of the leadership in Hanoi were greater than expected. A bombing campaign was intended to break that will, but restraint on the exercise of our capability, namely our air power, to break that will, was too much and it was lifted too late.' ('Vietnam in Perspective' in Patrick J. Hearden (ed.), *Vietnam: Four American Perspectives* (West Lafayette, IN: Purdue University Press, 1990), p. 42.)
10. Keith Payne makes a useful differentiation in regard to such matters: 'I distinguish here between being 'rational' and being 'sensible' or 'reasonable'. Rational refers to a method of decision-making: taking in information, prioritizing values, conceptualizing various options, and choosing the course of action that maximizes value. In contrast, sensible refers to whether one is perceived as behaving in ways that are understandable to the observer, and may therefore be anticipated. This may involve having goals, a value hierarchy, and behavior patterns that, if not shared, are familiar to the observers. One can be quite rational within one's own decision-making framework, yet grossly outside the observer's understanding or norm. One can be quite rational within one's own framework of values, but be viewed as unreasonable and not sensible by an opponent.' (*Deterrence in the Second Nuclear Age* (Lexington, KY: University Press of Kentucky, 1996), pp. 52–3.) This precisely describes the discontinuity between American observations of North Vietnamese behavior, and Hanoi's perception of its own behavior. Hanoi had a clear value hierarchy, a rational decisionmaking process, and so forth, but US policymakers found it difficult to accept that what they considered to be unreasonable behavior was, by Hanoi's standards, entirely sensible. US leaders did not want to acknowledge that the North Vietnamese communists would endure almost any damage to their homeland, no matter how severe, so long as there remained a reasonable prospect of eventual victory.
11. Colin S. Gray, *Explorations in Strategy* (Westport, CT: Greenwood, 1996), pp. 99–103.
12. Ibid., p. 99.
13. Philip Anthony Towle, *Pilots and Rebels: The Use of Aircraft in Unconventional Warfare 1918–1988* (London: Brassey's, 1989), p. 157.
14. Ibid.
15. The contrast between French and US use of airpower in Indochina is interesting. The French use of airpower reflected some ideas similar to those later implemented by the United States, but the French effort was hampered by a shortage of aircraft and other factors. The most notable example of the failure of French airpower was when General Navarre attempted both to 'protect Laos and to lure the insurgents into a trap by occupying the valley of Dien Bien Phu near the Laotian frontier in November 1953' (ibid., p. 108), but was unable to keep the base adequately supplied by air. This mis- calculation played a key role in a humiliating French loss. When the Americans were

similarly surrounded at Khe Sanh in 1968, however, they easily defended their base and in doing so inflicted terrible losses on the attacking North Vietnamese forces. On the French use of airpower see ibid., pp. 106–16, and Bernard Fall, *Hell in a Very Small Place: The Siege of Dien Bien Phu* (Oxford: Pall Mall, 1967), *passim*. On airpower in the siege of Khe Sanh see John Prados and Ray W. Stubbe, *Valley of Decision: The Siege of Khe Sanh* (New York: Dell, 1993), *passim*.

16. It should be noted that the distinction between 'tactical' and 'strategic' applications of airpower is problematic, as the US use of airpower in Vietnam well demonstrated. See Gray, *Explorations in Strategy*, pp. 61–2.

17. This problem was not by any means unique to Vietnam. During the Malayan Emergency, the British were conscious of this 'public relations' consideration, and took pains to avoid causing civilian deaths by bombing. See Raphael Littauer and Norman Uphoff (eds), *The Air War in Indochina* (rev. edn, Boston, MA: Beacon, 1972), pp. 212–13.

18. One of the primary reasons the mining of the North Vietnamese harbors was rejected was because of fear that the Soviet Union would find its inability to supply its client embarrassing and might undertake an attempt to reopen the ports or initiate another intemperate course of action. See Senator Mike Gravel (ed.), *Pentagon Papers*, vol. 4 (Boston, MA: Beacon, 1972), p. 147.

19. In 1966, the United States did make a concerted effort to attack Hanoi's POL reserve, but with generally disappointing strategic results. See John T. Smith, *Rolling Thunder: The Strategic Bombing Campaign Against North Vietnam 1964–68* (Walton on Thames, UK: Air Research Publications, 1994), pp. 100 and 112–13. This effort was, however, still restricted; for example, the USSR continued to deliver oil to Haiphong. Moreover, an isolated anti-POL campaign was not a fair test of the potential efficacy of bombing: a well-devised air campaign against North Vietnam would have been an holistic effort that attacked many vital points, not just POL stocks.

20. The American public wisely displayed skepticism concerning the value of bombing halts. In a survey taken from 1 to 6 February 1968 Gallup pollsters asked the following question: 'Some people say that a halt in bombing will improve our chances in Vietnam for meaningful peace talks. Others say that our chances are better if the bombing is continued. With which group are you more inclined to agree?' An overwhelming 70 per cent of respondents favoured continuation of the bombing, 15 per cent supported a bombing halt, and 15 per cent were undecided. This is especially surprising when one considers that the Tet Offensive was ongoing during the period the survey was taken. There is little evidence for the popular myth that Americans somehow realized after the beginning of Tet that the war was 'unwinnable'. During the February 1968 survey, pollsters also asked: 'How do you think the war in Vietnam will end – in an all-out victory for the United States and the South Vietnamese, in a compromise peace settlement, or in a defeat for the United States and the South Vietnamese.' Of those surveyed, 61 per cent believed compromise most likely, 20 per cent thought all-out victory probable, 14 per cent had no opinion, and only 5 per cent thought that the United States and South Vietnam would be defeated. (George H. Gallup, *The Gallup Poll, Public Opinion 1935–1971*, vol. 3, 1959–1971 (New York: Random House), pp. 2105–6.)

21. Richard M. Nixon, *No More Vietnams* (New York: Avon, 1985), p. 163.

22. See Kenneth P. Werrell, 'Did USAF Technology Fail in Vietnam?: Three Case Studies', *Airpower Journal*, 12, 1 (Spring 1998), pp. 93–6.

23. See Guenter Lewy, *America in Vietnam* (New York: Oxford University Press, 1980), pp. 411–14; Nixon, *No More Vietnams*, pp. 146 and 157–8; and Henry Kissinger, *White House Years* (Boston, MA: Little, Brown, 1979), pp. 1190–1 and 1452–5.

24. Kissinger, *White House Years*, p. 1099.
25. On US Marine efforts in the Easter Offensive see G.H. Turley, *The Easter Offensive: Vietnam, 1972* (Novato, CA: Presidio, 1985), and Charles D. Melson and Curtis G. Arnold, *US Marines in Vietnam: The War in Vietnam: The War That Would Not End, 1971–1973* (Washington, DC: History and Museums Division, Headquarters, USMC, 1991), pp. 35–88.
26. Kissinger, *White House Years*, p. 1113.
27. Nixon, *No More Vietnams*, p. 145.
28. Bernard C. Nalty (ed.), *The Vietnam War: The History of America's Conflict in Southeast Asia* (New York: Smithmark, 1996), p. 294.
29. A.L. Gropman, 'The Air War in Vietnam, 1961–73' in R.A. Mason (ed.), *War in the Third Dimension: Essays in Contemporary Air Power* (London: Brassey's, 1986), p. 55.
30. Richard M. Nixon, *RN: The Memoirs of Richard Nixon* (New York: Grosset & Dunlap, 1978), pp. 606–7. Italics in original.
31. For a sampling of statements by high communist officials publicly disseminated by the DRV in 1966–67 see Patrick J. McGarvey (ed.), *Visions of Victory: Selected Vietnamese Communist Military Writings, 1964–68*, Hoover Institution Publications, 81 (Stanford, CA: Stanford University Press, 1969), pp. 61–251.
32. It should be noted that Nixon did not commit to a strong bombing policy when he first took office – there was a lapse of over three years from his inauguration to the beginning of Linebacker I. This is representative both of tentativeness on his part and, more favorably, of his capacity for strategic learning. These issues are explored in greater detail below.
33. Nixon, *No More Vietnams*, p. 148.
34. Ibid., p. 149.
35. Kissinger, *White House Years*, p. 1073.
36. See ibid., pp. 1174–86; Nixon, *RN*, pp. 601–2.
37. See Peter B. Mersky and Norman Polmar, *The Naval Air War in Vietnam* (2nd edn, Baltimore, MD: Nautical & Aviation Publishing Co. of America, 1986), pp. 198–9.
38. Nixon, *No More Vietnams*, p. 149.
39. Qiang Zhai, *China and the Vietnam Wars, 1950–1975* (Chapel Hill, NC: University of North Carolina Press, 2000), pp. 204–5, and Kissinger, *Diplomacy*, p. 691.
40. Qiang, *China and the Vietnam Wars*, p. 206.
41. Mason, *War in the Third Dimension*, p. 56.
42. Lewy, *America in Vietnam*, p. 412. On the damage to Hanoi and Haiphong also see U.S. Grant Sharp, *Strategy for Defeat: Vietnam in Retrospect* (Novato, CA: Presidio, 1989), pp. 252–4.
43. Mason, *War in the Third Dimension*, p. 56.
44. Tilford, *Crosswinds*, p. 165.
45. Ibid., p. 167.
46. Ibid.
47. Ibid., p. 169.
48. Mason, *War in the Third Dimension*, p. 56.
49. Unless the United States used nuclear weapons to devastate North Vietnamese society. Although militarily viable (indeed, virtually effortless), this of course would have been a totally unacceptable solution to the Indochina problem.
50. For an alternative view of the likely effectiveness of an interdiction-based strategy during the Johnson years, see Pape, *Bombing to Win*, pp. 174–210. However, it should be noted that this analysis considers airpower in isolation; the likely effect of combining airpower with ground interdiction in Laos, Cambodia, and the northern RVN is not considered in detail.

51. Preventing the DRV from receiving seaborne supplies in the mid-1960s would no doubt have angered the communist great powers and resulted in strong protests and threats. It is, however, unlikely that such an action would have resulted in a wider war. A Chinese or, particularly, Soviet military response to the laying of mines would have been grossly disproportionate to the nature of the action, and it is unlikely that either power would have sought a military confrontation with the United States over this issue. After all, mining North Vietnam's ports would not have imperiled that regime's survival or threatened Chinese territory. Soviet and Chinese ships would obviously have been endangered by US mines – a great concern to the Johnson administration – but the United States could have dealt with that problem by providing reasonable notice to those powers. At any rate, it is highly unlikely that the PRC or USSR would have intervened in Indochina because of mine damage to one of their vessels.

52. See Jeffrey Record, *The Wrong War: Why We Lost in Vietnam* (Annapolis, MD: Naval Institute Press, 1998), pp. 181–2.

53. It is, however, possible that the destruction of North Vietnam's dikes might not have had a catastrophic effect on the rice crop. See Pape, *Bombing to Win*, p. 194.

54. McMaster, *Dereliction of Duty*, pp. 143 and 148.

55. Clodfelter, *The Limits of Air Power: The American Bombing of North Vietnam* (New York: Free Press, 1989), p. 126. There was also some question as to how difficult it would be to destroy the dikes and dams. In separate interviews conducted several years after the decisionmaking on the issue, Chief of Staff John McConnell and Air Force Maj.-Gen. Robert Ginsburgh expressed differing opinions on the question: the former thought that bombing the dikes would have been 'a pretty fruitless operation', while the latter believed that B-52s attacking during high-water periods could have successfully demolished the dikes.

56. Ibid.

57. Lewy, *America in Vietnam*, p. 399.

58. After stating his belief that 'attacks on industrial targets are not likely to contribute either to interdiction or to persuasion of the regime', McNaughton suggests: 'Strikes at population (*per se*) are likely not only to create a counterproductive wave of revulsion abroad and at home, but greatly to increase the risk of enlarging the war with China and the Soviet Union. Destruction of locks and dams, however – if handled right – might (perhaps after the *next* Pause) offer promise. It should be studied. Such destruction does not kill or drown people. By shallow-flooding the rice, it leads after time to widespread starvation (more than a million?) unless food is provided – which we could offer to do "at the conference table".' (Gravel (ed.), *Pentagon Papers*, vol. 4, p. 43.)

59. In early 1967, the CIA noted that by bombing the Red River dikes and causing large crop losses, the United States would force North Vietnam to devote much of its transportation capacity to the movement of imported food and that '[d]epending on the success of interdiction efforts, such imports might overload the transportation system'. The CIA noted, however, that '[t]he levees themselves could be repaired in a matter of weeks' and that 'any military effects of bombing them would be limited and short-lived'. (Ibid., p. 140.) While overloading the transportation infrastructure would have been harmful to the DRV's military effort, this would merely have been a temporary setback for the communists – and the United States would have inflicted great misery on the civilian population of North Vietnam in exchange for this small benefit. It is representative of the peculiar nature of US strategy in Vietnam that policymakers considered such options when the obvious alternative of directly attacking the transportation grid, which would have been both more effective militarily and more humane, was available.

60. Exceptions to this general rule are possible: most notably, the surrender of Japan in 1945

perhaps directly resulted from blockade and aerial bombardment, which together made successful Japanese defense of the home islands implausible. However, even this is a controversial point. Some authors would claim that seapower alone was key to the destruction of the Japanese Empire and that it 'was not defeated by aerial bombardment. It was defeated by unrestricted submarine warfare, which strangled Japan's factories long before air power tried to knock them out.' (George Friedman and Meredith Lebard, *The Coming War with Japan* (New York: St Martin's Press, 1991), p. 334.)

61. Also, North Vietnam should never have been allowed to build its comprehensive air defense network: the suppression of air defenses and the destruction of SAM assembly facilities (regardless of their location) should have been an ongoing high priority mission for US pilots. The enormous aircraft losses in the war were not necessary and the fact that the United States allowed the DRV to construct a first-class air defense network is illustrative of the self-defeating nature of US military strategy in Indochina. Many US aviators were killed, wounded, or captured (the latter then being used as hostages by Hanoi) and billions of dollars worth of equipment were lost because Washington refused to suppress North Vietnam's air defenses.

7

Endgame:
Nixon's Peace and the
Abandonment of South Vietnam

It is generally accepted that 1968 was the year in which the inevitability of the eventual US defeat in Vietnam became evident. This, however, is inaccurate: although Tet and its aftermath demonstrated many of the weaknesses of the US effort, it by no means became immediately obvious that the United States was 'destined' to lose. Although alarmists in the media pointed to the Tet Offensive as proof that the United States was not gaining, and was indeed losing, ground in its struggle to create a stable South Vietnam capable of self-defense, most knowledgable observers correctly saw Tet as an operational catastrophe for the communists. The NLF's intelligence network had been shattered and the NLF itself had taken enormous casualties in its misguided bid to conquer the RVN's cities and incite a rebellion of the South Vietnamese citizenry.

The South Vietnamese public's distaste for 'popular' rebellion demonstrated convincingly that, contrary to the claims of Vietnamese communists and many figures within the American antiwar movement, the majority of the South Vietnamese population was not desperate for communist rule. After Tet, the burden of the war in the RVN was increasingly borne by the NVA: North Vietnamese had to be brought South in large numbers in order to keep the war, which was progressively losing its revolutionary aspect, active. Indeed, if control of eastern Laos and Cambodia had not long since been ceded to the communists, the revolution in the South might well have sputtered out and become little more than a minor irritant. The main challenge for the United States would then have been to build up the ARVN to the point where it could, with confidence, smash any invasion across the DMZ and, eventually, completely take over interdiction operations in eastern Laos and Cambodia.

By 1968, however, the United States had made several poor choices that assured that maintaining a non-communist government in Saigon would not be an uncomplicated task. Because of this history, the American public was losing patience with the war, there was a vocal antiwar movement both in Congress and on the streets that was constantly attacking government policy, and the pressures for a US withdrawal from Indochina were rapidly increasing. In addition, the ARVN had been to a great degree ignored by the US armed forces (who found it easier to conduct operations with minimal ARVN involvement; this brought short-term benefits but did little to improve the South Vietnamese military over the long term) and the process of making South Vietnam responsible for its own defense was not as advanced as it might have been.

In November 1968, one of the potentially most important events of the war occurred: in a very close race, Vice-President Hubert Humphrey lost the presidency to Richard Nixon. As a Republican with no association with the outgoing administration, Nixon was untainted by Vietnam. He had been marginally involved in Vietnam decisionmaking during the Eisenhower years, but this connection was trivial; Nixon had not made any decisions on the prosecution of the war and the private counsel he had offered had been largely ignored by the Kennedy and Johnson administrations. Moreover, Nixon made no specific campaign promises on how he would end the war in Vietnam: having offered no details of how he intended to terminate the war he could take practically any action and not convincingly be accused of betraying the public trust. Nixon entered office with certain inherent difficulties – he was, after all, burdened with an ongoing commitment that offered multitudinous difficulties but was nevertheless not easily resolved – but enjoyed considerable flexibility in his options about how to conduct the closing period of the US effort in Vietnam.

For his first months in office, Nixon made few substantive decisions concerning Indochina. The administration cautiously explored the Vietnam problem, eventually arriving at the uninspired conclusion that the 'Vietnamization' of the war, as rapidly as prudence allowed, should be the policy of the United States. Since the stated position of the United States had always been that US armed forces were merely assisting an ally facing foreign aggression, this was not a profound change of declaratory policy. Nonetheless, the new focus on Vietnamization did provide some intellectual focus to the drifting US effort, and at least properly diagnosed the fundamental problem Saigon faced: South Vietnam was not capable of defending itself against the North without US military assistance, and it needed to acquire the ability to do so as quickly as possible. Vietnamization was, however, a weak and belated corrective for a potentially fatal malady.

It was not inevitable that Nixon would choose to more-or-less preserve the policies of his predecessor. Given that his political base consisted of the more conservative, generally hawkish elements of the electorate and Congress, and that he personally possessed strong anticommunist credentials, his reticence is slightly puzzling. In the closing years of the US involvement, Nixon would repeatedly display a thirst for decisive action and a willingness to accept risks; his cooperation with the ARVN invasion of Laos, his initiation of Linebacker I and II, and the bombing of Cambodia are all examples of bold, controversial policy moves. In 1969, however, Nixon was hesitant, which was certainly an understandable reaction – he had, after all, witnessed and benefited from the war's political destruction of his predecessor – but nevertheless consumed valuable time. Most importantly, Nixon squandered his 'honeymoon period' of bipartisan goodwill (such as it was, given the antipathy many Democrats felt toward him personally) and allowed 'Johnson's war' to become 'Nixon's war' without any essential changes in the way the United States conducted the conflict.

Nixon assumed that he had little opportunity to 'reinvent' the conflict in Vietnam. On the one hand, he was unwilling simply to withdraw all US troops and allow Saigon to collapse. This was not, however, the impression of many antiwar activists, some of whom (with wishful thinking) had taken his campaign pledge to 'end the war' to mean that he would withdraw immediately.[1] Their belief was not entirely without foundation. Although Nixon would later point out that he had never claimed to have a 'secret plan' to end the war, this was only accurate in the strict sense. He had certainly hinted that his administration would institute some great change in Vietnam policy and rumors abounded that if Nixon were elected the war would be ended on a six-month timetable; the conclusion that the forthcoming great change would be US withdrawal came naturally to those who disdained Nixon, believing that he was 'not even sincere in his anti-Communism, [and] saw no anomaly in the prospect of a cynical betrayal of everything he had always stood for'.[2] This ploy certainly helped Nixon achieve the presidency, and may even have been critical to the unusually close 1968 election because it helped spur the Democratic left to desert Humphrey, but it also served as a constraining factor on the new president once he entered office.

Nixon refused to abandon South Vietnam completely, but also chose not to escalate the war rapidly in the hope of a 'knockout blow'. While acknowledging that '[t]he opinion polls showed a significant percentage of the public favored a military victory in Vietnam', Nixon writes that 'most people thought of a military victory in terms of gearing up to administer a knockout blow that would *both end the war and win it*'.[3] He believed 'that there were only two such knockout blows available to me', and he refused to consider either of them: the bombing of North Vietnam's irrigation dikes and the use of tactical nuclear weapons.[4] The new president's refusal to pursue either of these options was correct, most importantly because neither of these options would likely have been successful over the long term. As was discussed above, simply flooding North Vietnam would have accomplished little of permanence. In desperation,

North Vietnam probably would have signed a treaty of peace, but once it had recovered its ability to wage war (no doubt with Chinese and Soviet assistance) it would again have pressured the RVN. The same would have been true of the use of tactical nuclear weapons, but with an even less enduring effect. The NVA would have been devastated temporarily, Hanoi probably would have signed a peace treaty, and the war in the South would soon have been restarted.

At the same time, however, Nixon also arbitrarily discarded options that might have provided for a termination of the war on acceptable conditions. In his writings, he acknowledges that there were military options that might have aided US victory, including the resumption of bombing over North Vietnam, a threat to invade the DRV that would have 'thereby tied down North Viet-namese forces along the demilitarized zone', the mining of Haiphong harbor, and the authorization of 'hot pursuit of Communist forces into their sanctuaries in Cambodia and Laos'.[5] He further acknowledges that the United States 'had the resources to pursue these tactics', but argues that 'while they might have brought victory, I knew it would probably require as much as six months and maybe more of highly intensified fighting and significantly increased casualties before the Communists would finally be forced to give up and accept a peace settlement'.[6] On balance, Nixon saw this as unacceptable. Given the question of 'whether I could have held the country together' during a period of intense, high-casualty war, the effect of such a policy on his attempt to create a better relationship with the PRC and Soviet Union, the fact that military victory would not assure South Vietnam's survival, and similar factors Nixon thought that military triumph could not be obtained.

By the time Nixon was elected, his personal vision of the war was infected with the sort of 'light defeatism' that had afflicted the Johnson administration: he saw victory as something that could be obtained at the negotiating table, but not won in the field.[7] He writes that:

> I began my presidency with three fundamental premises regarding Vietnam. First, I would have to prepare public opinion for the fact that total military victory was no longer possible. Second, I would have to act on what my conscience, my experience, and my analysis told me was true about the need to keep our commitment. To abandon South Vietnam to the Communists now would cost us inestimably in our search for a stable, structured, and lasting peace. Third, I would have to end the war as quickly as was honorably possible. Since I had ruled out a quick military victory, the only possible course was to try for a fair negotiated settlement that would preserve the independence of South Vietnam. Ideally the war could be over in a matter of months if the North Vietnamese truly wanted peace. Realistically, however, I was prepared to take most of my first year in office to arrive at a negotiated agreement.[8]

In the first months of the Nixon administration, a five-point strategy to obtain an acceptable peace was developed.[9] Its components included: 'Vietnamization' of the conflict and improvement in the quality of the ARVN, comprehensive pacification of the countryside, diplomatic isolation of the DRV from the communist great powers, serious pursuit of peace negotiations, and gradual withdrawal of all US combat troops.[10] Some of these ideas had merit and one, the upgrading of the ARVN, was vital to the long-term survival of South Vietnam. Nonetheless, the five-point plan did not form a convincing strategy for securing an acceptable peace in Vietnam. These were measures characteristic of a government seeking a dignified disengagement from a troublesome venture, not of one vigorously pursuing political–military victory.

The Vietnam effort had always been pursued half-heartedly, and the limited enthusiasm for the war had long since dissipated. Nixon chose to accept this reality, and work within its bounds rather than to attempt to alter it: like Johnson, he attempted to seek a diplomatic solution for a problem that seemed to defy military solution. Thus, the Nixon administration's involvement in Vietnam was marked by diplomatic maneuver and the long, slow US military withdrawal from Indochina. Ironically, however, in the last months before the Paris Peace Agreement was signed, Nixon displayed reckless brilliance and qualities of leadership that might, if applied earlier and more consistently, have made the US withdrawal from Vietnam triumphal.

While Nixon hoped to wrap up the Vietnam conflict in under a year, he instead spent his entire first term of office and more seeking a negotiated end to US involvement. Nixon's error was to assume that Hanoi would settle for any terms that would not leave it in a position to conquer the RVN, and would do so without the incentive of new and extraordinary pressures; but if Johnson could not wring a peace agreement from North Vietnam, there was little reason to assume that a new president could do so without a fundamental shift in US policy. Unlike Johnson, however, Nixon proved capable of strategic learning, and hence deserves to be considered as an enormously better military–strategic leader than his predecessor. As Nixon grew comfortable exercising his powers as commander-in-chief (and became increasingly annoyed with Hanoi's intransigence), he was progressively emboldened and thus eventually proved capable of daring and successful moves like the mining of Haiphong.

With hindsight, the barrier to greater success was that Nixon allowed caution to override his bolder (and better) instincts for too long. The new president entered office with the grave handicap imposed by Johnson's handling of the war, and there was little room for error or hesitation. Johnson had years to overcome his errors of 1964–65, but the time was useless to him because he refused to question his assumptions and radically alter his strategy. Nixon did not have the luxury of time: he could have won an acceptable peace for the United States if he had been as daring in 1969 as he was in 1972,[11] but during the crucial first months of his presidency he was tentative.

THE LOSING OF THE PEACE

Even if Nixon can be criticized for incertitude at a crucial period, however, it is vital to note that his conservative, plodding strategy of Vietnamizing the war almost worked.[12] The conventional wisdom that the ARVN was always a poor force, and that the Saigon government was so unstable and unpopular that it was incapable of self-defense, is false. Under Thieu, the South Vietnamese government attained a reasonable measure of stability, and with Vietnamization the United States managed to create a fairly competent South Vietnamese military force.

The ARVN was not, of course, especially good by US military standards, but that was not essential: it merely needed to be good enough to battle the ongoing insurgency and to defend South Vietnam against invasion by the DRV. To judge Vietnamization a failure because the ARVN was not turned into a first-class army is unfair: contrary to mythology, the NVA was not an army of supermen. With assistance from US airpower and a very small number of US ground troops, the ARVN proved capable of defending South Vietnam against the Easter Offensive, and generally performed well in engagements with NVA troops despite the fact that there were very few Americans on the ground. In 1972, the ARVN was good enough. In 1975 it was perhaps an even better force but, denied US airpower and desperately undersupplied because of the US Congress, it collapsed.

The conquest of South Vietnam, however, proved little about the general quality of the 1975 ARVN, which had been trained by the United States to fight more-or-less in the US style, complete with copious use of airpower and artillery. Some authors would argue that the very fact that South Vietnam was conquered proved the low quality of the ARVN. This standard is, however, fatuous: an army that has better trained personnel may be defeated by a foe that is superior in equipment and/or numbers. In 1975, the NVA had an enormous material advantage over the ARVN; isolated, underequipped ARVN units had insufficient logistical and air support and were unable to resist the North Vietnamese.[13] As more and more of the South fell under the control of Hanoi, the offensive gathered great momentum. There is, however, no compelling reason to believe that the NVA would have been able to destroy a well-equipped ARVN that enjoyed ample air support.[14]

When the fickle US Congress reduced South Vietnam's military aid to a tiny fraction of what it had been a few years before, the ARVN, unsurprisingly, was not capable of rapidly adapting and fighting a 'poor man's war'. As history played out, Nixon's strategy in Vietnam was almost, but not quite, good enough. If there had been no Watergate scandal the Nixon strategy probably would have been adequate and the Republic of Vietnam would today be a functioning state.[15] Petty events are often the catalysts for grand ones, and a burglary in a Washington hotel might well have set in motion a specific chain of events that culminated in the conquest of Saigon by the NVA.

Perhaps the best example of how close Nixon came to preserving the RVN is unwittingly provided by George Ball who, when a Johnson administration policymaker, was skeptical of the war and subsequently was fiercely critical of the Nixon policy. Shortly after the fall of Saigon, Ball writes:

> By leaving a North Vietnamese army holding enclaves all over South Vietnam in juxtaposition with the armies of the south, [Nixon] sought to freeze a situation that could not possibly lead to peace but, at the most, to a protracted struggle with an almost certain Saigon defeat at the end of the road. Would anyone argue, for example, that there would have been a 'secure peace' with the Confederate States of America if a cease-fire had been arranged in the spring of 1864, leaving both sides fully armed, with elements of the Union Army occupying strong enclaves at New Orleans, Jacksonville, and other points along the coast, while Confederate guerrilla forces held considerable areas of Tennessee and Missouri – particularly if the South continued to have its arms resupplied by Great Britain ... There is ample reason to believe that, had Mr. Nixon not been deposed, our embroilment in South Vietnam might still be continuing at a renewed high level of intensity – unless of course, Congress had put its foot down.[16]

Furthermore, Ball reminds readers that Nixon sent Thieu letters dated 14 November 1972 and 5 January 1973, which were intended to convince the latter to sign the Paris Peace Agreement. In the 5 January letter, Nixon informed Thieu that '[s]hould you decide, as I trust you will to go with us, you have my assurance of continued assistance in the post-settlement period and that *we will respond with full force* should the settlement be violated by North Vietnam'.[17]

Ball is correct that Nixon's peace would not have been stable, and that the military contest for control of South Vietnam would have continued for years. Yet, while the American Civil War is in most ways not comparable to the Vietnam conflict, Ball's comparison of the 1973 Vietnam situation to the American Civil War is an interesting one, and it indirectly undermines his contention that the eventual defeat of South Vietnam would be 'almost certain'.

If, to use Ball's example, the United States and the Confederate States had initiated a cease-fire and the latter had enjoyed constant access to foreign military supplies, the Confederacy might today be an extant state. Conflict would certainly have continued for a time, but the pre-eminent national goal of President Jefferson Davis and his government would probably have been achieved. An amply supplied Confederate Army would have been able to fight much more effectively than an impoverished one could, and over time the will of the North to carry on the fight would have waned (perhaps Lincoln would even have lost the election of November 1864, leading to a McClellan government eager to grant independence formally to the Confederate States).

The critical mission of the Saigon government, like that of the Richmond government, was national survival. Even though it contained numerous provisions that Saigon found objectionable, the Paris Peace Agreement did not undermine that purpose fundamentally. If the United States had carried out the Agreement in the spirit in which Nixon signed it, the RVN would have continued to exist: the Agreement, after all, effectively banned any North Vietnamese invasion of the RVN. (The 1975 invasion was the last of a long string of violations of the Agreement.)

The purpose of the United States effort in Vietnam was *not* to bring peace *per se*. Because Hanoi was unwilling to accept a non-communist government in Saigon, immediate peace was only possible if South Vietnam capitulated. A peace purchased at the price of a communist conquest of the RVN was, however, not acceptable to Nixon. Instead, the Nixon program assumed that relative peace was to come over time, as Hanoi's challenge to the RVN was progressively subdued.

NIXON TAKES THE HELM

As Richard Nixon took over the White House, the Vietnam situation appeared to be at a crossroads. A bombing halt over North Vietnam had been in place since 1 November 1968, while the Paris peace talks were finally ready to begin after a 'three month haggle over the shape of the table, which was really a dispute over the status of [the NLF]',[18] and the antiwar movement was restless but relatively quiet – any assertive action by the new president would likely initiate a wave of protest, but caution in Vietnam would ease the new administration's 'protest problem' at home.

The one major adjustment that Nixon almost immediately initiated was a change in the policy regarding bombing in Cambodia. He was prompted partly by the February 1969 offensive launched by the North Vietnamese. In 'an act of extraordinary cynicism', the DRV launched the offensive before any important negotiating sessions in Paris with the new US delegation; moreover, 'the offensive began the day before a scheduled Presidential trip overseas, thus both paralyzing [the US] response and humiliating the new President'.[19] Nixon was outraged, and '[a]ll his instincts were to respond violently',[20] but his desire to ensure the success of his first foreign trip as president caused him to hesitate. Fear of domestic protest dissuaded the president from ordering a resumption in the bombing of North Vietnam.[21] He did, however, order the bombing of communist sanctuaries in eastern Cambodia; the bombing campaign was kept secret both to prevent domestic upheaval and to assure that Prince Sihanouk was not placed 'in a perilous position', since Cambodia was tacitly neutral.[22]

The bombing of Cambodia was militarily and politically sensible (although the wisdom of attempting to keep such a large operation secret is questionable), but it was nevertheless an inadequate response to the provocation presented to the new president. North Vietnam was challenging the Nixon administration to react assertively, and it did not do so. This signaled weakness *and continuity*, since it indicated that the circumspection and desperation for a settlement which marked the late Johnson administration was unchanged; the United States demonstrated that it would continue to be a paper tiger. This was an inauspicious fashion in which to begin the Paris negotiations and, unsurprisingly, the North Vietnamese proved intransigent for several years. The DRV adopted the simple, but essentially sound, tactic of striking a stubborn negotiating stance and waiting for the US position to erode. This sensible strategy was only interrupted much later by Nixon's assertive use of force against the North Vietnamese homeland.

NIXON AND BELATED DECLARATION OF WAR

When Nixon was elected president in November 1968, the conflict in Vietnam was not yet 'Nixon's war'. He had the option of rejecting the war as fought and turning the problem over to Congress. Nixon could have announced that, given that the Constitution of United States invests Congress with the power to declare war, he was requesting that Congress declare war against North Vietnam and its agents or explicitly reject the further use of force in Indochina (a 'declaration of peace') once certain conditions were met, chiefly the return of US prisoners of war. While he could have enunciated his support for the former option, the decision of Congress ultimately would have decided the question.

If Congress had declared war, Nixon would have been free to prosecute the conflict in a zealous manner (the invasion of North Vietnam would not just have been accepted, it would have been expected), while the antiwar movement would have been legally silenced; protesters would clearly have been 'providing aid and comfort to the enemy' and committing a felonious act. The North Vietnamese leadership undoubtedly (and rightfully) would have been terrified by this development, and Hanoi's negotiating strategy would likely have undergone considerable adjustment. In short, if Congress declared war on North Vietnam, the political conditions for victory in Indochina would have been created.

If, however, Congress chose not to declare war, the demise of South Vietnam would almost have been guaranteed. For good reason, few observers doubted in 1968–69 that the immediate withdrawal of US forces would quickly lead to the collapse of the RVN. Saigon was not then ready to provide for its own defense, and was both psychologically and militarily heavily dependent on its superpower protector. If Congress decided to liquidate the US commitment to Vietnam, however, the president would have been obliged to comply – Nixon could not have asked the legislative branch for a judgment on the Indochina question and then refused to accept that decision.

When the volatility of the era and the wrath that surrounded the Vietnam issue are considered, it is unsurprising, perhaps even admirable, that Nixon chose not to seek a declaration of war. Even in retrospect it is difficult to ascertain how Congress, and the country as a whole, would have responded to the proposal. While Johnson likely could have secured a declaration of war in the wake of the Gulf of Tonkin incident, it is by no means certain that Nixon could have obtained one. Certainly, one of the most acrimonious political fights in American history would have followed the president-elect's request for a policy ruling. Worse still, Congress might not have voted promptly on the question; a long period of uncertainty would have been disastrous for the morale of US and South Vietnamese troops.

Thus, it is only in relation to what actually occurred in Vietnam in 1975 that the pursuit of a declaration of war by Nixon appears prudent. At the time, the president-elect chose the appropriate path. This is not to say that he would not have been able promptly to secure a declaration of war against North Vietnam – he might have succeeded in this, and if so the United States in all probability would have promptly defeated the DRV and imposed appropriate terms on Hanoi. Notwithstanding this fact, it would have been irresponsible for Nixon to seek a declaration of war; clearly, if he had failed to obtain such a declaration, the effect on the US undertaking in Vietnam, and to the reputation of the United States as a protecting power, would have been catastrophic.

Options less extraordinary than a request for an act of war were also closed, for all practical purposes, to Nixon. Henry Kissinger argues cogently, but ultimately unconvincingly, that the president should have taken his plan for the conduct of the war to the Congress and the people:

> Faced with violent demonstrations, Congressional resolutions progressively edging toward unilateral withdrawal, and the hostility of the media, Nixon should have gone to the Congress early in his term, outlined his strategy, and demanded a clear-cut endorsement of his policy. If he could not obtain that endorsement, he should have asked for a vote to liquidate the war and made the Congress assume responsibility ... Nixon rejected such advice because he felt that history would never forgive the appalling consequences of what he considered an abdication of executive responsibility. It was an honorable – indeed, a highly moral and intellectually correct – decision. But in the American system of checks-and-balances, the burden which Nixon took upon himself was not meant to be borne by just one man.[23]

Kissinger is correct that the burden Nixon shouldered was not intended for one man, but the errors of his predecessor and the peculiar circumstances of the times conspired to give the president no responsible option but to accept it. Just as Franklin Roosevelt felt morally and strategically obligated to nudge the United States toward involvement in a war unwanted by a clear majority of the American people and Abraham Lincoln was forced to accept even graver burdens (and occasionally to act against the spirit of the US Constitution so as to recreate national unity),[24] Nixon had to act alone as commander-in-chief if he were to proceed responsibly. Presenting executive policy on Vietnam to Congress for its approval would have carried most of the disadvantages of requesting an act of war and few of the potential benefits.

WATERGATE AND THE DEATH OF THE RVN

The greatest error that Richard Nixon made in relation to Vietnam was not, in the usual sense of the terms, tactical, operational, or even strategic. In fact, it had nothing to do with Indochina, except incidentally: the series of events that are commonly lumped together under the term 'Watergate' set in motion an historical process that left South Vietnam defenseless at a critical point in its history. Watergate resulted in the overthrow of a flawed but strong president and the immense weakening of the executive branch of the US government. At the time of South Vietnam's 'moment of truth' in 1975, the president did not even have the option to intervene, because Congress had effectively barred further US military intervention in Vietnam by banning the use of appropriated funds for combat operations in Indochina after 15 August 1973 (a constitutionally dubious formulation, since it indirectly constrained the power of the commander-in-chief, but one to which Nixon – deeply wounded by Watergate and besieged by antiwar critics – consented). Almost simultaneously, the Khmer Rouge consolidated its hold on Cambodia.

Once it became clear how desperate the situation was in South Vietnam – and by 5 April, US Army Chief of Staff Weyand warned the president that the situation in Vietnam 'was very critical' and that $722 million worth of supplies were immediately needed 'if [South Vietnamese] efforts were to have any chance of success'[25] – the president should have been able to take action to prevent the collapse of the RVN. The likely method would have been fairly simple: air support to the ARVN combined with a surge in supplies to South Vietnam (a 'Linebacker III' operation against North Vietnam would have been militarily desirable, but not strictly necessary).[26] Indeed, a major invasion might never have been launched in 1975 had Watergate not occurred: the weakness of the executive branch was obvious, and this no doubt had an impact on North Vietnam's behavior.[27] If Nixon had been undistracted, he would probably have been able to rally the hawks and win the battle against the antiwar forces who wished to tie his hands in 1973,[28] thus enabling enforcement of the Paris Peace Agreement and US fulfillment of its solemn obligation.[29]

142

None of this occurred, however, because Watergate destroyed the Nixon administration. On 9 August 1974, Nixon was succeeded by Vice-President Gerald Ford, a well-meaning but ineffectual caretaker president. Even a president as talented as Lincoln would have been hard-pressed to revive South Vietnam's prospects after Watergate had lamed the executive branch – the power of the presidency was clearly at its lowest ebb since Franklin Roosevelt took office in 1933. Despite the fact that he had been a long-serving member of the House of Representatives, House minority leader, and was untainted by Watergate (except by his pardon of Nixon, a statesmanlike act that created rumors of a 'deal' between the two men),[30] Ford was able to make no noticeable impact on the anti-RVN stance of Congress.

Nevertheless, it is difficult to criticize Ford for his ineffectiveness, because in 1974 the American electorate, embittered by Watergate and suspicious of Republicans, elected numerous candidates who were strongly opposed to further aid to South Vietnam, thus strengthening the already-dominant anti-Saigon feeling within Congress. (The Democratic Congressional leadership was vocally antiwar and had little affection for the Thieu government.) The South Vietnamese were not naive, and realized that their protecting power was turning against them; this damaged ARVN morale, and created further instability in the RVN.[31] South Vietnamese national morale was always fragile, and, as the fact of United States abandonment of Saigon became clearer, defeatism increased.

In spring 1975, South Vietnam was conquered outright by the NVA. At the beginning of 1975, the North Vietnamese leadership was by no means certain that this would be the year in which the South would be assimilated. Indeed, it was thought more likely that the war would continue until 1976 or 1977,[32] but, as the ARVN defenses folded while the Americans did nothing, it became increasingly clear that Saigon was doomed. Desperate South Vietnamese leaders attempted to create a defensible rump RVN, surrendering the northern provinces while retaining control of the southern part of the country, but this effort failed disastrously.[33]

While ARVN resistance collapsed, the Ford administration quibbled with Congress over small amounts of military aid and questions related to the treatment of refugees. Congress, which had expended many billions of dollars and well over 50,000 American lives on the Vietnam enterprise, refused to provide South Vietnam with more than tiny amounts of aid. At the time, this attitude was accepted as perfectly logical by most decisionmakers, but in retrospect it seems bizarre. Having, with great difficulty, secured a withdrawal from Indochina while at the same time not appearing to have deserted its weak and often difficult Vietnamese ally, it was relatively easy for Washington to enforce that peace or at least provide generous military assistance to the ARVN, yet the United States chose to do neither.

The reluctance of Congressional and other policymakers to return troops to

Vietnam itself, or even to enforce the peace with US airpower, was under-standable (although, in the latter case, unwise), but the refusal to provide South Vietnam with adequate aid was simply illogical. After the United States had fought so many years and expended vast resources to secure its reputation as a reliable protector, it was not sensible to provide less-than-generous aid to South Vietnam. The cost of doing so was minimal compared to the cost of the war and, even if the RVN disintegrated, the United States would have done much to maintain its reputation – in McNaughton's phrase from March 1965, before US combat units entered the ground war and about eight years before the Paris Peace Agreement – 'as a good doctor' who had 'kept promises, been tough, taken risks, gotten bloodied, and hurt the enemy very badly'.[34] The United States had done all that, and had even shown admirable persistence, but after the Agreement many policymakers – and much of the American public – were willing to discard hard-fought gains for no prudent reason.

The difficult economic conditions of the early 1970s were often cited as a reason to cut aid to Saigon, but this was so weak a rationale as to be absurd: inflation and unemployment were serious but hardly crippling, and by any economic standard the burden South Vietnam placed on the United States was a small fraction of what it had been in the mid- to late-1960s. The United States had sunk tens of billions of dollars into the Vietnam project, and that money was justified largely as an expense that had to be paid if the United States were to maintain its reputation as a reliable guarantor of the security of its allies. This concern was as important (if not more important considering, among other factors, the greater size and quality of the Soviet nuclear arsenal) in the 1970s as it was in the 1960s.

Ultimately, economic and strategic factors did not motivate Congress to decrease RVN aid to a trickle. The anti-Saigon element in Congress considered economic and strategic issues, at least in regard to Indochina, to be secondary to 'moral' concerns. Narrowly framed ethical questions and antipathy for Saigon dictated their behavior, and the notion that other democratic governments might be endangered by a communist victory in Vietnam was not taken seriously or was accepted as a necessary cost for achieving the supposed greater good of ending the Vietnam conflict forever. Strongly anti-Saigon leaders were in turn aided by the aversion that less radical policymakers had for further discussion of the Vietnam question. Most Americans, both inside and outside of government, were simply tired of Vietnam and wanted the problem to go away.

CONCLUSION: A VERY CLOSE ISSUE

The US war in South Vietnam was lost by a hairsbreadth. In early 1973, Saigon had fulfilled, or was on the way to fulfilling most of the requirements for long-term success. The RVN had an economy that was enormously vibrant in comparison to that of the North, an army that was fairly good and getting better (fighting, one notes, an insurgency that had several years before lost its native character and was now conducted almost entirely by foreign troops; by the mid-1970s, the internal revolutionary movement was well past its peak), and had achieved relative political stability under Thieu. Given time, the RVN would probably have developed in a pattern similar to that of South Korea, the Republic of China, or many other formerly authoritarian but non-communist countries, enjoying a growing economy and progressive democratization.[35] As South Vietnam developed, the population would likely have felt a progressively greater stake in the survival of governmental institutions, and, as the ARVN improved, the external threat from the relatively backward DRV would have faded.

When the outcome of the war is treated as an inevitability, the worries of the North Vietnamese themselves are ignored. Hanoi was not ignorant of the South Korean precedent, and knew when it signed the Paris Peace Agreement in 1973 that if Saigon could survive its first 'post-American' years, it might well survive indefinitely. Even earlier, it was apparent to discriminating observers that South Vietnam was becoming an adequately successful state:

> As Hanoi took stock in the spring and summer of 1971, it could perceive a gradual strengthening of South Vietnamese military and economic capacity and a consolidation of Thieu's administrative structure deep into the countryside. While the South Vietnamese election of October 1971 was imperfectly democratic in American eyes, it was, in Vietnamese terms, a demonstration of Thieu's strength. The military and political capacity of the Viet Cong was progressively eroding ... Both of the critical variables appeared to be moving against Hanoi as Vietnamization progressed: the strains on American political life of protracted war were easing; and South Vietnam was consolidating its nationhood. Evidently, a blow that would destroy the South Vietnamese military and political structure, discredit Nixon's Vietnamization policy, and bring men into power in Washington already committed to abandon US commitments in Southeast Asia seemed attractive to Hanoi.[36]

Hence, North Vietnamese leaders decided to launch the 1972 Easter Offensive. Hanoi promptly suffered an inglorious defeat, thereby demonstrating the success of the Nixon policy and the progress of Vietnamization. North Vietnam's failure to conquer Saigon in 1972 provides strong support for the contention that Nixon's Vietnam policy was prudent, and it provided clear instruction as to how the United States could maintain a non-communist government in South Vietnam.

With hindsight, it is remarkable how little impact the events of 1972 had on Congressional and public opinion; after all, the ARVN, with negligible US assistance on the ground, had defeated the NVA in open combat on a large scale. US policy was vindicated, and defeatists arguing that the Vietnam situation was hopeless were shown to be wrong. The South Vietnamese were not utterly inept, and could defend themselves quite competently without a half-million US troops, *if* the United States were willing to support Saigon, just as Hanoi was receiving vast amounts of aid from the Soviet Union and the PRC. Hanoi had great-power patrons who were (at least for the time being) willing to bankroll its war, and if South Vietnam were to survive it needed continuing support from the United States. When Hanoi's army broke through ARVN defenses, it did so with Soviet and Chinese equipment. At the same time Saigon, which had been starved of aid for two years, received little assistance from the United States; much of the RVN air force could not fly because of shortages of parts, its artillery was deprived of shells, and so forth.

If Washington simply had continued to follow the logic of the Nixon policy the Republic of Vietnam almost certainly would exist today. Moreover, given the history of South Korea and other non-communist Asia–Pacific countries with close ties to the United States, it is likely that the RVN would be democratic and reasonably prosperous. Furthermore, the Khmer Rouge likely would not have conquered Cambodia and murdered millions of their compatriots: Nixon favored continuing aid and assistance to Lon Nol's government, and South Vietnam had an ongoing interest in assuring that Cambodia was ruled by a non-communist government. Cambodia's genocide was a side effect of Congress's decision to relinquish responsibility for the fate of Indochina; in the early 1970s Cambodia was completely cut off from US aid, 'with the argument that it would help save lives – a euphemism for abandonment, and a grim joke in light of the genocide that followed'.[37]

The decision to leave Indochina to its fate was the final modification in Vietnam policymaking. Instead of continuing with a policy course that had a record of success, the United States chose to extricate itself from Southeast Asia, discarding nearly all the gains it had made over the previous decades. Although it is one of the least studied aspects of US decisionmaking on Vietnam, it is worthy of careful study, because it was the most perverse. The Kennedy, Johnson, and Nixon administrations all made errors in their Vietnam policy, and some of the errors of the former two were grievous, but they were mistakes made for rational reasons and generally in good faith. Kennedy administration policymakers did not want to fight a difficult war in Laos and, albeit wrongly, believed that South Vietnam could be defended more easily by fighting the insurgency internally. The Johnson administration adopted a graduated response primarily out of a desire to avoid a wider war in Indochina. The Nixon administration could have drifted less in its early years, and probably obtained both an acceptable peace treaty and a 'Vietnamized ARVN' sooner, but there was honest puzzlement over how best to extract US troops from South Vietnam while also securing the ongoing independence of that country. Nixon could also, even more importantly, have avoided the Watergate scandal, but that was a domestic error of a singular kind that was only indirectly linked to Vietnam. These were all serious errors, but they are all explicable.

The 'Indochina endgame' policy of the United States is not easily explainable in rational-actor terms, because it was not fundamentally based on responsible calculations of national interest and was even illogical. The United States discarded considerable tangible gains in Vietnam (including the survival of an ally that, while still weak, retained a non-communist government), as well as the intangible benefits it derived from having been a reliable protecting power, in exchange for nothing. Thus, the US enterprise in Indochina unnecessarily ended with public embarrassment and shame – including the pitiable sight of US Marines struggling to prevent would-be refugees from overrunning the US embassy – when it might instead have been vindicated.

NOTES

1. Norman Podhoretz, *Why We Were in Vietnam* (New York: Simon & Schuster, 1982), p. 135.
2. Ibid.
3. Richard M. Nixon, *RN: The Memoirs of Richard Nixon* (New York: Grosset & Dunlap, 1978), p. 347. Emphasis added.
4. Ibid.
5. Richard M. Nixon, *No More Vietnams* (New York: Avon, 1985), p. 102.
6. Ibid.
7. For a very different perspective, see Spencer C. Tucker, *Vietnam* (Lexington, KY: University Press of Kentucky, 1999), pp. 154–5.
8. Nixon, *RN*, p. 349.
9. While allowing that many 'details of implementation' remained when Nixon actually assumed the presidency, Jeffrey Kimball argues that the essential components of Nixon's plan to end the war were in place before he took office and that efforts to convince North Vietnamese leaders that Nixon was inclined to vigorous military action and was dangerously unpredictable, if not mentally unstable (the 'madman theory'), were key to the implementation of Nixon's program. See *Nixon's Vietnam War* (Lawrence, KS: University Press of Kansas, 1998), p. 98. Nixon certainly believed that unpredictability was vital to successful negotiation. However, if he had possessed a truly clear scheme to end the war, it is probable that he would have undertaken assertive action immediately upon becoming president rather than allowing a lengthy period of practical inaction and apparent bureaucratic indecision. On balance, it appears likely that in January 1969 Nixon did not have a clear plan on how to end the Vietnam conflict, although he surely had some general ideas on how to do so in an acceptable fashion.
10. Nixon, *No More Vietnams*, pp. 104–6.
11. Even in early 1970 Nixon showed a considerable appetite for risk. US–RVN ground operations in Cambodia were launched on 30 April, and, although their military necessity was apparent, they generated great antagonism toward the Nixon administration. Bui Diem writes that he reported to Thieu that '[o]n the internal political scene it is obvious that [Nixon] is running a lot of risk because the decision has not only provoked a split among the Republicans, it can also rekindle the blaring national debate that

seemed to have faded'. The ambassador was correct about the political risk, and on 4 May the Kent State incident occurred. By 9 May, an estimated 100,000 protesters were gathered near the White House and 'the president himself was under siege'. (*In the Jaws of History* (Boston, MA: Houghton Mifflin, 1987), p. 274.)

12. It is often charged that the negotiations with North Vietnam and the Vietnamization process were merely intended to provide time for a 'decent interval' between the withdrawal of US troops from South Vietnam and the inevitable fall of that country. Such a viewpoint is overly cynical. Although Kissinger tended to be skeptical about whether Vietnamization would ultimately succeed, Nixon apparently had considerable faith in the likelihood that it would produce a South Vietnam fundamentally capable of self-defense. See Nixon, *No More Vietnams*, pp. 103–5, and Podhoretz, *Why We Were in Vietnam*, p. 148. On Kissinger's doubts about Vietnamization see Walter Isaacson, *Kissinger: A Biography* (New York: Touchstone, 1992), pp. 236–7.

13. Even in early 1974, the ARVN was forced to placed severe restrictions on the use of ammunition and by April 1974 'South Vietnam's supply situation became critical'. (Nixon, *No More Vietnams*, pp. 186–7.)

14. Zumwalt argued that the ARVN was 'pretty good overall', and noted that 'they fought courageously when the enemy seized Hue ... When [the South Vietnamese] finally folded, it was after a year of [the United States] refusing to carry out [its] secret commitment to provide equipment to them to replace their losses and President Nixon and later Ford's inability to use airpower because Congress was insisting ... they not use it ... [despite so many US mistakes throughout the war], we still had a two Vietnam solution and we lost it over here with Watergate'. (Interview with author, 4 September 1997, Rosslyn, VA.)

15. As Summers convincingly asserted, 'Watergate was a disaster for [the RVN] ... I think Nixon would have stood by his word whether Congress liked it or not – and gotten away with it, probably'. (Interview with author, 9 September 1997, Bowie, MD.)

16. George W. Ball, *Diplomacy for a Crowded World: An American Foreign Policy* (Boston, MA: Little, Brown, 1976), p. 79.

17. Quoted in ibid., p. 80. Ball's italics. Ball then questions what the meaning of the phrase 'full force' is, ominously writing: 'Nuclear bombs? No one will ever know.' It is, however, extremely improbable that Nixon meant to imply that nuclear weapons usage by the United States was an acceptable option. In all likelihood, he simply wished to reassure Thieu that the United States would continue as the guarantor of South Vietnam's political existence. A longer excerpt from the 5 January 1973 letter is in Kissinger, *White House Years* (Boston, MA: Little, Brown, 1979), p. 1462. Also, Kissinger notes that the letter was staff-drafted, which further indicates that the actual phrase 'full force' was not particularly significant.

18. Kissinger, *White House Years*, p. 237.

19. Ibid., p. 242.

20. Ibid., p. 243.

21. Nixon, *No More Vietnams*, pp. 107–8.

22. Ibid., p. 108.

23. Kissinger, *Diplomacy* (New York: Simon & Schuster, 1994), p. 700.

24. A contrary view on the question of whether Lincoln heeded the spirit of the Constitution is provided in Arthur M. Schlesinger, Jr, 'War and the Constitution: Abraham Lincoln and Franklin D. Roosevelt', in Gabor S. Boritt (ed.), *War Comes Again: Comparative Vistas on the Civil War and World War II* (New York: Oxford University Press, 1995), pp. 143–65.

25. Gerald R. Ford, *A Time to Heal* (New York: Berkley, 1980), p. 246.

26. The main practical difficulty with resumed bombing of the North, aside from the

obvious domestic problems, would have concerned the question of downed US fliers. The return of US prisoners of war had been secured in the Paris Peace Accords but, if the United States resumed the bombing of North Vietnam at any time thereafter, more prisoners would presumably have been taken. This would have been a difficult problem, but not necessarily an insoluble one: for example, once policymakers were satisfied that a renewed campaign had achieved its goals, the United States could have demanded the return of all prisoners and stated that bombing would continue until the POWs were returned.

27. However, even after Watergate, Hanoi was not certain that the United States would not respond with airpower to a large-scale invasion of the RVN, and its initial probes in 1975 were cautious. See Robert Conquest, 'Rules of the Game: Why West is Down and East is Up', in James E. Dornan, Jr (ed.), *United States National Security Policy in the Decade Ahead* (London: MacDonald & Jane's, 1978), p. 107.

28. Nixon himself actually tends to disagree with this, writing that '[w]ithout Watergate we [the Administration] would have faced the same opposition to our use of military power to enforce an agreement that would bring peace to Vietnam'. (*No More Vietnams*, p. 182.) Certainly it is true that Nixon would have faced opposition to any attempt to enforce the Paris Accords. Nonetheless, the former president (who was perhaps inclined to rewrite history to demonstrate that his political demise was not vital to the demise of South Vietnam) understates the degree to which Watergate had dissipated his energy and undermined his foreign policy leadership. For instance, on 30 April 1973 Nixon delivered the speech in which he announced the resignation of Haldeman and Ehrlichmann, 'my closest aides' (*RN*, p. 848). Afterward, the Watergate situation only deteriorated further for the Nixon administration. On 30 June, as the Nixon presidency was approaching 'terminal meltdown', he signed the bill including the 15 August cut-off date. During the months that led to that critical event, Nixon and those around him were distracted and harassed; meanwhile, the president's political standing was being demolished by domestic events. If there had been no Watergate, those months might have been very different – after all, in early 1973, Nixon had finally succeeded in ending US participation in the conflict on reasonably honorable terms, a feat that many of his critics had said was impossible. A confident president, flush with a recent devastating election victory over an antiwar opponent and the successful withdrawal of US ground forces, would have been a much more difficult target for figures such as Senators Kennedy and Mansfield.

29. On the Nixon administration's intent to support the RVN against an invasion by the North, see Henry Kissinger, *Years of Renewal* (New York: Simon & Schuster, 1999), p. 470.

30. See Ford, *A Time to Heal*, pp. 174–7.

31. See Robert D. Schulzinger, *A Time for War: The United States and Vietnam, 1941–1975* (New York: Oxford University Press, 1997), pp. 318–19.

32. Kissinger, *Years of Renewal*, p. 481.

33. See Philip B. Davidson, *Vietnam at War: The History, 1946–1975* (Novato, CA: Presidio, 1988), pp. 695–700.

34. Quoted in William Conrad Gibbons, *The US Government and the Vietnam War, Executive and Legislative Roles and Relationships*, Part III: January–July 1965 (Princeton, NJ: Princeton University Press, 1996), p. 158.

35. It is often ignored, but in its later years South Vietnam had numerous quasi-liberal institutions; Thieu's government was not an authoritarian one of the sternest kind. While there indubitably was some electoral fraud, 'elections were held with international observers present, and opposition Buddhists almost won control of the National Assembly'. Furthermore, the South Vietnamese enjoyed substantial religious, economic,

and political freedom, and could choose from 'three television stations, twenty radio stations, and twenty-seven daily newspapers, all of which were free to express dissenting views within certain bounds'. (Nixon, *No More Vietnams*, p. 205.) As was obvious at the time (and had been obvious for decades), the North Vietnamese enjoyed none of these freedoms. To reasonable observers, there was no question as to whether citizens enjoyed more liberties within the RVN or the DRV. Furthermore, there was no reason for anti-Saigon activists to think that North Vietnam was anything other than a totalitarian regime with a clear record of internal repression or to believe that, after conquering the South, Hanoi would not engage in crude reprisals against those who had expressed opinions of which it did not approve.

36. W.W. Rostow, *The Diffusion of Power: An Essay in Recent History* (New York: Macmillan, 1972), pp. 556–7.
37. Kissinger, *Diplomacy*, p. 697.

Conclusion: A Wealth of Failures

The Vietnam conflict has consistently been the most strategically misappraised of all US conflicts and with few exceptions the Vietnam literature has been a poor strategic teacher. There has been a decided tendency to view operational difficulties – such as the perseverance of the communists or the lack of North Vietnamese industrial infrastructure 'worthy' of bombing – as insurmountable barriers to US victory. At the same time, there has been a reluctance to acknowledge that the United States had compensating advantages that could have made a decisive difference in the outcome of the war. As this work has demonstrated, the United States was not predestined to fight and lose in Indochina.

Indeed, US decisionmakers enjoyed a large number of military options and had an unusually long time in which to shape an appropriate strategy, but made numerous poor decisions and thus squandered their opportunity to dominate the conflict. These errors occurred over more than a decade, from before the United States actively entered the war until after it disengaged militarily.

Given the information which they possessed, and the suppositions which they could reasonably draw from that knowledge, Washington's overall record of strategic decisionmaking on Vietnam is extraordinarily poor while MACV's is, at best, mediocre. Nevertheless, despite myriad errors, the United States almost succeeded in achieving its goals. By the time that the last US combat troops left Vietnam, the GVN had become tolerably stable, the ARVN was a reasonably competent force, the internal communist revolution was on the wane (although not totally expunged), and there were many other indications that South Vietnam was a developing country with good long-term prospects.

THE WAGES OF CIRCUMSPECTION

Eventually, the errors of US policy came full circle. Policymakers felt they needed to be in Indochina both because the area had strategic value (at least to a limited degree) and because US behavior in that region would send messages to both allies and enemies. Nevertheless, US leaders were unwilling to pursue military–political options that were perceived to carry a high risk of causing a great-power confrontation. They opted for war but attempted to limit their liability. Once US ground units entered combat, however, the stakes for the United States in Indochina increased exponentially. At that point, US prestige was clearly committed to such a degree that there should have been no further discussion of extraordinary restrictions on warmaking. Even if the RVN had little inherent strategic value, the 'commitment of the flag' made it unacceptable to lose in Vietnam.

US policymakers trapped their country in a losing cycle because they were *unwilling to take risks or make an effort commensurate with the importance of their commitment.* The decision to involve US forces in combat in Vietnam was questionable, but once taken the national interest, as well as the moral obligation to US troops at risk in the RVN, required that the venture be pursued with conviction. (Moreover, the American public was willing to support strong action in Vietnam.) The risk of war with China or other difficulties were an inherent part of the Vietnam endeavor, and the attempt to make the war 'escalation-proof' unacceptably warped and weakened the undertaking.

Throughout history there have been occasions in which great powers have lost small wars without substantial detriment to their overall foreign policy, but the United States was not in that position in Vietnam in the 1960s. The nature of its domestic politics and the character of its contest with the Soviet Union meant that a failure in Indochina would be a great one, not necessarily because of South Vietnam's inherent value, but because of the damage to the general reputation of the United States as an ally and protecting power. This injury to the standing of the United States, in turn, could (and arguably did) cause subsequent negative effects, but fortunately for the United States and its allies, the overall damage caused by Vietnam was limited.[1] The foreign policy of the United States was temporarily weakened,[2] and many US policymakers demonstrated knee-jerk opposition to any foreign involvement which they imagined might lead to 'another Vietnam',[3] but the ability and will of the United States to serve as a credible protecting power was not destroyed. This does not, however, retroactively vindicate US policymakers. The results of their actions could have been disastrous, and, at the time, they could not know that would not in fact be the case; poor decisions are not justified merely because they do not have apocalyptic results.

BREAKING THROUGH THE MYTHS OF VIETNAM

The major myths of Vietnam have been categorized and attacked herein in order to demonstrate that, if it had used its military power more judiciously, Washington could have succeeded in attaining its goals in Indochina at a reasonable price and in a timely manner. The preservation of the RVN was not an impossible goal or, compared to many other military–political enterprises undertaken by great powers, even a particularly difficult one.

North Vietnam could not escape the fact that relative to the United States it was a small, poor, and militarily weak state. Hanoi was ruled by a clique possessed of above-average strategic talent, but comparative weakness was an inescapable given for the DRV. It was the prerogative of the United States to shape the conflict, but Washington ceded its opportunity to control the war, instead acting tentatively and failing to make good use of its advantages. North Vietnam, on the other hand, maintained a clear focus on its primary goal of national unification and displayed admirable nerve in its conduct of the war.[4] The United States conducted itself like a confused country trapped by circumstance instead of an assertive superpower fighting a medium-sized expeditionary war in the pursuit of distinct goals. The US government failed in Vietnam chiefly because, although it possessed overwhelming means, Lyndon Johnson and his key advisors lacked the strategic judgment to use wisely the assets at their disposal.

In order to avoid ignominy in Vietnam, it was not sufficient for the United States to be a good doctor that attempted to help a deeply flawed client but failed to succeed. That was a more desirable reputation than the one that the United States earned itself in the mid-1970s by acting perfidiously, but 'losing well' was still an unattractive outcome for the United States. Given the perceived relative power of the two states, the United States had to win, and preferably do so impressively, in order to reflect a properly imposing image to its friends and foes.[5] The more complete and speedily obtained the victory over North Vietnam, the more it in turn would have benefited the United States in the attainment of its larger strategic goals. (Although, of course, even an uninspiring success which achieved enforcement of the Paris Peace Agreement would have been enormously preferable to actual defeat.)

If the time before the United States entered combat in Vietnam had been used well, the general debate over how to win in Vietnam would have been concluded before US units engaged in ground combat. Indeed, before the United States even dropped one bomb on the DRV, Washington should have settled on a strategy for successfully terminating the conflict in a timely fashion. Bombing North Vietnam and slowly pouring troops into South Vietnam in the hope of eventually convincing Hanoi to abandon its war aims was not an acceptable substitute for sound military–political thinking.

When policymakers chose to enter the war in Vietnam, the US military should have been given the resources and freedom to conduct military operations in a responsible manner. Basic operational issues such as whether to mine North Vietnam's ports, to wage a vigorous air campaign against the DRV, and operate as needed in Laos and Cambodia should have been considered settled in the affirmative, for such actions were prerequisite to effective warmaking in Indochina. Placing grave and unusual constraints on the US military effort was an act of hubris for which the United States and, especially, South Vietnam in the end paid dearly.

THE MIASMA OF ERROR

There was no single, key error that fundamentally undermined the American effort in Vietnam. Neither the Johnson administration policy on the use of strategic bombing, US decisions regarding Laos and Cambodia, nor any other single error doomed the US effort. The United States might have prevailed if it had merely made essentially correct choices about any of the three major warfighting areas discussed herein. If the United States had exerted rigorous control over access to eastern Laos and Cambodia, pursued an appropriate policy of strategic bombing, *or* conducted its war in South Vietnam differently (creating a combined command, instituting longer tours of duty for officers, and so forth), it is probable that Washington would have succeeded in securing the long-term independence of the RVN. If US policymakers had made correct decisions in regard to two of these three areas, it is very likely indeed that Saigon would have retained its independence.

Even though US policymakers misjudged Beijing's military capabilities and fretted too much about PRC intervention, there were still options available to the United States that – unlike an invasion of the Red River Delta[6] – carried little risk of large-scale Chinese intervention. To grasp how poorly the US government conducted the war (and how fully Johnson and some of his advisors were ruled by a mixture of fear of Beijing and reluctance to commit fully to the task at hand) it is essential to understand that US policymakers still possessed plausible options for timely victory even if they were highly wary of the PRC. Simple miscalculation of the intentions and capabilities of the PRC was important but not, by itself, decisive to the outcome of the war – it required heroic intellectual exertion on the part of American civilian leaders to convince themselves that almost every sensible strategic option was likely to bring about a war with China or have other serious detrimental effects.[7]

As the table below illustrates, there were reasonable solutions to all the major challenges faced by the United States. Accepting these solutions did not require great perceptiveness on the part of US policymakers, yet they were all rejected.

The first great US failure was primarily one of logic. The United States could have avoided major risk entirely simply by avoiding combat involvement in the region. Although the demise of the RVN would then have been almost inevitable, there was no overriding national interest that *required* the United States to be in Vietnam; the option of non-involvement was open to policymakers. The United States would have suffered a loss of face, but it would have been insignificant compared to the humiliation of defeat (especially if the RVN

Table 3: Solutions to Challenges Facing the United States in Indochina, 1962–75

Problem	Solution
Unwillingness of US policymakers to undertake a substantial military effort	No combat involvement in Indochina; 'cut losses'
Fear of Chinese intervention	Reasonable analysis of Chinese capabilities and intentions
Need to isolate communist insurgency in South Vietnam	Avoid false 'neutralization' of Laos; operate freely in Laos and Cambodia
Need to coerce North Vietnam; damaging North Vietnamese warmaking capabilities	Measures discussed throughout, including vigorous use of airpower against the DRV and, if desired, limited invasion of that country
Need to make effective use of US forces in South Vietnam; ensuring that the RVN was capable of energetic self-defense	Actions discussed in Chapter 3, including instituting a combined allied command and providing MACV with sufficient forces to operate against both main-force and smaller enemy units
Ensuring that the RVN survived after the Paris Peace Agreement – 'winning the peace'	Military enforcement of the Paris Peace Agreement; continuing large-scale military and other aid to the RVN and Cambodia for as long as necessary

were renounced before the fall of Diem). Over the long term non-involvement was probably not a judicious option – indeed, it might have given communist elements the momentum to take control of other Southeast Asian countries such as Indonesia and Singapore,[8] a clearly disastrous result.[9] Nevertheless, it would have been one solution to the United States' 'Indochina problem': the United States did not have to be in Vietnam,[10] and it was not prudent to engage there if US policymakers were not serious about achieving victory. The explanation by President Johnson and other policymakers that they felt they needed to support Saigon so as to avoid a 'who lost Vietnam' debate is not an acceptable excuse: a perilous political–military enterprise should either be undertaken seriously or not at all.

The second great US failure was analytical (and strongly related to the aforementioned logical error): Washington's estimation of the likelihood and magnitude of Chinese intervention. The belief of US policymakers that the PRC might intervene in Vietnam was understandable; given the knowledge that they possessed, it was reasonable for them to consider the possibility that a Sino–American conflict might occur in Vietnam.

Nevertheless, the fear of Chinese intervention expressed by figures such as Johnson and McNamara was exorbitant. Policymakers possessed reasonable estimates from trustworthy sources that indicated that Vietnam was not 'just like Korea'. Indeed, many key differences – such as the fact that North Korea bordered vital industrial areas and that Beijing itself was within realistic striking distance for US forces – were obvious. The PLA clearly did not possess the ability to bring massive force to bear in Indochina, and by all appearances it wished to avoid ground combat against US forces.

If the key US policymakers had integrated reasonable assumptions about China's capabilities and intentions into their decisionmaking, it would have been clear to them that the United States could reasonably risk conflict with Beijing and could, if necessary, defeat PLA expeditionary forces. This, in turn, would have given the assurance that they could risk energetic action in Laos and (at least from the air) against the DRV. While US leaders should have avoided combat in Vietnam if they were not serious, a proper analysis of Chinese capabilities and intentions would have demonstrated to them that they could 'afford to be serious'. Because key US leaders did not employ reasonable estimates of China's military potential and political intent, the entire US effort in Indochina was needlessly distorted and enfeebled. (Indeed, many policymakers perhaps did not wish to integrate reasonable assumptions about Chinese power into their thinking, preferring to be constrained by a 'Beijing bogeyman' as an excuse that conveniently explained why their options had to be so limited.)

Another key error was the decision to 'neutralize' Laos and to continue treating Laos and Cambodia as neutral states long after it became publicly apparent that North Vietnam was making use of those countries. It was naïve of policymakers to believe that the Laos Accords would meaningfully curtail North Vietnamese infiltration of that country and obtuse of Washington to continue to pretend that Laos was a neutral country long after extensive North Vietnamese use of that state was obvious. The United States attempted to guarantee that Indochina would not be a unified theater, but even the most cursory examination of Hanoi's behavior should have made it obvious that the North Vietnamese were too shrewd strategically to obey the Laos Accords. Moreover, there was only a negligible probability of a serious Chinese response to US action in the southern portion of Laos. If the Kennedy administration had displayed appropriate respect for the intelligence of the communists and appreciation for the vital importance of geography in the Vietnam conflict,[11] the United States would never have attempted to neutralize areas which were (given the seriousness of the enemy) inherently beyond neutralization.

Another broad area of US error was in its warfighting strategy against the DRV. As discussed above, the theory of graduated pressure was flawed: slowly increasing pressure on Hanoi both failed to coerce the North Vietnamese leadership and undermined the military effectiveness of the strategic air campaign. Indeed, timid US targeting and frequent bombing pauses likely encouraged the North Vietnamese in their belief that the United States wanted a quick settlement to the Vietnam problem – and therefore could be defeated by a tenacious enemy. However, American leaders could have pursued an energetic bombing campaign against North Vietnam that would have certainly damaged the DRV's ability to carry on the war in the South (without, it should be noted, substantially increasing the risk of large-scale Chinese intervention in Vietnam). Although it is unlikely, this might have motivated Hanoi to abandon its military drive for the unification of Vietnam.[12]

The next general area of US error was in its warfighting strategy in South Vietnam; both Washington and MACV made numerous errors. Washington's mistakes, particularly the slow build-up in Vietnam troop levels, damaged the military effort. MACV's errors were more forgivable, but nevertheless it made several major mistakes, such as pursuing large-unit operations in rural areas to the exclusion of other military efforts and refusing to create a unified multinational military command. The most important effects of MACV's operational errors were indirect, and would have made little difference if civilian policymakers had been wiser strategically. Nevertheless, as events transpired the fact that these policies hindered the qualitative improvement of the ARVN and slowed the pacification of the Vietnamese countryside was important to the survival of the GVN. If MACV had been more deft in its handling of the war in South Vietnam, it might have made good most of the errors of its civilian masters; however, it lacked the creativity to do so and thus failed to save Washington from itself.

The final basket of errors occurred in the period after the signing of the Paris Peace Agreement: the United States discarded the opportunity to enforce the Paris treaty and thereby to buttress the long-term survival of the GVN. Instead of supporting South Vietnam generously, the United States progressively curtailed military aid to Saigon. The ARVN, whose development as a fighting force had been shaped by the US military, was increasingly forced to fight a 'poor man's war' against an NVA that had been generously rearmed by the Soviet Union and PRC after its 1972 invasion of the South.

The remedy for this mistake is obvious: at minimum, the United States should have continued to aid the GVN generously. Preferably, the United States could also have enforced the Paris Peace Agreement rigorously from the date of its signing – which might have deterred the North Vietnamese from their 1975 invasion of South Vietnam – and if necessary resumed its use of airpower against North Vietnam. The Watergate scandal and the resulting political environment made the latter action unlikely, but the refusal to provide South Vietnam with ample material support was politically perverse. In essence, the United States chose to undermine South Vietnam at the time when it was finally prepared to do precisely what Washington had always hoped it would: defend itself competently without the aid of US troops.[13]

THE SUPERPOWER THAT DEFEATED ITSELF

Vietnam is perhaps most instructive strategically as a demonstration of how a great, or even a super-, power can discard its military and political leverage, failing more because of the poverty of its strategic thinking than the power of its enemy. It is impossible to discern useful lessons of Vietnam unless it is first acknowledged that the government of the United States committed political–military suicide in Indochina; Washington could have won, but willingly and repeatedly rejected options that would have made that possible. A critical flaw in most of the Vietnam literature has been to emphasize the difficulty of the US task in Vietnam while understating the overall military superiority which the United States enjoyed.

The Vietnam enterprise was a failure for the United States because US policymakers committed and persisted in gross error. Presented with a variety of choices, they stubbornly chose options contrary to their interests, often with full or partial knowledge that they were doing so; for example, it was obvious that refusing to bomb key North Vietnamese targets or to operate in Laos and Cambodia was damaging to the military effort. Many US policymakers appear to have believed this restraint to be politically sophisticated – that a limited conflict called for limited means and (preferably very) limited risks. As events demonstrated, however, they were not astute judges of how to balance ends and means. US policymakers were good at avoiding wider war, less-than-successful at limiting the commitment of US military resources to Indochina, and very bad indeed at ensuring the independence of South Vietnam.

To believe that success was impossible for the United States in Vietnam requires a wilful ignorance of military and political history. Many vastly more difficult endeavors have been undertaken, and the truly spectacular feats of human history speak for themselves. The destruction of Persia by Alexander the Great, the toppling of the Aztec Empire by Hernando Cortés, and the expansion of Mongol power under Genghis Khan and his successors presented far more difficult challenges then the ones the United States faced in Vietnam. Indeed, the United States had done many things more difficult than ensuring the survival of a weak client against the encroachments of a small antagonist. The War of Independence, the Civil War, and the Second World War all presented Washington with far more daunting military problems than Vo Nguyen Giap could ever hope to devise. The United States did not lose in Vietnam because it could not win: it lost because, even though it possessed enormous advantages over its enemy, its policymakers lacked the wisdom to construct a strategy for victory.

NOTES

1. However, it is notable that the Soviet Union believed Vietnam had greatly damaged the United States and thus interpreted Washington's détente strategy as a reflection of American weakness. See Ben B. Fischer, *A Cold War Conundrum: The 1983 Soviet War Scare*, Reference no. CSI97-10002 (Langley, VA: Central Intelligence Agency, Center for the Study of Intelligence, September 1997), p. 3.
2. Robert Jervis is no doubt correct when he observes that 'the American experience in Vietnam shaped policy for the succeeding decade'. ('US Grand Strategy: Mission

Impossible', *Naval War College Review*, 51, 3 (Summer 1998), p. 33.)

3. See Robert Conquest, 'Rules of the Game: Why West is Down and East is Up', in James E. Dornan, Jr (ed.), *United States National Security Policy in the Decade Ahead* (London: MacDonald and Jane's, 1978), p. 106.

4. When Nguyen Ngoc Hoa, the onetime commander of Transport Unit 559 was asked by an American journalist in 1989 whether he had been envious of the equipment the Americans possessed, he sagely replied: 'Yes, I was jealous every day, especially of the C-130s, the big transport planes, and the Chinook helicopters. The Americans could move more supplies and men in an hour than I could move in a month. But you see it made no difference in the end. I think we understood our limitations better than you understood your advantages.' (Morley Safer, *Flashbacks: On Returning to Vietnam* (New York: St Martin's, 1991), p. 87.)

5. Great powers, in this respect, operate under a handicap when they battle lesser opponents. For example, the USSR was unquestionably the ultimate victor in the 1939–40 Winter War, but the Finnish effort is (rightly) better respected, and the Red Army's desultory performance in that contest encouraged the belief of Hitler and other observers that the Soviet Union could be quickly conquered. See Desmond Seward, *Napoleon and Hitler: A Comparative Biography* (New York: Viking, 1988), pp. 192–3, and Gerhard L. Weinburg, *A World At Arms: A Global History of World War II* (New York: Cambridge University Press, 1994), p. 180.

6. It should be emphasized that an invasion of the DRV was not a prerequisite to US success in Indochina. There are certainly arguments in favor of such a move, but there were also 'victory options' that did not require that North Vietnam territory be threatened.

7. For instance, while campaigning for election in 1964, Johnson commonly would speak of his desire to avoid war with China. Notes by an aide indicate that he frequently made comments to the effect that 'we could get tied down in a land war in Asia very quickly if we sought to throw our weight around'. On 21 October in Akron, Ohio, Johnson made the preposterous claim that the PRC had 'over 200 million men in their army'. (Eric F. Goldman, *The Tragedy of Lyndon Johnson* (New York: Alfred A. Knopf, 1969), pp. 235–7.)

8. It has occasionally been argued that US intervention in Vietnam provided other Southeast Asian countries such as Singapore, Indonesia, Thailand, and Malaysia with a badly needed respite from communist pressure and that this was necessary in order for them to build stable governments and prosperous economies. Whether or not this is true is beyond the scope of this work, but the argument certainly bears serious consideration. Furthermore, it is notable that, if this view is correct, the United States achieved important gains in Asia despite the US government's strategic mismanagement of the Vietnam conflict. As Jim Rohwer argues, 'notwithstanding the almost universal view of Americans themselves to the contrary, America was not only right about Vietnam, but the sacrifices it made there, far from being in vain, accomplished in a spectacular way the broader aims of Asian stability and prosperity that the intervention was intended to secure'. (*Asia Rising: How History's Biggest Middle Class Will Change the World* (London: Nicholas Brealey, 1996), p. 307.)

9. When considering the question of whether a war with the PRC was an acceptable price to pay for the preservation of South Vietnam, it is worth noting that the majority of observers who say 'no' would likely admit nevertheless that preserving the independence of South Korea was worth the price of a war with China – a war which, for reasons cited above, was far more costly for the United States than a US–PRC war in Indochina in the mid-1960s likely would have been.

10. Long before US entry into the war, in the early and mid-1950s, some figures (such as Chairman of the JCS Adm. Arthur Radford) worried that the fall of South Vietnam might indirectly result in communist rule in Japan and have other extraordinary ripple

effects. See Barbara W. Tuchman, *The March of Folly: From Troy to Vietnam* (New York: Ballantine, 1985), pp. 251 and 261. By the mid-1960s, however, it was clear to thoughtful observers that such extreme outcomes were highly unlikely.

11. For an examination of the enduring importance of geographical considerations in strategy, see Colin S. Gray, 'The Continued Primacy of Geography', *Orbis*, 40, 2 (Spring 1996), pp. 247–59.

12. It is worth bearing in mind that the failure of the United States to compel North Vietnam does not prove definitively that Hanoi could not under any circumstances be compelled. As Gray observes, 'North Vietnam's leaders in the 1960s and 1970s were certainly not beyond deterrence. But, the United States of that era failed to pose a sufficiently deterring threat. The fact that Washington performed execrably in attempts at intra-war deterrence and violated all of the principles of war, does not speak badly for deterrence theory. That US failure does speak badly for the deterrence theory that was fashionable in Washington in the 1960s, and it speaks volumes to the lack of grasp of strategy by Lyndon Johnson's White House ... but deterrence theory *per se* was not missing in action in Vietnam'. ('The Definitions and Assumptions of Deterrence', *Journal of Strategic Studies*, 13, 4 (December 1990), pp. 7–8.)

13. See Ronald H. Spector, *Advice and Support: The Early Years of the US Army in Vietnam, 1941–1960* (New York: Free Press, 1985), p. 375.

Select Bibliography

BOOKS

Alexander, Bevin, *The Stranger Connection: US Intervention in China, 1944–1972*, Contributions to the Study of World History, 34 (New York: Greenwood, 1992).

Anderson, David L., *Trapped by Success: The Eisenhower Administration and Vietnam, 1953–1961*, Contemporary American History Series (New York: Columbia University Press, 1991).

Armbruster, Frank E., Raymond D. Gastil, Herman Kahn, William Pfaff, and Edmund Stillman, *Can We Win in Vietnam?: The American Dilemma*, Hudson Institute Series on National Security and International Order, 2 (London: Pall Mall, 1968).

Asprey, Robert B., *War in the Shadows: The Classic History of Guerrilla Warfare from Ancient Persia to the Present* (rev. edn, Boston, MA: Little, Brown, 1994).

Avant, Deborah D., *Political Institutions and Military Change: Lessons from Peripheral Wars*, Cornell Studies in Security Affairs (Ithaca, NY: Cornell University Press, 1994).

Ball, George W., *Diplomacy for a Crowded World: An American Foreign Policy* (Boston, MA: Little, Brown, 1976).

——, *The Past Has Another Pattern: Memoirs* (New York: W.W. Norton, 1982).

Bannan, John F. and Rosemary F., *Law, Morality and Vietnam: The Peace Militants and the Courts* (Bloomington, IN: Indiana University Press, 1974).

Baritz, Loren, *Backfire: A History of How American Culture Led Us into Vietnam and Made Us Fight the Way We Did* (New York: Ballantine, 1985).

Bergerud, Eric M., *Red Thunder, Tropic Lightning: The World of a Combat Division in Vietnam* (Boulder, CO: Westview, 1993).

Blair, Anne E., *Lodge in Vietnam: A Patriot Abroad* (New Haven, CT: Yale University Press, 1995).

Bui Diem, *In the Jaws of History* (Boston, MA: Houghton Mifflin, 1987).

Butler, David, *The Fall of Saigon: Scenes from the Sudden End of a Long War* (New York: Dell, 1985).

Buzzanco, Robert, *Masters of War: Military Dissent and Politics in the Vietnam Era* (New York: Cambridge University Press, 1996).

Cassinelli, C.W., *Total Revolution: A Comparative Study of Germany Under Hitler, the Soviet Union Under Stalin, and China Under Mao* (Santa Barbara, CA: Clio, 1976).

Castle, Timothy N., *At War in the Shadow of Vietnam: US Military Aid to the Royal Lao Government, 1955–75* (New York: Columbia University Press, 1993).

Chen Jian, *China's Road to the Korean War: The Making of the Sino–American Confrontation*, The US and Pacific Asia: Studies in Social, Economic, and Political Interaction (New York: Columbia University Press, 1994).

'Cincinnatus' [Cecil B. Currey], *Self-Destruction: The Disintegration and Decay of the United States Army During the Vietnam Era* (New York: W.W. Norton, 1981).

Clifford, Clark, with Richard Holbrooke, *Counsel to the President: A Memoir* (New York: Random House, 1991).

Clodfelter, Mark, *The Limits of Air Power: The American Bombing of North Vietnam* (New York: Free Press, 1989).

Cohen, Eliot A. and John Gooch, *Military Misfortunes: The Anatomy of Failure in War* (New York: Free Press, 1990).

Corr, Gerard H., *The Chinese Red Army: Campaigns and Politics Since 1949* (New York: Schocken, 1974).

Currey, Cecil B., *Victory At Any Cost: The Military Genius of Viet Nam's Gen. Vo Nguyen Giap* (Washington, DC: Brassey's, 1997).

Davidson, Philip B., *Vietnam at War: The History, 1946–1975* (Novato, CA: Presidio, 1988).

Dulles, Foster Rhea, *American Foreign Policy Toward Communist China, 1949–1969* (New York: Thomas Y. Crowell, 1972).

Ebert, James R., *A Life in a Year: The American Infantryman in Vietnam, 1965–1972* (Novato, CA: Presidio, 1993).

Fall, Bernard, *Hell in a Very Small Place: The Siege of Dien Bien Phu* (Oxford: Pall Mall, 1967).

——, Roger M. Smith (ed.), *Anatomy of a Crisis: The Laotian Crisis of 1960–1961* (Garden City, NY: Doubleday, 1969).

Ferguson, Niall (ed.), *Virtual History: Alternatives and Counterfactuals* (London: Papermac, 1997).

Foot, Rosemary, *The Practice of Power: US Relations with China Since 1949* (Oxford: Clarendon, 1995).

Ford, Gerald R., *A Time to Heal: The Autobiography of Gerald R. Ford* (New York: Berkley, 1980).

Friedman, George and Meredith, *The Future of War: Power, Technology, and American World Dominance in the 21st Century* (New York: Crown, 1996).

Fulbright, J. William, with Seth P. Tillman, *The Price of Empire* (New York: Pantheon, 1989).

Gaiduk, Ilya V., *The Soviet Union and the Vietnam War* (Chicago, IL: Ivan R. Dee, 1996).

Gallup, George H., *The Gallup Poll, Public Opinion 1935–1971*, vol. 3, 1959–1971 (New York: Random House, 1971).

Gelb, Leslie H., with Richard K. Betts, *The Irony of Vietnam: The System Worked* (Washington, DC: Brookings Institution, 1979).

Gettleman, Marvin E., Jane Franklin, Marilyn B. Young, and H. Bruce Franklin (eds), *Vietnam and America: A Documented History* (rev. 2nd edn, New York: Grove, 1995).

Gibbons, William Conrad, *The U.S. Government and the Vietnam War: Executive and Legislative Roles and Relationships*, four vols (Princeton, NJ: Princeton University Press, 1986–95).

Goldman, Eric F., *The Tragedy of Lyndon Johnson* (New York: Alfred A. Knopf, 1969).

Goncharov, Sergei N., John W. Lewis, and Xue Litai, *Uncertain Partners: Stalin, Mao, and the Korean War* (Stanford, CA: Stanford University Press, 1993).

Gravel, Senator Mike (ed.), *The Pentagon Papers*, four vols (Boston, MA: Beacon, 1971–72).

Gray, Colin S., *War, Peace, and Victory: Strategy and Statecraft for the Next Century* (New York: Simon & Schuster, 1990).

——, *Explorations in Strategy* (Westport, CT: Greenwood, 1996).

Haig, Alexander M., with Charles McCarry, *Inner Circles: How America Changed the World: A Memoir* (New York: Warner, 1992).

Halberstam, David, *The Making of a Quagmire* (London: Bodley Head, 1965).

——, *The Best and the Brightest* (New York: Penguin, 1972).

Hearden, Patrick J. (ed.), *Vietnam: Four American Perspectives* (West Lafayette, IN: Purdue University Press, 1990).

Hendrickson, Paul, *The Living and the Dead: Robert McNamara and Five Lives of a Lost War* (London: Papermac, 1996).

Hennessy, Michael A., *Strategy in Vietnam: The Marines and Revolutionary Warfare in I Corps, 1965–1972*, Praeger Studies in Diplomacy and Strategic Thought (Westport, CT: Praeger, 1997).

Herring, George C., *LBJ and Vietnam: A Different Kind of War*, An Administrative History of the Johnson Presidency Series (Austin, TX: University of Texas Press, 1994).

Higgins, Marguerite, *Our Vietnam Nightmare* (New York: Harper and Row, 1965).

Hilsman, Roger, *To Move a Nation: The Politics of Foreign Policy in the Administration of John F. Kennedy* (New York: Delta, 1967; first published 1964).

Hood, Stephen J., *Dragons Entangled: Indochina and the China–Vietnam War* (Armonk, NY: M.E. Sharpe, 1992).

Hoopes, Townsend, *The Limits of Intervention: An Inside Account of How the Johnson Policy of Escalation in Vietnam was Reversed* (rev. edn, New York: David McKay, 1973).

Hunt, Richard A., *Pacification: The American Struggle for Vietnam's Hearts and Minds* (Boulder, CO: Westview, 1995).

Iklé, Fred Charles, *Every War Must End* (rev. edn, New York: Columbia University Press, 1991).

Isaacson, Walter, *Kissinger: A Biography* (New York: Touchstone, 1996).

Johnson, Chalmers, *Autopsy on People's War* (Berkeley, CA: University of California, 1973).

Johnson, Lyndon Baines, *The Choices We Face* (New York: Bantam, 1969).

——, *The Vantage Point: Perspectives on the Presidency, 1963–1969* (New York: Popular Library, 1971).

Kagan, Donald, *On the Origins of War and the Preservation of Peace* (London: Pimlico, 1997; originally published 1995).

Kahin, George McT., *Intervention: How America Became Involved in Vietnam* (New York: Alfred A. Knopf, 1986).

—— and John W. Lewis, *The United States in Vietnam* (rev. edn, New York: Delta, 1969).

Kaiser, David, *American Tragedy: Kennedy, Johnson, and the Origins of the Vietnam War* (Cambridge, MA: Belknap Press/Harvard University Press, 2000).

Karnow, Stanley, *Mao and China: From Revolution to Revolution* (New York: Viking, 1972).

——, *Vietnam: A History* (New York: Penguin, 1984).

Kendrick, Alexander, *The Wound Within: America in the Vietnam Years, 1945–1974* (Boston, MA: Little, Brown, 1974).

Kennedy, John F., Allan Nevins (ed.), *The Burden and the Glory* (London: Hamish Hamilton, 1964).

Kimball, Jeffrey, *Nixon's Vietnam War* (Lawrence, KS: University Press of Kansas, 1998).

Kissinger, Henry, *American Foreign Policy* (expanded edn, New York: W.W. Norton, 1974).

——, *White House Years* (Boston, MA: Little, Brown, 1979).

——, *Years of Upheaval* (Boston: Little, Brown, 1982).

——, *Diplomacy* (New York: Simon & Schuster, 1994).

——, *Years of Renewal* (New York: Simon & Schuster, 1999).

Kolko, Gabriel, *Anatomy of a War: Vietnam, the United States, and the Modern Historical Experience* (New York: The New Press, 1995; originally published 1985).

Krepinevich, Andrew F., Jr, *The Army and Vietnam* (Baltimore, MD: Johns Hopkins University Press, 1986).

Krulak, Victor H., *First to Fight: An Inside View of the US Marine Corps* (Annapolis, MD: Naval Institute Press, 1984).

Lewy, Guenter, *America in Vietnam* (New York: Oxford University Press, 1980).

Leys, Simon, trans. Carol Appleyard and Patrick Goode, *The Emperor's New Clothes: Mao and the Cultural Revolution* (London: Allison & Busby, 1977).

Li Zhisui, trans. Tai Hung-chao, *The Private Life of Chairman Mao* (New York: Random House, 1994).

Lind, Michael, *Vietnam: The Necessary War: A Reinterpretation of America's Most Disastrous Military Conflict* (New York: Free Press, 1999).

Macdonald, Peter, *Giap: The Victor in Vietnam* (London: Fourth Estate, 1993).

MacFarquhar, Roderick (ed.), *The Politics of China: The Eras of Mao and Deng* (2nd edn, Cambridge: Cambridge University Press, 1997).

Mailer, Norman, *The Armies of the Night: History as a Novel, The Novel as History* (New York: Signet, 1968).

Mayers, David Allan, *Cracking the Monolith: US Policy Against the Sino–Soviet Alliance*, Political Traditions in Foreign Policy (Baton Rouge, LA: Louisiana State University Press, 1986).

McCullough, David, *Truman* (New York: Simon & Schuster, 1992).

McGarvey, Patrick J. (ed.), *Visions of Victory: Selected Vietnamese Communist Military Writings, 1964–68*, Hoover Institution Publications, 81 (Stanford, CA: Stanford University Press, 1969).

McMaster, H.R., *Dereliction of Duty: Lyndon Johnson, Robert McNamara, the Joint Chiefs of Staff, and the Lies that Led to Vietnam* (New York: Harper-Collins, 1997).

McNamara, Robert S., with Brian VanDeMark, *In Retrospect: The Tragedy and Lessons of Vietnam* (New York: Vintage, 1996).

——, James G. Blight, and Robert K. Brigham, with Thomas J. Biersteker and Herbert Y. Schandler, *Argument Without End: In Search of Answers to the Vietnam Tragedy* (New York: Public Affairs, 1999).

Mersky, Peter B. and Norman Polmar, *The Naval Air War in Vietnam* (2nd edn, Baltimore, MD: Nautical & Aviation Publishing Co. of America, 1986).

Moore, Harold G. and Joseph L. Galloway, *We Were Soldiers Once ... And Young: Ia Drang: The Battle that Changed the War in Vietnam* (Shrewsbury, UK: Airlife, 1994).

Morris, Roger, *Uncertain Greatness: Henry Kissinger and American Foreign Policy* (London: Quartet, 1977).

Morrison, Wilber H., *The Elephant and the Tiger: The Full Story of the Vietnam War* (New York: Hippocrene, 1990).

Mueller, John E., *War, Presidents, and Public Opinion* (New York: John Wiley & Sons, 1973).

Nalty, Bernard C. (ed.), *The Vietnam War: The History of America's Conflict in Southeast Asia* (New York: Smithmark, 1996).

Newman, John M., *JFK and Vietnam: Deception, Intrigue, and the Struggle for Power* (New York: Warner, 1992).

Nitze, Paul H., with Anne M. Smith and Stephen L. Rearden, *From Hiroshima to Glasnost: At the Center of Decision – A Memoir* (New York: Grove Weidenfeld, 1989).

Nixon, Richard M., *RN: The Memoirs of Richard Nixon* (New York: Grosset & Dunlap, 1978).

——, *The Real War* (New York: Warner, 1981).

——, *No More Vietnams* (New York: Avon, 1985).

Nolan, Keith William, *Into Laos: The Story of Dewey Canyon II/Lam Son 719, Vietnam 1971* (New York: Dell, 1986).

Nolting, Fredrick, *From Trust to Tragedy: The Political Memoirs of Fredrick Nolting, Kennedy's Ambassador to Diem's Vietnam* (New York: Praeger, 1988).

Oberdorfer, Dan, *Tet!* (New York: Da Capo, 1984; originally published 1971).

Olson, James S. and Randy Roberts, *Where the Domino Fell: America and Vietnam, 1945–1995* (2nd edn, New York: St Martin's, 1996).

Palmer, Bruce, Jr, *The 25-Year War: America's Military Role in Vietnam* (Lexington, KY: University Press of Kentucky, 1984).

Palmer, Dave Richard, *Summons of the Trumpet: A History of the Vietnam War from a Military Man's Viewpoint* (New York: Ballantine, 1984; originally published 1978).

Pape, Robert A., *Bombing to Win: Air Power and Coercion in War*, Cornell Studies in Security Affairs (Ithaca, NY: Cornell University Press, 1996).

Payne, Keith, *Deterrence in the Second Nuclear Age* (Lexington, KY: University Press of Kentucky, 1996).

Perret, Geoffrey, *A Country Made By War: From the Revolution to Vietnam – The Story of America's Rise to Power* (New York: Random House, 1989).

Perry, Mark, *Four Stars* (Boston, MA: Houghton Mifflin, 1989).

Peterson, Michael E., *The Combined Action Platoons: The US Marines' Other War in Vietnam* (New York: Praeger, 1989).

Podhoretz, Norman, *Why We Were in Vietnam* (New York: Simon & Schuster, 1982).

Powell, Colin L., with Joseph E. Persico, *A Soldier's Way: An Autobiography* (London: Hutchinson, 1995).

Prados, John, *Keepers of the Keys: A History of the National Security Council from Truman to Bush* (New York: William Morrow, 1991).

—— and Ray W. Stubbe, *Valley of Decision: The Siege of Khe Sanh* (New York: Dell, 1993).

Prochnau, William, *Once Upon a Distant War* (New York: Times, 1995).

Qiang Zhai, *China and the Vietnam Wars, 1950–1975* (Chapel Hill, NC: University of North Carolina Press, 2000).

Raskin, Marcus G. and Bernard B. Fall (eds), *The Viet-Nam Reader: Articles and Documents on American Foreign Policy and the Viet-Nam Crisis* (rev. edn, New York: Vintage, 1967).

Reeves, Richard, *President Kennedy: Profile of Power* (London: Papermac, 1994).

Reischauer, Edwin O., *Beyond Vietnam: The United States and Asia* (New York: Alfred A. Knopf, 1968).

Rohwer, Jim, *Asia Rising: How History's Biggest Middle Class Will Change the World* (London: Nicholas Brealey, 1996).

Rostow, W.W., *The Diffusion of Power: An Essay in Recent History* (New York: Macmillan, 1972).

——, *The United States and the Regional Organization of Asia and the Pacific, 1965–1985*. Ideas and Action Series, No. 6 (Austin, TX: University of Texas Press, 1986).

Safer, Morley, *Flashbacks: On Returning to Vietnam* (New York: St Martin's, 1991).

Scales, Robert H., Jr, *Firepower in Limited War* (rev. edn, Novato, CA: Presidio, 1995).

Schell, Jonathan, *The Real War: The Classic Reporting on the Vietnam War* (New York: Pantheon, 1987).

Schultz, Richard H., *The Secret War Against Hanoi: The Untold Story of Spies, Saboteurs, and Covert Warriors in Vietnam* (New York: Perennial, 1999).

Schulzinger, Robert D., *A Time for War: The United States and Vietnam, 1941–1975* (New York: Oxford University Press, 1997).

——, "'It's Easy to Win a War on Paper': The United States and Vietnam, 1961–1968' in Diane B. Kunz (ed.), *The Diplomacy of the Crucial Decade: American Foreign Relations During the 1960s* (New York: Columbia University Press, 1994), pp. 183–218.

Schwarzkopf, H. Norman, with Peter Peret, *It Doesn't Take a Hero: The Autobiography* (New York: Bantam, 1993).

Sharp, U.S. Grant, *Strategy for Defeat: Vietnam in Retrospect* (Novato, CA: Presidio, 1978).

Shawcross, William, *Sideshow: Kissinger, Nixon and the Destruction of Cambodia* (New York: Pocket, 1979).

Sheehan, Neil, *A Bright Shining Lie: John Paul Vann and America in Vietnam* (London: Jonathan Cape, 1989).

Small, Melvin, *Johnson, Nixon, and the Doves* (New Brunswick, NJ: Rutgers University Press, 1989).

——, *Covering Dissent: The Media and the Anti-Vietnam War Movement*, Perspectives on the Sixties (New Brunswick, NJ: Rutgers University Press, 1994).

Smith, John T., *Rolling Thunder: The Strategic Bombing Campaign Against North Vietnam 1964–68* (Walton on Thames, UK: Air Research Publications, 1994).

Smith, R.B., *An International History of the Vietnam War*, vols 1–3 (London: Macmillan, 1983–91).

Snepp, Frank, *Decent Interval: An Insider's Account of Saigon's Indecent End Told by the CIA's Chief Strategy Analyst in Vietnam* (New York: Vintage, 1978).

Sorley, Lewis, *A Better War: The Unexamined Victories and Final Tragedy of America's Last Years in Vietnam* (New York: Harcourt, 1999).

Spector, Ronald H., *Advice and Support: The Early Years of the US Army in Vietnam, 1941–1960* (New York: Free Press, 1985).

——, *After Tet: The Bloodiest Year in Vietnam* (New York: Free Press, 1993).

Stanton, Shelby L., *The Rise and Fall of an American Army: US Ground Forces in Vietnam, 1965–1973* (Stevenage, UK: Spa, 1989).

Summers, Harry G., Jr, *On Strategy: A Critical Analysis of the Vietnam War* (Novato, CA: Presidio, 1982).

——, *On Strategy II: A Critical Analysis of the Gulf War* (New York: Dell, 1992).

Taylor, A.J.P., *From Napoleon to the Second International: Essays on Nineteenth-century Europe* (London: Penguin, 1995).

Taylor, Maxwell D., *The Uncertain Trumpet* (New York: Harper & Brothers, 1960).

Thee, Marek, *Notes of a Witness: Laos and the Second Indochinese War* (New York: Random House, 1973).

Thompson, Sir Robert, *Make for the Hills: Memories of Far Eastern Wars* (London: Leo Cooper, 1989).

Tilford, Earl J., Jr, *Crosswinds: The Air Force's Setup in Vietnam*, Texas A&M University Military History Series (College Station, TX: Texas A&M University Press, 1993).

Tolson, John J., *Airmobility in Vietnam: Helicopter Warfare in Southeast Asia* (New York: Arno, 1981).

Towle, Philip Anthony, *Pilots and Rebels: The Use of Aircraft in Unconventional Warfare, 1918–1988* (London: Brassey's, 1989).

Truman, Harry S., *Years of Trial and Hope, 1946–1953* (London: Hodder & Stoughton, 1956).

Tuchman, Barbara W., *The March of Folly: From Troy to Vietnam* (New York: Ballantine, 1985).

Turley, G.H., *The Easter Offensive: Vietnam, 1972* (Novato, CA: Presidio, 1985).

VanDeMark, Brian, *Into the Quagmire: Lyndon Johnson and the Escalation of the Vietnam War* (New York: Oxford University Press, 1991).

Weinburg, Gerhard L., *A World At Arms: A Global History of World War II* (New York: Cambridge University Press, 1994).

Wells, Tom, *The War Within: America's Battle Over Vietnam* (New York: Henry Holt, 1994).

Westmoreland, William C., *A Soldier Reports* (New York: Da Capo, 1989; originally published 1976).

White, Theodore H., *The Making of the President 1968* (New York: Pocket, 1970).

Whiting, Allen S., *The Chinese Calculus of Deterrence: India and Indochina* (Ann Arbor, MI: University of Michigan Press, 1975).

Wolff, Tobias, *In Pharaoh's Army: Memories of a Lost War* (London: Picador, 1994).

Zumwalt, Elmo R., Jr, *On Watch: A Memoir* (New York: Quadrangle, 1976).
—— and Elmo Zumwalt III, with John Pekkanen, *My Father, My Son* (New York: Dell, 1987).

ARTICLES

Armstrong, Hamilton Fish, 'Power in a Sieve', *Foreign Affairs*, 46, 3 (April 1968), pp. 467–75.
Beckett, Ian F.W., 'Robert Thompson and the British Advisory Mission to South Vietnam, 1961–1965', *Small Wars and Insurgencies*, 8, 3 (Winter 1997), pp. 41–63.
Brandon, Henry, 'The Dilemma of SE Asia', *Survival*, 7, 1 (January–February 1965), pp. 38–40.
Bredo, William, 'Agrarian Reform in Vietnam: Vietcong and Government of Vietnam Strategies in Conflict', *Asian Survey*, 10, 8 (August 1970), pp. 738–50.
Bullington, James R. and James D. Rosenthal, 'The South Vietnamese Countryside: Non-Communist Political Perceptions', *Asian Survey*, 10, 8 (August 1970), pp. 651–61.
Bundy, William P., 'The Path to Viet Nam: Ten Decisions', *Orbis*, 11, 3 (Fall 1967), pp. 647–63.
Burke, Arleigh, 'Alternatives in Vietnam', *Ordnance*, 50, 3 (May–June 1966), pp. 611–13.
Chen Jian, 'China's Involvement in the Vietnam War, 1964–69', *China Quarterly*, 141 (June 1995), pp. 356–87.
Clifford, Clark, 'A Viet Nam Reappraisal: The Personal History of One Man's View and How it Evolved', *Foreign Affairs*, 47, 4 (July 1969), pp. 601–22.
——, with Richard Holbrooke, 'Annals of Government: Serving the President: The Vietnam Years II', *New Yorker* (13 May 1991), pp. 45–83.
Cooper, Chester L., 'The Complexities of Negotiation', *Foreign Affairs*, 46, 3 (April 1968), pp. 454–66.
Dean, Robert D., 'Masculinity as Ideology: John F. Kennedy and the Domestic Politics of Foreign Policy', *Diplomatic History*, 22, 1 (Winter 1998), pp. 29–62.
Denno, Bryce F., 'Military Prospects in Vietnam', *Orbis*, 9, 2 (Summer 1965), pp. 411–17.
Divine, Robert A., 'Historiography: Vietnam Reconsidered', *Diplomatic History*, 12, 1 (Winter 1988), pp. 79–93.
Duncanson, Dennis J., 'Vietnam and Foreign Powers', *International Affairs*, 45, 3 (July 1969), pp. 413–23.
Fall, Bernard B., 'The Second Indochina War', *International Affairs*, 41, 1 (January 1965), pp. 59–73.
——, 'Vietnam in the Balance', *Foreign Affairs*, 45, 1 (October 1966), pp. 1–18.

——, Richard N. Goodwin, George McGovern, and John P. Roche, 'Containing China: A Round-Table Discussion', *Commentary*, 41, 5 (May 1966), pp. 23–41.

Freedman, Lawrence, 'Vietnam and the Disillusioned Strategist', *International Affairs*, 72, 1 (January 1996), pp. 133–51.

Garson, Robert, 'Lyndon B. Johnson and the China Enigma', *Journal of Contemporary History*, 32, 1 (January 1997), pp. 63–80.

Garver, John W., 'The Chinese Threat in the Vietnam War', *Parameters*, 22, 1 (Spring 1992), pp. 73–85.

——, 'Little Chance', *Diplomatic History*, 21, 1 (Winter 1997), pp. 87–94.

Gelber, Lionel, 'History and the American Role', *Orbis*, 11, 1 (Spring 1967), pp. 199–209.

Gilpatric, Roswell L., 'Vietnam and World War III', *Survival*, 7, 5 (August 1965), pp. 192–5.

Goodman, Allan E., 'South Vietnam: War Without End?', *Asian Survey*, 15, 1 (January 1975), pp. 70–84.

Gray, Colin S., 'Looking Back on a Lost Opportunity', *National Review* (12 May 1978), pp. 580–3.

——, 'The Definitions and Assumptions of Deterrence: Questions of Theory and Practice', *Journal of Strategic Studies*, 13, 4 (December 1990), pp. 1–18.

He Di, 'The Most Respected Enemy: Mao Zedong's Perception of the United States', *China Quarterly*, 137 (March 1994), pp. 144–58.

Hess, Gary R, 'The Military Perspective on Strategy in Vietnam: Harry G. Summers's *On Strategy* and Bruce Palmer's *The 25-Year War*', *Diplomatic History*, 10, 1 (Winter 1986), pp. 91–106.

Hilsman, Roger, 'Must We Invade the North?', *Foreign Affairs*, 46, 3 (April 1968), pp. 425–41.

Hoopes, Townsend, 'Legacy of the Cold War in Indochina', *Foreign Affairs*, 48, 4 (July 1970), pp. 601–16.

Hunter, Robert E. and Philip Windsor, 'Vietnam and United States Policy in Asia', *International Affairs*, 44, 2 (April 1968), pp. 202–13.

Huntington, Samuel P., 'The Bases of Accommodation', *Foreign Affairs*, 46, 4 (July 1968), pp. 642–56.

Johnson, Robert H., 'Vietnamization: Can it Work?', *Foreign Affairs*, 48, 4 (July 1970), pp. 629–47.

Kahn, Herman, 'If Negotiations Fail', *Foreign Affairs*, 46, 4 (July 1968), pp. 627–41.

Kissinger, Henry A., 'The Viet Nam Negotiations', *Foreign Affairs*, 47, 2 (January 1969), pp. 211–34.

Kristol, Irving, 'American Intellectuals and Foreign Policy', *Foreign Affairs*, 45, 4 (July 1967), pp. 594–609.

Lacouture, Jean, 'From the Vietnam War to an Indochina War', *Foreign Affairs*, 48, 4 (July 1970), pp. 617–28.

Langland, Stanley G., 'The Laos Factor in a Vietnam Equation', *International Affairs*, 45, 4 (October 1969), pp. 631–47.

Lansdale, Edward G., 'Still the Search for Goals', *Foreign Affairs*, 47, 1 (October 1968), pp. 92–8.

Lichtheim, George, 'Vietnam and China', *Commentary*, 39, 5 (May 1965), pp. 56–9.

Lockhart, Greg, 'Constructing the Vietnam War: A Review Article', *Contemporary Southeast Asia*, 18, 3 (December 1996), pp. 320–36.

MacFarquhar, Roderick, 'Mao's Last Revolution', *Foreign Affairs*, 45, 1 (October 1966), pp. 112–24.

Michael, Franz, 'The Stakes in Vietnam', *Orbis*, 12, 1 (Spring 1968), pp. 121–31.

Morgenthau, Hans J., 'War With China?', *Survival*, 7, 4 (July 1965), pp. 155–9.

——, 'To Intervene or Not to Intervene', *Foreign Affairs*, 45, 3 (April 1967), pp. 425–36.

Naughton, Barry, 'The Third Front: Defense Industrialization in the Chinese Interior', *China Quarterly*, 115 (June 1988), pp. 351–86.

Nixon, Richard M., 'Asia After Viet Nam', *Foreign Affairs*, 46, 1 (October 1967), pp. 111–25.

Osgood, Robert E., 'The Reappraisal of Limited War', in 'Problems of Modern Strategy: Part One', *Adelphi Papers*, 54 (February 1969), pp. 41–54.

Owens, Mackubin Thomas, 'Mr McNamara's *Apologia*: Still Missing the Point About Vietnam', *Strategic Review*, 23, 3 (Summer 1995), pp. 5–6.

Possony, Stefan T., 'Mao's Strategic Initiative of 1965 and the US Response', *Orbis*, 11, 1 (Spring 1967), pp. 149–81.

Pye, Lucian W., 'China in Context', *Foreign Affairs*, 45, 2 (January 1967), pp. 229–45.

Race, Jeffery, 'How They Won', *Asian Survey*, 10, 8 (August 1970), pp. 628–50.

Record, Jeffrey, 'The Critics Were Right', *US Naval Institute Proceedings*, 122, 11 (November 1996), pp. 64–8.

Rostow, W.W. ', The Case for the Vietnam War', *Parameters*, 26, 4 (Winter 1996/97), pp. 39–50.

Schwartz, Benjamin, 'Chinese Visions and American Policies', *Commentary*, 41, 4 (April 1966), pp. 53–9.

Shaplen, Robert, 'Viet Nam: Crisis of Indecision', *Foreign Affairs*, 46, 1 (October 1967), pp. 95–110.

——, 'Our Involvement in Laos', *Foreign Affairs*, 48, 3 (April 1970), pp. 478–93.

Sorley, Lewis, 'To Change a War: General Harold K. Johnson and the PROVN Study', *Parameters*, 28, 1 (Spring 1998), pp. 93–109.

Thayer, Carlyle A., 'Vietnam: A Critical Analysis', *Small Wars and Insurgencies*, 2, 3 (December 1991), pp. 89–115.

Thompson, Sir Robert, 'Squaring the Error', *Foreign Affairs*, 46, 3 (April 1968), pp. 442–53.

Waldron, Arthur, '"Eat People" – A Chinese Reckoning', *Commentary*, 104, 1 (July 1997), pp. 28–33.

Walton, C. Dale, 'Vietnam: Avoidable Tragedy or Prudent Endeavor?' Review essay, *Comparative Strategy*, 19, 4 (October–December 2000), pp. 355–60.

Wiarda, Jonathan S., 'The US Coast Guard in Vietnam: Achieving Success in a Difficult War', *Naval War College Review*, 51, 2 (Spring 1998), pp. 30–46.

Wirtz, James J., 'Deception and the Tet Offensive', *Journal of Strategic Studies*, 13, 2 (June 1990), pp. 82–98.

Xiaoming Zhang, 'The Vietnam War, 1964–1969: A Chinese Perspective', *Journal of Military History*, 60, 4 (October 1996), pp. 731–62.

Young, Kenneth T., 'American Dealings with Peking', *Foreign Affairs*, 45, 1 (October 1966), pp. 77–87.

Zagoria, Donald S., 'Communism in Asia', *Commentary*, 39, 2 (February 1965), pp. 53–8.

GOVERNMENT PUBLICATIONS

Heiser, Joseph, *Logistic Support*, Vietnam Studies, CMH Pub 90-15 (Washington, DC: Department of the Army, 1991).

Lamy, Perry L., *Barrel Roll 1968–73: An Air Campaign in Support of National Policy* (Maxwell Air Base, AL: Air University Press, 1996).

Palmer, Bruce, Jr, 'Commentary' in John Schlight (ed.), *Second Indochina War Symposium: Papers and Commentary*, CMH Pub 103-1 (Washington, DC: US Army Center of Military History, 1986).

Sharp, U.S. Grant and William C. Westmoreland, *Report on the War in Vietnam* (Washington, DC: US Government Printing Office, 1968).

Spurgeon, Neel, *Medical Support of the US Army in Vietnam, 1965–1970*, Vietnam Studies (Washington, DC: Department of the Army, 1991).

Starry, Donn A., *Mounted Combat in Vietnam*, Vietnam Studies (Washington, DC: Department of the Army, 1978).

Stolfi, Russel H., *US Marine Corps Civic Action Efforts in Vietnam, March 1965–March 1968* (Historical Branch, G-3 Division, Headquarters, US Marine Corps, 1968).

US Department of State, *Foreign Relations of the United States, 1958–1960*, vol. 19, *China* (Washington, DC: GPO, 1996).

——, *Foreign Relations of the United States, 1961–1963*, vol. 24, Laos Crisis (Washington, DC: GPO, 1994).

——, *Foreign Relations of the United States, 1964–1968*, vol. 1, *Vietnam 1964*; vol. 2, *Vietnam January–June 1965*; vol. 3, *Vietnam June–December 1965*; vol. 4, *Vietnam 1966* (Washington, DC: GPO, 1992–1998).

West, Francis J., Jr, *Small Unit Action in Vietnam, Summer 1966* (Washington, DC: History and Museums Division; Headquarters USMC, 1977; originally published 1967).

OTHER SOURCES

Banner, Gregory T., 'The War for the Ho Chi Minh Trail', MA thesis, US Army Command and General Staff College, 1993.

Brush, Peter, 'Civic Action: The Marine Corps Experience in Vietnam', *Vietnam Generation Journal* on line, 5, 1–4 (March 1994), <http://jefferson.village. virginia.edu/sixties/HTML_docs/Texts/Scholarly/Brush_CAP_01.html>.

Eun Ho Lee and Yong Soon Yim, *Politics of Military Civic Action: The Case of South Korean and South Vietnamese Forces in the Vietnam War*, Asian Studies Monograph Series (Hong Kong: Asian Research Service, 1980).

Shulimson, Jack, 'The Marine War: III MAF in Vietnam, 1965–71'. Paper delivered at the 18–20 April 1996 Vietnam Symposium at the Texas Tech University Center for the Study of the Vietnam Conflict, <http://www.ttu. edu/~vietnam/96papers/marwar.htm>.

Index